Uniting Hearts, Igniting Change

The Journey of Connection

Brian Mosley

This book is a message of hope to everyone doing their best in tough circumstances. Please pass it on.

"Here's to the bridge-builders, the hand-holders, the light-
bringers, those extraordinary souls wrapped in ordinary
lives who quietly weave threads of humanity into an
inhumane world.
They are the unsung heroes in a world at war with itself.
They are the whisperers of hope that peace is possible.
Look for them in this present darkness.
Light your candle with their flame.
And then go.
Build bridges.
Hold hands.
Bring light to a dark and desperate world.
Be the hero you are looking for.
Peace is possible. It begins with us." – L.R. Knost

ISBN-13: 979-8-33631-545-5
Imprint: Independently published

1st September 2024

Acknowledgements

"It takes a village to raise a child."

This book was made possible by so many unique, beautiful, creative people who have given their time, love, support and inspiration through my life. I must acknowledge my family who gave me a loving and secure childhood in stormy times.

To my wife, Karen, my children and grandchildren who fill me with love and sustain me through every creative project.

To my sister Sheila, and the many close friends who I admire for their passion, spirit and wisdom, who helped me with proof reading, suggestions for improvements and ongoing support and encouragement. And to my community of Love Sheffield, you never cease to amaze and inspire me to further connection.

Thank you so much, words will never be enough to convey my feelings of love and respect.

Finally, to my mum, Norma who remains with me in spirit today, closer than ever - she would be happy that I did my best.

Contents

Preface: Call of Nature

Towards the end of 2016, as I approached my 50th birthday, a pivotal moment dramatically altered the course of my life. On a bright sunny day in Sheffield, while driving to work along Penistone Road, I noticed something jarring. The central reservation, usually lined with beautiful trees, now displayed a row of ugly stumps where those trees had once stood.

The sight was like a sudden and unexpected slap across the face. I was taken aback by the intensity of my reaction – a mixture of sadness, anger and disgust that welled up inside me. The emotional impact was so strong that I had to pull over. That moment of shock awakened something deep within me and set in motion a strange series of events that would open up a dramatic new pathway for my life.

For years, I'd been living a life out of balance, a common plight for a self-employed professional engineer. My work kept me away from home during the week, leaving Karen, my wife, to care for our three young children back in Sheffield. I'd been glad they had family nearby, good schools, and lots of friends, but being apart felt like I was doing time in a luxurious open prison. The work was challenging and interesting, but the sense of isolation and lack of purpose were ever-present. I was only ever truly happy over the weekend when I could be with my beautiful young family.

I'd tried to find ways to keep myself grounded and to combat the imbalance while I was away from home – practical psychology, meditation, photography, mountain biking and running were all things I tried, to ease the stress and loneliness. During periods between serious projects, I had the delight of working from home, developing a second business as a health coach, time with my family, taking our kids to school, and practising photography. This is when I first began posting on discussion forums around digital photography, and brought my first community together, the Olympus Photo Safari Group – which was a great learning experience and allowed me to enjoy socialising in service to a community.

Inevitably though, I always had to return to working away from home to earn a substantial income. As time passed, I grew increasingly aware of the 'transactional relationships' that pervaded professional environments – the cliques, the power games, the politics, the inflated egos, and the deep-seated insecurities. I found myself reluctantly drawn into the midst of this petty conflict, feeling my authentic self – dissolve away in the process.

The sight of those tree stumps starkly brought these feelings to the surface, revealing my deep longing for genuine connection and a more balanced life. This book is the result of my journey from that pivotal moment. It explores the deep truth of connection – how it allows life force to flow through our lives, bringing our inner selves to engage with reality.

I've come to understand that connection is far more than a social nicety; it is a fundamental aspect of human existence, woven into the very fabric of life. It serves as our gateway to a deeply fulfilling life, rich with meaning.

Through my experiences with the Sheffield tree dispute and the growth of our 24,000 strong 'Love Sheffield' community, I've witnessed firsthand the transformative power of connection. I've discovered simple concepts which make connecting with people a joy. I've gone on to discover that bringing people together with shared values of kindness, compassion and creativity, we can magnify compassion, create vibrant communities, and ignite positive change on every level.

This book is for anyone who senses the profound importance of human connection in our increasingly fragmented world. Whether you're a community builder, a business leader, an educator, or simply someone yearning for more meaningful relationships, you'll find here a compass to guide you towards deeper personal growth and positive societal change.

Our journey will take us through the varied landscapes of connection, from the intimacy of self-reflection to the vast horizons of global transformation. My hope is that these pages will spark your own journey of connection, revealing new pathways for creating the compassionate, vibrant communities we all long for. Together, let's explore how we can create a more connected, compassionate, and fulfilling life.

With heartfelt gratitude,

Brian Mosley
Founder of Love Sheffield

1. Introduction: The Essence of Connection

"Connection allows life energy, experienced as love,
to bring our inner selves to engage with reality."
– Brian Mosley

What if I told you that our current understanding of connection only hints at its true significance? It's more than a way to engage; it's how our inner selves come alive and interact with the world around us.

Connection allows life energy, experienced as love, to bring our inner selves to engage with reality. This isn't mere speculation, but a fundamental truth unearthed through my own transformative journey. This book will guide you through an enlightening exploration where connection becomes the key to unlocking a life of deep meaning and far-reaching impact.

Imagine Connection

That moment of seeing the destroyed trees became a turning point, a catalyst for understanding that connection is not just about human relationships, but about how we interact with the entire fabric of reality. This realisation set me on a path to discover how connection can transform not just individual lives but entire communities, and onwards to global impact.

In the following chapters, I offer you a journey – one that has transformed my life and that holds immense potential for every one of us. We will explore a path of connection from sub-atomic to cosmic scale. This knowledge will recognise the power you have to create unlimited positive change in the world. Yet, I offer this not as an absolute truth, but as my personal perspective, distilled from many years of study, personal experience and reflection. Take what resonates, leave what doesn't, and know that even the ideas that don't immediately make sense may resurface over time, perhaps offering unexpected insights in the future. It is my hope that you will become a co-explorer in this adventure of connection.

Together, we'll explore the landscapes of reality, personal growth, community building, and global transformation. We'll draw wisdom from ancient teachings and cutting-edge science, forming a solid understanding that bridges past and present to empower our future. Through the lens of connection, we'll reimagine our relationships, our communities, and our very purpose in this interconnected world.

Are you ready to uncover the true meaning and depth of connection? Let me share a moment that brought home the concept of connection for me. During our Love Sheffield Artists Exhibition, I had invited Angela, a friend from our online community, to visit. Angela, a former primary school teacher and artist, had been quite isolated for some time. When she arrived, beautifully dressed but visibly anxious, I sensed her determination to make a real-world connection.

As we began to chat, my wife Karen mentioned our growing concern about her parents, who were in their 80s and possibly showing early signs of dementia. Angela's eyes lit up with recognition and compassion. She shared that she had cared for her father through his journey with dementia until the end.

What unfolded was incredible. The energy between Karen and Angela was palpable as they exchanged experiences, fears, and hopes. Angela spoke of the challenges she had faced, but more importantly, of the deep love and precious moments she had shared with her father. Her words were a comfort to Karen's worries, offering both practical wisdom and emotional strength.

In that moment, I witnessed two women from different walks of life find strong common ground. Their faces glowed with warmth and understanding as they spoke. It was as if a current of life itself flowed between them, dissolving their differences and creating an instant, meaningful bond.

As you move through your own experiences, think of connection as the channel through which life energy brings your inner self into harmony with the world. By understanding and allowing this energy to flow, you can transform your relationships, your community, and ultimately, your entire life.

Quotes and Book References

I love quotes. I think they align us with people who have often lived rich lives of connection with their passion and offer us a symbol of collective wisdom in an inspiring insight. I've used quotes to introduce each section of my book, to help me focus and to convey key points of wisdom. I've created an index of quotes which will hopefully help you to quickly review or navigate the concepts throughout this book.

Another way to tap into the power of collective intelligence, is to ground my work in science and deep thinking by people who have given their lives to their passion and written important, influential books on related ideas. You'll find references to highly regarded and influential books throughout my work, and I've created an index of books also, for you to explore your own related interests in more depth. I really hope this helps you to pursue your own curiosity in depth where it grabs you.

The Journey of Connection

"The most powerful agent of growth and transformation is something much more basic than any technique: a change of heart." – John Welwood

This journey of connection goes beyond learning. It's about seeing ourselves and others differently, with open minds and caring hearts. This simple shift can transform everything.

Our exploration unfolds across eight levels, each building on the last. Each of these eight levels is a step on your journey towards a life where connection fuels personal growth, strengthens relationships, and creates a powerful legacy. By the end of this journey, you will have a deeper understanding of how to harness the power of connection to achieve lasting fulfilment and make a meaningful impact in the world.

The connection compass illustrates the directions in which we may become more energised. You decide where you wish energy to flow, remembering that meaningful connection feels like love.

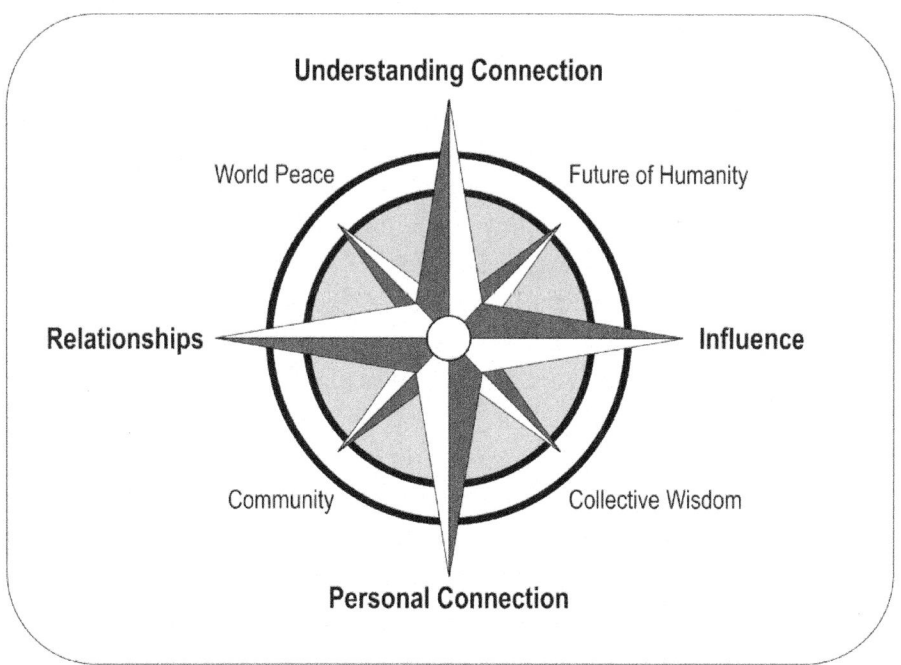

Figure 1. Connection Compass

1. **Understanding Connection**: We start by looking at what connection really means – its roots, how it spreads intelligence, and how understanding it can change the way we see the world. This first step opens our eyes to a new way of being.
2. **Personal Connection**: Next, we turn inwards, exploring how we align with ourselves. We'll learn about self-awareness and managing our emotions. This inner work is the foundation for all other connections.
3. **Relationships**: We then widen our view to look at relationships – extending beyond people to include places, technology, nature, and ideas. We'll explore how our bonds with these different aspects of life shape our understanding of the world. This broader view helps us see how all these connections come together to create our personal life story.
4. **Influence**: As we go deeper, we'll discover how authentic connections naturally lead us to make positive changes around us. From our close relationships to our wider community, we'll see how genuine connection can spark real change.
5. **Collective Wisdom**: We'll then explore collective wisdom – how connection lets us share insights across cultures and generations. This shows us the true power of our shared intelligence, and how each of our experiences adds to a bigger picture.
6. **Community**: Next, we bring connection into the world of business. We'll see the huge benefits of running a business with a strong sense of community and shared purpose.
7. **World Peace**: Near the end of our journey, we'll imagine how deep, widespread connection could bring about global harmony. We'll look at world peace not as a far-off dream, but as something that could naturally grow from truly connected societies.

8. **Future of Humanity**: Finally, we'll look to the future. We'll think about how new forms of connection, especially through technology and AI, might shape humanity's path forward. We'll consider how these advances could enhance our ability to engage with reality and each other. This invites us to envision and help create a future where authentic connection is at the heart of how we live and grow.

Throughout this exploration, we'll draw on personal stories, scientific findings, ancient wisdom, and new ideas. Each level offers both understanding and practical ways to deepen our interconnectedness in all areas of our lives.

Are you ready to explore The Journey of Connection? This path offers more than knowledge; it reveals a new way of living - one where interconnection guides us towards love and fulfilment.

In Sheffield, we've witnessed this journey unfold in remarkable ways, from personal transformations in local initiatives to city-wide attitude shifts. Our community's special character provides fertile ground for connection to flourish.

As we begin this journey together, reflect on your own experiences of connection. Consider a time when you felt deeply connected, a place that brings you a sense of belonging, and an area of your life where you'd like to improve your relationships. These reflections will be your starting point, and I encourage you to revisit them as we progress, noting how your views evolve.

The Interconnected Web of Life

"In nature we never see anything isolated, but everything in connection with something else which is before it, beside it, under it and over it." – Johann Wolfgang von Goethe

Goethe's insight about life and nature reveals that connection is life's purpose. We inhabit a world where nothing stands alone. Everything interacts with everything else, creating a living network of connections. This sets the stage perfectly for our exploration of how life weaves itself together, from the tiniest cell to the grandest ecosystem. We're invited to open our senses and minds to the countless links that surround us, often unseen but always vital.

Connection is an intrinsic part of being alive, embedded in the very fabric of life itself. Every cell in our body relies on intricate interactions to survive and fulfil its purpose. This molecular-scale world mirrors the broader human need for connection. Just as a tree's strength comes from its intricate root system, hidden beneath the surface yet vital for growth, our wellbeing depends on the often-unseen network of our sensory, social and emotional bonds.

In my experience, the way intelligence scales is through connection; in fact, all intelligence is distributed. In networks, whether neural or social, the power and capability of the system are amplified through interactions. This collective intelligence emerges from the exchanges and collaborations among individuals, communities, and even nations, enhancing our ability to innovate and adapt.

This scaling of collective intelligence mirrors the butterfly effect in nature. Just as a butterfly's wings can theoretically influence weather patterns across the globe, a single person's impact can cascade through humanity's collective consciousness. Our smallest actions, therefore, carry the potential for far-reaching transformation.

Historical and Cultural Perspectives

"The threads of human connection weave a tapestry far richer than any one culture can produce alone." – Zora Neale Hurston

People who have travelled well, and experienced diverse cultures often grasp connection's importance more deeply. Their insights reveal how different societies understand and value human bonds, offering a richer view of connection's role in our shared history.

Connection has always been at the heart of human societies. It's woven into our stories, rituals, and philosophies, shaping how we understand ourselves and our place in the world. From the wisdom of indigenous peoples to the teachings of Eastern and Western thinkers, the importance of connection echoes through time.

Indigenous cultures often see the world as a web, where every part touches all others. Eastern philosophies speak of harmony and balance. Western traditions explore how our bonds with others shape who we are. In Sheffield, our industrial past shows how shared knowledge and collaboration sparked innovation and growth to create global impact.

Modern-Day Relevance: Bridging the Gap in a Disconnected World

"We are all living in cages with the door wide open."
– George Lucas

From childhood, we're guided to fit into the society in which we are born, often adopting self-limiting beliefs. Yet, we have the power to recognise and release ourselves from these weights we carry, blending the boundless creativity of our youth with the wisdom of our experiences. This fusion unveils new pathways for connection and positive change in our world.

Today, we find ourselves in a world of constant noise and endless demands on our attention. Meaningful connections often fade into the background, replaced by fleeting interactions. Many feel isolated in a sea of faces, their phones full of contacts but their hearts yearning for genuine connection.

In Love Sheffield, we've witnessed this play out in our community. Yet, we've also seen how individuals recognise that a simple hello, a shared moment, can begin to mend these frayed bonds. Ironically, we've used social media to remind ourselves that real-world connection is always possible, always within reach. Individuals seeking better relationships, simply by embodying our core values of kindness, compassion, and creativity, become powerful advocates for the transformative power of connection.

Johan Hari, in *Lost Connections*, explores how our modern world has led to widespread feelings of isolation. David Bradford and Carole Robin, in *Connect*, show us how authenticity and vulnerability can build strong relationships, even in today's fast-paced environment.

To make deeper connections, we can start small. Being genuine in our interactions, truly listening to others, and finding a balance between our digital and face-to-face worlds – these simple steps can lead to more fulfilling relationships.

As we continue our journey of connection, we'll draw on diverse insights – from personal to global, from ancient wisdom to modern challenges. Each step will offer both understanding and practical ways to improve our relationships across all areas of our lives.

The Magic of Community

"We are like islands in the sea, separate on the surface but connected in the deep." – William James

Beneath the surface, we share deep connections that often go unnoticed. In Love Sheffield, we've observed how these subtle bonds cascade through our community, often beyond our conscious awareness. When we inspire others with kindness and creativity, these hidden links spring to life, revealing a vibrant network of human potential.

This effect materialises in remarkable ways. As people unite around shared values, everyday life takes on an extraordinary quality. It's like watching a garden burst into bloom, with each person bringing their own gifts to enrich the collective soil. From this fertile ground, a living community emerges, where ideas intermingle and flourish in unexpected ways.

Support flows naturally, finding those who need it most. Solutions to tough problems sprout from unlikely places. Our community grows stronger with each challenge, bending like a tree in the wind – flexible yet firmly rooted. We saw this strength in action during the pandemic, as neighbours reached out to each other, shared resources, and found new ways to stay connected.

In the warmth of true connection, people feel safe to grow beyond their usual limits. An artist's view improves an engineer's design. A carer's insight sparks an entrepreneur's new venture. Each person's contribution feeds the whole, creating a harvest richer than anyone could cultivate alone.

This living fabric of connection we're creating in Sheffield has the potential to spark a global movement. As we become a vibrant community of communities, we're laying the groundwork for a worldwide shift in how people relate and work together. This book itself is an expression of this emerging reality, born from the growth and strengthening of bonds across our community.

Conclusion: A Call to Connection

"The greatest thing in this world is not so much where we stand as in what direction we are moving." – Johann Wolfgang von Goethe

Our journey into connection is all about the way we choose to move. The true value lies in the path we walk together and the love we share with our fellow travellers along the way. This exploration is a compass guiding us towards our authentic selves and our place in the universe.

The chapters ahead will offer practical insights for improving relationships across all spheres of life - from our innermost selves to the global community. We'll uncover how seemingly small adjustments in our relationships can begin significant transformations, not just in our personal lives, but in our communities and the wider world.

2.   Level 0 – Understanding Connection

"The quality of your life is the quality of your relationships." – Anthony Robbins

---

Our connections, in their breadth and depth, deeply shape our lives and wellbeing. By viewing the world through a 'connection lens', we can uncover our purpose, which often emerges from these relationships. This perspective naturally guides us towards a life rich in meaning and fulfilment.

Our early years are typically spent exploring and experiencing connections, while later in life, we often find our purpose through these established bonds, continuing to deepen our connections as we grow.

My childhood in Crookesmoor, Sheffield, was more than just an adventure; it was an early lesson in the power of connection. The freedom to explore not only the streets but also the bonds with friends and community planted the seeds for my later understanding of how these relationships form the basis of a purposeful life.

My family home felt like a castle, where I was loved, protected, and learned a sense of survival. Family drama led to a move across Sheffield and a new community for my pre-teens onwards in Wisewood. This was a nicer area with a better school, but different enough to make me stand out – never ideal for any teenager.

I've never sought to accumulate friends – my focus has always been on work and family, and naturally assumed that was normal – so didn't expect any deep and lasting friendships. Over the last 8 years, as I've discovered my own journey of connection, that has gradually changed and now I can think of many friends that I really care about. It's not something I've forced, it's taken time and gentle, authentic interaction with kindness, compassion and creativity being a part of every interaction.

Many of the ideas I'll discuss in this book may seem quite abstract, but they are deeply rooted in life experience, a lifetime of study, practise and observation. I'm blessed to serve a large community of friends who Love Sheffield, and this book is a result of the distributed intelligence, or collective wisdom of many thousands of friends.

Connection is the very essence of what it means to be human. It's the invisible thread that binds us to ourselves, to others, and to the world around us. More than just engagement, it's the way life energy flows, creating unity, understanding, and shared experience. At its core, connection is the vital force that brings life to our interactions, creating emotional bonds and a deep sense of belonging. As you become more connected, you'll discover that your path to fulfilment unfolds naturally. Each new link you form adds richness and purpose to your life, helping you realise your full potential.

"The way we talk to our children becomes their inner voice."
– Peggy O'Mara

Our capacity for connection begins to take shape in our earliest years, perhaps even before birth. The environments we experience as children deeply influence our ability to form relationships throughout life. The stark contrast between nurturing and harmful early experiences reveals how crucial these formative years are in shaping our openness to connection.

In a loving home, children breathe in trust and security as naturally as air. These become the foundation of all their future relationships. They naturally learn empathy and communication by watching and mirroring caring adults. In these conditions, authenticity flourishes. Children learn the delicate dance of intimacy and self-protection, guided by gentle boundaries.

But not all children are so fortunate. In homes where love is scarce or twisted, the natural flow of connection is disrupted. Trust, which should be as natural as breathing, becomes a foreign concept. These children learn early that the world is not a safe place, and this knowledge shapes how they interact with others throughout their lives. Empathy might not develop fully, and communication often becomes a tool for survival rather than connection.

To start improving our relationships today, we might try this: spending a few minutes each day in quiet reflection, focusing on understanding our emotions. Then, in our next conversation, practise being fully present – listen without interrupting, and speak our truth with kindness. These small steps will gradually transform our interactions and deepen our connections.

As we look for a deeper understanding of connection, we realise it extends beyond our relationships with other people. It includes how we relate to everything – nature, our communities, the entire world. We're part of a vast, interconnected web of life, each of us playing our unique role in the shared consciousness of existence.

"We don't see things as they are, we see them as we are."
– Anaïs Nin

Our perception – the way we see things through filters of belief drastically influences how we experience the world around us. By choosing to view the world through a 'connection lens', we can uncover new layers of meaning in our everyday experiences. A chat with a neighbour outside school becomes a chance for real human contact. A walk in the park turns into a deep experience of nature.

On our journey, big insights often come from surprising places – when we approach these everyday moments of connection with open minds, they can lead to deep understanding.

Let's keep this sense of wonder as we explore connection. Whether we're having a deep talk with a friend, joining a community event, or just sitting quietly, we can admire the web of connections that make our lives richer.

By becoming lifelong learners, we abandon the idea of perfection and instead enjoy continuous growth – the result is wisdom, happiness, and the chance to pay it forward. Each small step towards deeper connection – with ourselves, others, and our world – makes our lives more meaningful. We're all on this journey together, each in our own way.

"The journey to connection is not a path we find, but one we create with every authentic step." – Maya Angelou

Our journey towards connection is an act of creation, a path we forge with each authentic step. As we engage genuinely with others and the world around us, we actively build and strengthen the bonds that enrich our lives. This process of connection, while simple in concept, holds immense potential to transform our relationships and reshape our society.

As we travel deeper into connection, we'll explore its many aspects. We'll confront the barriers our modern world erects against authentic relationships. We'll relate timeless philosophical ideas that have shaped how we understand human bonds. We'll see how connection empowers us to create change, rippling out from our personal lives to touch the whole of humanity.

This exploration will take us from the intimacy of self-reflection to the vast scale of our species' future. At each step, we'll uncover connection's transformative power. It's a force that doesn't just enrich our individual lives, but has the potential to reshape the very fabric of human society.

Through it all, we'll find that connection is both simpler and more powerful than we might have imagined. It's as immediate as a genuine smile, yet as vast as our collective human potential. Let's continue this journey with open hearts and curious minds, ready to discover the true depth of our interconnectedness.

The Neuroscience of Connection

"The brain is wider than the sky, For, put them side by side, The one the other will include With ease, and you beside."
– Emily Dickinson

The human brain, with its vast complexity, continues to amaze and perplex scientists. As we consider the neuroscience of connection, we're going where the boundaries between biology and experience, between the physical and the metaphysical, begin to blur.

Have you ever wondered what happens in our brains when we connect with others? As we live our lives, creating bonds and experiencing communities, it's fascinating to consider the biological underpinnings of these experiences. Science, in its ongoing quest to understand our world, is gradually uncovering the intricate workings of human connection.

Imagine, if you can, the neural symphony that plays when we interact with others. At the heart of this orchestra are mirror neurons – special cells that fire both when we act and when we observe others acting. It's as if our brains are quietly mirroring the actions and emotions of those around us, laying the groundwork for empathy and understanding.

Then there's oxytocin, often called the 'bonding hormone'. When we share a warm embrace or engage in a heartfelt conversation, our brains release this signature chemical, promoting trust and deepening our connections. It's nature's way of rewarding us for coming together, reminding us of the deep impact our relationships have on our wellbeing.

But the story doesn't end there. Recent scientific explorations are venturing into realms that seem more like science fiction than reality. Some researchers are exploring how the strange world of quantum physics might play a role in our consciousness and connections. It's fascinating to think that the same principles governing subatomic particles might influence how we think and relate to each other.

While these cutting-edge theories are still being tested, they remind us of the basic interconnectedness of all things. From the firing of neurons to the release of hormones, from our conscious thoughts to the intricate interplay in our brain cells, our very biology seems exquisitely tuned for connection. In Sheffield, we feel these features in action during events like the Tramlines music festival. The shared excitement and joy of the crowd creates a palpable energy that seems to flow between fans, demonstrating how our brains are wired for collective experiences.

Of course, science is still catching up with what many have intuitively felt for years – that we are deeply, intrinsically connected beings. The warmth of a friend's smile, the comfort of a supportive community, the joy of shared experiences – these are truths we've lived long before any laboratory could confirm them.

As we continue our journey of connection, let's carry this sense of wonder with us. Whether we're engaged in a heartfelt conversation with a neighbour, participating in a community event, or simply sitting in quiet contemplation in one of our beautiful parks, we can marvel at the intricate processes that make these experiences possible.

Relationalism and Connection

"The world is not a collection of things, it is a collection of events."
– Carlo Rovelli

Our understanding of reality is being reshaped by insights from quantum physics. As we look deeper into the nature of connection, we're led to question not just how we relate to one another, but the very fabric of existence itself.

Relationalism, a concept from the philosophy of physics, offers a fascinating way to understand our interactions. Imagine reality as a web of relationships rather than a collection of isolated objects. Just as a spider's web vibrates with every touch, so too does our world respond to every connection we make, illustrating how deeply intertwined we all are.

Let's consider how this view might reshape our understanding of our communities and our actions within them. Imagine a city more than a collection of buildings and people, see a vibrant network of relationships and interactions, constantly shifting and evolving. In this light, every conversation, shared project, and moment of kindness goes beyond being a discrete event. Instead, each becomes an integral part of the living, ever-evolving reality we create together.

When we gather for a community event in a local park, or when neighbours unite to support a local initiative, we go beyond mere participation in isolated activities. We're co-creating a living, breathing network of connections that extends far beyond the immediate moment. The warmth, creativity, and sense of belonging that emerge from these interactions stem not from any individual, but from the dynamic interplay between us all.

This perspective fundamentally reframes our role in shaping our communities and our world. When we offer a helping hand to a neighbour, or share an idea in a community meeting, we do more than affect a single interaction. We send ripples through an intricate web of relationships, with the potential to cascade into far-reaching changes that extend well beyond our immediate surroundings.

In essence, we go beyond building communities in the traditional sense. We're continuously shaping our shared reality, where every act of kindness, every creative expression, every genuine connection contributes to the emergence of a new way of being together. It's a thrilling and humbling realisation - that through our everyday actions, we're playing a part in reshaping how people may connect worldwide.

This relational view invites us to see our city as a living, evolving story we're all writing together. Our daily interactions - a friendly nod, a shared laugh, a moment of mutual support - aren't throw away lines, but vital chapters in this unfolding tale. Thinking of it this way, we might find ourselves moving through our city with a renewed sense of purpose and wonder. Each connection we make, each small kindness we offer, contributes to the ever-changing rhythm of our shared urban life. It's a powerful reminder that in any city, we're more than mere inhabitants - we're contributors to a shared story.

The Toxic Fishtank

"The real problem of humanity is the following: we have Paleolithic emotions, medieval institutions, and god-like technology." – E.O. Wilson

Our modern world presents a distinct challenge: we are ancient beings in a swiftly changing world, grappling with our own chaotic growth. This tension forms the backdrop of our societal fishtank.

Imagine our society as a vast aquarium. We're all swimming in it together, each special in our own way. The water we swim in is our shared culture, our collective beliefs and ways of being. But like any living system, our tank can become polluted, clouding our wellbeing and our ability to truly connect with each other.

The contaminants in our societal waters often sneak in quietly, masquerading as progress. Rampant consumerism and materialism cloud the water, distorting what we hold dear. The ceaseless flow of information creates a sort of information overload, obscuring our view. Media and advertising cast unrealistic ideals, like warped mirrors in our tank.

Technology has introduced a powerful new current, opening channels for global connection but bringing its own set of pollutants. As our digital interactions increase, genuine face-to-face connections often dwindle. Many feel isolated despite being more 'connected' than ever. Social media's highlight reels fuel constant comparison, breeding a nagging sense of inadequacy.

In our societal aquarium, different groups face distinct challenges. Our elders often find themselves in quieter corners, isolated by reduced mobility and the loss of companions. Those living with chronic illnesses swim against a strong current of physical limitations, their ability to engage socially often hampered. Neurodiverse individuals navigate these waters with a different set of fins, their particular way of perceiving the world sometimes making social communication challenging. Meanwhile, geographically isolated individuals circle in small eddies, cut off from the broader currents of cultural and educational resources.

Despite the crucial role of social connection in our wellbeing, there's often a lack of political will to prioritise it. We see this in underfunded community spaces, urban planning that neglects communal areas, and education policies that undervalue social-emotional learning.

Addressing these issues requires a shift in our priorities. We need to recognise connection not as a luxury, but as a fundamental human need, crucial for a thriving society. We need a holistic approach to policymaking that considers the intricate web of interactions sustaining us all.

The key lies in balance – learning to swim mindfully in these complex waters. We must develop digital literacy and use technology to improve relationships, not replace them. By creating clearer currents in our tank, we can foster environments where authentic interactions flourish.

In Love Sheffield, we've seen how small actions can create ripples that cascade into waves of positive change. Whether it's organising community events or simply choosing to engage in genuine, face-to-face conversations, each of us has the power to contribute to cleaner, clearer waters.

As we navigate life's currents, we recognise ourselves as integral parts of a vast, interconnected ecosystem. By caring for our shared environment and for each other, we create a world where all can flourish.

The Crisis of Purpose

"Those who have a 'why' to live, can bear with almost any 'how'."
– Viktor E. Frankl

Finding meaning in life isn't a luxury – it's a fundamental human need. This truth hits harder as we face the complexities of our modern world. The search for purpose lies at the heart of our existence, giving us the strength to endure life's challenges and find fulfilment in our daily lives.

Today, many of us feel lost, searching for meaning in a world that often seems to care more about what we do than who we are. As machines get smarter and take over more jobs, we're left wondering: what's our purpose?

Yuval Noah Harari, in his book *21 Lessons for the 21st Century*, points out that as AI and robots do more of our work, we may lose more than our jobs – we might lose our sense of purpose. If we can't make money, are we worth less? Society encourages us to equate earning potential to human worth, which is total nonsense, and yet it persists.

This loss of purpose is a very real and growing problem. Johan Hari, in *Lost Connections*, shows how feeling disconnected from meaningful work, from nature, from each other, and from hope for the future can make us feel deeply unhappy. Many of us feel this in our bones – a sense that something important is missing.

In recent years, we've witnessed how this disconnection from purpose can be channelled into divisive action. Individuals with significant social media influence, often detached from the real-world impact of their words, may use technology primarily for personal gain. This showcases the amplifying effect of new technologies - if we're not grounded in our core values and intentional about using technology to enhance human connection, we risk being overwhelmed by harmful ideologies.

Here in Sheffield, we've seen how community initiatives like Mums United and Love Sheffield work to counteract these divisive forces. By fostering face-to-face connections and promoting shared experiences across diverse groups, we're building resilience against the spread of disconnection and intolerance.

"The two most important days in your life are the day you are born and the day you find out why." – Mark Twain

But here's the thing: this crisis also gives us a chance to rethink what really matters. As the old ways of finding purpose become less reliable, we're challenged to find new ones. The key to this lies in how we connect – with ourselves, with others, and with the world around us.

I believe our sense of purpose emerges from connection. As we become more connected on every potential level, we become aware of and feel affinity for some aspect of concern to our community. We are naturally drawn to bring our unique, creative energy towards a solution. This becomes our naturally emergent and powerful feeling of purpose. In Love Sheffield, we've witnessed this happen firsthand. When individuals come together to support their neighbours, collaborate on community projects, or simply share their stories, they often discover a renewed sense of meaning. These relationships, grounded in kindness and creativity, offer a powerful response to the emptiness many of us grapple with in our modern world.

Our approach to connection addresses the crisis of purpose whilst revealing the timeless value of human bonds in our increasingly automated age. As artificial intelligence and robots absorb more routine tasks, our capacity for empathy, creativity, and authentic human interaction grows ever more precious. By deepening our connections, we do more than seek personal fulfilment; we rediscover the essence of our humanity in a rapidly changing world. This path of connection gives us deep sources of purpose, helping us face life's challenges with resilience and hope.

As we progress, Kai-Fu Lee, in AI *Superpowers*, suggests that jobs involving human-to-human interaction will become more common and more prized. Our capacity for empathy, creativity, and genuine connection – these are the things that make us profoundly human.

As we continue exploring connection, it's exciting to realise the massive power and relevance of relationships. We're doing something important – we're rediscovering what it means to be human in a world that's changing faster than ever before. By deepening our connections, we create sources of meaning that can sustain us through whatever the future brings.

In the face of this crisis of purpose, connection offers us a way forward. It invites us to find meaning not in what we produce or buy, but in how we relate – to ourselves, to each other, and to the world around us. As we move on to explore the philosophical foundations of connection, let's consider how these ideas might guide us towards a future where we all have a strong 'why' to live for.

Philosophical Foundations

"Everything we hear is an opinion, not a fact. Everything we see is a perspective, not the truth." – Marcus Aurelius

Our understanding of the world and our connections within it is uniquely shaped by our individual perspectives. As we consider the insights of great thinkers on the nature of connection, we find ourselves treading paths well-worn by centuries of philosophical inquiry. These timeless ideas offer us fresh lenses through which to view our own experiences.

Think of René Descartes' famous words: 'I think, therefore I am.' It's like that moment when we first notice our own thoughts. This awakening helps us see the same light in others, planting the seeds of empathy and real connection.

Plato's cave story makes us question what we think is real. He describes prisoners held in a cave all their lives, seeing only shadows and thinking that's all there is to reality. When one escapes, initially blinded by sunlight but then sees more of the world illuminated, he struggles to convince the others. This story asks us: Are we settling for shadows on a wall when there's a whole world outside? In our modern lives, are we mistaking likes and small talk for true connection?

Aristotle talks about different kinds of friendship. He suggests there are friendships based on usefulness, pleasure, and virtue. The deepest kind, he says, is based on shared goodness. It's not about what we can get, but about truly seeing and appreciating each other's character. This idea invites us to consider: Are we seeking these deeper connections in our own relationships?

Eastern ideas add another layer. Buddhism teaches that everything is connected, depending on many causes and conditions. Our very essence is interconnected, rather than being separate entities forming connections

Taoism suggests that our deepest connections might come not from trying hard, but from letting things flow naturally. It's about aligning with the rhythm of the universe.

These ideas help us see connection as more than just a personal or social thing. It becomes a way of being, a state of harmony with life's deepest truths. It's both who we are and why we're here.

Modern thinkers add their own nuance to this perspective. They challenge us to talk more genuinely, to see connection as essential to our growth, and to widen our circle of care to include all of humanity and beyond.

By blending old wisdom with new insights, we get a richer picture of connection. It becomes a guiding star for our actions, a force that shapes our societies, and a beacon for our shared future. When we embrace connection, we go beyond choosing a personal philosophy – we uncover a basic truth about who we are and who we can become. Sheffield's own philosophy, often described as 'gritty realism', reflects this interconnectedness. Our city's ethos of practical support and community action, seen in initiatives like the Sheffield Mutual Aid groups, embodies the idea that we're all in this together.

At the heart of our exploration of connection lies a fundamental truth: kindness, compassion, and creativity align with the very essence of our existence. When we embody these qualities, we become conduits for life energy, bringing more love into the world and deepening our connections with ourselves, others, and the universe at large.

Agency and Influence

"The only way to deal with an unfree world is to become so absolutely free that your very existence is an act of rebellion."
– Albert Camus

Our power to shape the world lies within us, becoming true through our choices and our way of being. This internal freedom allows us to influence our surroundings, even in tough circumstances. When we fully embrace this power, our very existence becomes a creative spark.

At its core, agency is our ability to act independently and make our own choices. When we think about connection, agency becomes our power to choose how we respond to events, how we relate to others, and how we engage with our communities. It's not about controlling everything around us, but about recognising our power to influence the flow of our shared reality.

Here in Sheffield, we see a clear example of how disconnection can erode our sense of agency. Our local council elections often see a turnout of only about 30%. This means our representatives are chosen by a majority of a minority – a stark illustration of political disengagement. But this disconnection from the democratic process points to a deeper issue. We've created a society that encourages us to behave more like consumers than active citizens.

Following government directives, our local councils now operate more like businesses. They outsource services and focus on managing budgets rather than engaging with us as active participants in governance. This approach reduces us to passive recipients of services, chipping away at our sense of agency and collective responsibility.

The impact of this shift reaches far beyond local governance. It seeps into our daily lives, colouring how we interact with our environment and each other. When we're treated as mere consumers of services rather than active participants in our community, we might lose sight of our power to create change.

To counter this, we need to create a culture that values civic engagement and recognises everyone as vital contributors to the democratic process. This shift begins with connection – to our communities, to our shared values, and to our collective power to effect change.

Our education system, too, plays a role in shaping our sense of agency. Often designed to produce employees rather than entrepreneurs, it can unintentionally dampen students' sense of agency and innovation. By prioritising conformity and job readiness over creativity and critical thinking, schools might limit young people's ability to see themselves as active creators of their futures.

Yet, by embracing connection – amongst students, across disciplines, and between schools and communities – we can inspire a sense of agency and purpose in our youth. We can empower young people to move beyond passive absorption of information. Instead, to question deeply, create boldly, and actively mould their own learning journeys.

In this context, influence isn't about manipulating others. It's about creating ripples that cascade into positive change through our authentic actions and connections. When we act from a place of genuine agency, in line with our values and connected to our community, our influence becomes a natural extension of who we are.

By recognising and growing our sense of agency, we open doors to deeper, more meaningful relationships. We become active co-creators of our shared reality, rather than passive consumers of a pre-determined world. This is the true power of connection – it allows us to reclaim our agency and use our influence to shape a more connected, compassionate world.

This concept of agency extends beyond individual actions to collective movements. When people connect around shared values and purpose, their collective agency can create fundamental societal shifts. We've seen this in grassroots movements that have reshaped political landscapes, in community initiatives that have transformed neighbourhoods, and in global campaigns that have influenced corporate behaviours.

In Sheffield, we've witnessed how small acts of connection can snowball into significant community changes. The Sheffield Trees Action Groups (STAG) demonstrate how individual agency can coalesce into significant influence. What began as a few concerned citizens grew into a movement that reshaped our nation's approach to urban forestry. These actions, born from genuine connection and a sense of agency, cascade out to influence wider society.

The digital age has added new dimensions to our understanding of agency and influence. Social media platforms offer unprecedented opportunities for individuals to share ideas and mobilise others around causes. However, this digital influence comes with its own challenges. The ease of online activism can sometimes lead to passive online support, where digital engagement replaces real-world action. The key lies in using digital tools to enhance, rather than replace, our physical world connections and actions.

Moreover, the rise of influencer culture significantly impacts young people's sense of agency and connection. Influencers often project idealised lifestyles and material success, creating unrealistic expectations and instilling a sense of inadequacy. This phenomenon can lead to decreased self-esteem and increased social anxiety, as young people compare their own lives to the seemingly perfect lives portrayed online.

Understanding connection enhances our sense of agency and influence. When we recognise how our actions are interconnected and impact others, we become more mindful and intentional in our behaviours. This awareness opens a sense of personal responsibility, as we understand that our choices contribute to the collective wellbeing. We can choose to engage with social media critically, to seek authentic relationships in the physical world, and to value our personal journey rather than comparing it to curated online personas.

The concept of collective agency is particularly relevant in our interconnected world. It refers to the capacity of a group to act together for a common purpose. Understanding collective agency can help us appreciate how connected communities can effect change on a larger scale than individuals acting alone.

In Sheffield, we can explore how collective agency has grown in community initiatives like the SSEN (Sheffield Social Enterprise Network), which provides a single point of contact for over 250 social enterprises across Sheffield. This organisation stepped up when central government phased out social enterprise business support contracts in 2011.

As we continue to navigate the complex interplay of agency and influence in our connected world, we must remain mindful of the power we hold. Every interaction, every choice, every connection we make has the potential to influence our shared reality. By embracing our agency and using our influence mindfully and compassionately, we can contribute to creating a more connected, empathetic, and vibrant world.

Distributed Intelligence

"None of us is as smart as all of us." – Ken Blanchard

Picture a symphony where each instrument contributes its distinct part, creating music more captivating than any solo performance. This illustrates how distributed intelligence works. It's not merely about individual brilliance, but how we harmonise our knowledge and experiences. Observing my grandchildren's development from birth has revealed this principle in action - their innate, effortless learning shows a form of intelligence that thrives on connection. When we pool our talents, intertwining our thoughts and emotions, we access a reservoir of wisdom far deeper than any individual could reach alone.

Nature offers stunning examples of this principle. Picture a flock of starlings in flight, creating mesmerizing patterns no single bird could conceive. This is distributed intelligence at work - countless individuals creating something far greater than themselves. At our best, human communities mirror this natural wonder.

Donald Hoffman, in his book *The Case Against Reality*, suggests our perceptions evolved not to show absolute truth, but to help us survive and thrive. This idea fits perfectly with distributed intelligence. Just as evolution shaped our individual views, our collective strengths emerge from the dance of our diverse perspectives and experiences.

Even our bodies demonstrate this concept. Dr. Michael Levin's research shows how cells, each with limited information, somehow work together to form complex structures. It's a tiny mirror of how we might collaborate on a larger scale.

In our daily lives, we can tap into distributed intelligence in simple ways. It might mean flattening workplace hierarchies or creating spaces for chance conversations. In our communities, it could involve designing public spaces that encourage spontaneous interactions – turning parks, cafes and community centres into hubs of our collective intelligence.

While digital tools have expanded our reach, we mustn't forget the irreplaceable value of face-to-face connections. Online platforms can support, but shouldn't replace the rich experiences that happen in person.

As we embrace this way of thinking, we start to see ourselves not as isolated individuals, but as vital parts of a larger, interconnected whole. It's an empowering shift, showing how even our smallest actions shape our shared reality.

In Sheffield, Kickback Recovery shows this principle in action. As a peer support group for those overcoming addiction, it taps into the power of shared experiences and collective wisdom. Each member brings their own journey, insights, and coping strategies to the group. Together, they create a supportive network that creates a powerful community for transformation. This approach recognises that recovery needs a community, where each person's struggles and triumphs contribute to a shared pool of knowledge and strength. By creating an environment of mutual support and understanding, Kickback Recovery taps into a source of distributed intelligence, turning individual challenges into collective solutions and hope.

The concept extends beyond humans. Swarm intelligence, inspired by insects like ants, shows how simple interactions between individuals can lead to complex, adaptive group behaviour. No single ant understands the big picture, yet together they solve intricate problems.

Love Sheffield shows distributed intelligence in action. As a city-wide social network, it uses leading-edge technology, including social media, mainstream media, and AI, to demonstrate the significance and power of human connection. This innovative approach transforms the entire city into a living example of collective wisdom, where each citizen becomes both a contributor to and beneficiary of shared knowledge and experience.

The University of Sheffield's Urban Flows Observatory is another prime example of distributed intelligence in action. Its primary goal is to understand and optimize the flow of energy and resources in urban environments to help cities thrive sustainably. By collecting data from across the city, it harnesses our collective knowledge to create solutions for urban challenges.

As we continue, let's consider how to grow distributed intelligence in our daily lives. How can we create spaces where diverse minds connect and collaborate? How might we redesign our institutions to better harness our collective wisdom?

By embracing distributed intelligence, we access a vast resource of creativity and resilience that exists not in any one person, but in the spaces between us all. Every conversation becomes a chance to tap into our collective strengths, every community project an opportunity to solve problems in ways no individual could have imagined alone.

Historical and Cultural Perspectives

"If you want to go quickly, go alone. If you want to go far, go together." – African Proverb

Throughout human history, the power of collective effort has been recognised as a fundamental force for progress and achievement. As our world becomes increasingly complex and interconnected, understanding how different cultures view and value connection is crucial for our peace today and for humanity to thrive in the future.

Connection has always been the pulse of human societies. It resonates through our stories, customs, and philosophies, shaping civilisations from ancient murmurs to modern debates. Indigenous wisdom offers powerful insights: the Australian Aboriginal practice of 'Dadirri' – deep, active listening to nature, others, and oneself – shows connection in its purest form. The Haudenosaunee people teach us to consider seven generations ahead, weaving our present actions into considered creation of the future.

From Africa comes "Ubuntu" – "I am because we are" – challenging us to see our humanity as inseparable from others. Eastern philosophies, like the Buddhist concept of dependent origination, remind us that nothing exists in isolation. Everything, everyone, every idea arises in concert, countless threads forming the intricate design of existence.

Western thought has also explored connection deeply. Aristotle's concept of "philia" highlights the deep friendship and mutual respect that form between individuals who share common values. The Greek term "Koinonia" captures a sense of community and shared purpose among people. During the Enlightenment, coffee houses became central to social life, serving as places where people gathered to exchange ideas and strengthen their relationships. These spaces played a crucial role in developing new forms of community and intellectual engagement.

Recent history illustrates connection's transformative power. United communities in the civil rights movement confronted deep-rooted injustices. The Berlin Wall's fall proved connection can transcend physical and ideological barriers. Our digital age brings new dimensions: the Arab Spring demonstrated how online networks can ignite real-world change. Yet these events also reveal that connection alone isn't sufficient – it needs to carry with it our understanding, empathy, and shared values to ignite positive change. The COVID-19 pandemic has etched a stark new chapter in our interconnected narrative, showing how local actions reverberate across the globe.

In Love Sheffield, we're growing our own living network of connection. Our community initiatives draw inspiration from diverse traditions, creating spaces where varied wisdom and experiences come together. This real world engagement strengthens our bonds and enriches our collective understanding.

These historical and cultural perspectives challenge us to think more broadly. They remind us that connection isn't just about personal relationships, but about our place in the grand movement of society, environment, and time. They urge us to look beyond the immediate, to consider how our actions today may influence the whole world tomorrow.

How might we apply these insights in our communities? Perhaps we could create spaces for deep listening, inspired by 'Dadirri'. Or make decisions with the "Seven Generations" principle in mind, considering their long-term impact. We could embrace "Ubuntu" by launching initiatives that prioritise collective wellbeing over individual gain.

The journey of connection never ceases. It evolves with each new challenge and opportunity. By bringing ancient wisdom to current understanding, we can create a future where connection isn't just an ideal, but a lived reality. In this world, we truly go far – because we journey together.

Interpreting Symbols in Present Reality

"Symbols are the imaginative signposts of life." – Margot Asquith

Symbols serve as powerful guides on our journey through life, shaping our understanding of the world and our place within it. As we look deeper into the nature of connection, we can see how these symbolic representations influence our reality, steer our paths, and strengthen our relationships with others.

We live in the present yet carry the past with us. Physical objects, cultural practices, and symbolic representations serve as bridges between then and now. These symbols compress vast spans of history into forms we can grasp today. Our link to the past lives in these symbols, challenging us to unravel their multifaceted meanings.

Consider the Yorkshire Rose. This elegant emblem has represented Yorkshire for centuries, its story stretching back to the Wars of the Roses. Today, it's more than a historical footnote – it's a living symbol connecting people to their heritage and each other. You'll spot it on cricket caps, business logos, even tattooed on skin. Each appearance reaffirms a sense of belonging and shared history.

But symbols are alive. They evolve as society changes. Look at Sheffield's coat of arms, with its hammer of Thor and sheaf of arrows. Once a nod to the city's metalworking past, it now embodies Sheffield's resilience and creativity. It reminds us that our interpretation of symbols adapts to our current needs and circumstances.

In healing spaces, symbols take on significant importance. Art therapy uses symbolic imagery to help people express complex emotions. Someone grappling with loss might find comfort in symbols of growth and renewal, like trees or butterflies. These symbols offer tangible paths to healing, resonating deeply on personal and cultural levels.

Bessel van der Kolk's work, *The Body Keeps the Score*, shows how past experiences live on in our bodies, affecting our ability to connect. His insights highlight the importance of engaging with symbols from our past to bridge the gap between old wounds and present healing. By working with these symbols, people can process stored emotions, growing personally and forming better relationships.

The flexibility of symbols allows us to reinterpret them for modern times, enriching our current experiences. The idea of 'Sheffield spirit' has evolved from being solely about industrial might to encompassing resilience, cultural vibrancy, and strong community bonds. This shift helps residents connect with their city's history while embracing its present and future.

Our collective memory, preserved in objects and patterns, doesn't just keep the past alive – it shapes our future. Sheffield's *Women of Steel statue* stands as a powerful reminder of the women who worked in steel factories during the World Wars. It honours their contribution and inspires future generations, ensuring that wisdom from the past continues to guide us. The statue in Sheffield city centre is more than just a monument. It's a powerful symbol of our city's resilience, work ethic, and the previously unsung contributions of women to our industrial heritage.

As we move forward, interpreting symbols brings both opportunities and responsibilities. We can create more inclusive communities by reimagining existing symbols and crafting new ones that reflect our evolving values. Yet we must be careful to remain true to our relationships, ensuring our symbolic interpretations enrich rather than overshadow our real-world experiences.

In Love Sheffield, our symbology speaks volumes about our vision for connection and transformation. It's a simple yet powerful image: a butterfly, a heart, and a tidal wave. The butterfly represents each beautiful, unique individual in our community, embodying personal transformation and the power of small actions. The heart at the centre symbolises the love binding us together, amplifying our individual efforts into collective momentum. The tidal wave illustrates the far-reaching impact of our combined energies – a surge of positive change cascading through our city and beyond. This symbol captures our core belief: every person, empowered by love and community, can create ripples of transformation that grow into waves of massive positive change.

As we continue our journey of connection, let's remain alert to the symbols around us. By thoughtfully engaging with these compressed messages from past and present, we can deepen our sense of connection and find new ways to create meaning together. In doing so, we honour our heritage while actively shaping the symbols that will guide future generations on their own journey of connection.

Understanding the Landscape for Positive In

*"If you think you are too small to make a difference, try slee
with a mosquito." – Dalai Lama*

In every seemingly small gesture, there lies an immense potential to influence the world around us. It's the recognition of this hidden power within us that serves as the foundation for true leadership.

Leadership, at its heart, is not about titles or positions. It's a quality that lives within each of us, often hidden beneath layers of societal expectations and peer pressure. When we recognise and reclaim this innate capacity, particularly the art of leading ourselves, we lay the groundwork for authentic connections. It's in realising our own agency that we take the first step towards influencing others and discovering shared purpose.

Sheffield brims with examples of this grassroots leadership in action. Consider Always an Alternative, a group that's transforming young lives through mentoring and positive activities. They go beyond offering support; they help shape brighter futures, build confidence and crucial skills in at-risk youth.

Kickback Recovery offers another powerful example of grassroots leadership. This peer support group initiative embodies the strength found in shared experience. By creating a safe space for individuals to connect, share their stories, and support one another in overcoming addiction, Kickback Recovery demonstrates how community-led efforts can address complex personal and social challenges. Their approach shows that some of the most effective change comes from those who have lived through the issues they're addressing, turning personal struggles into a source of hope and healing for others.

The Hope Community Foundation shows us how deep community engagement can create resilience and growth. Their "Community Champions" programme doesn't just solve problems; it weaves a stronger social fabric, creating a network of neighbours supporting neighbours.

The Sheffield Creative Guild demonstrates how uniting individuals around a shared passion can elevate an entire city. By connecting and supporting creative practitioners, they've helped cement Sheffield's reputation as a hub of innovation and artistic expression.

These local initiatives reflect a broader truth: global consciousness often emerges from individual insights. When people understand how their actions ripple through larger networks, potentially cascading into broader impacts, they're more likely to engage in practices that support sustainability, social justice, and community resilience. The Sheffield Climate Alliance embodies this principle, helping individuals see how their local efforts contribute to global climate goals.

Seth Godin's *Tribes* and Peter Block's *Community* offer valuable perspectives on leading and connecting groups. Godin explores the power of small, united groups to drive change, while Block emphasises structures that enhance belonging. These ideas help us build communities capable of tackling complex challenges.

Voluntary Action Sheffield breathes life into these principles, magnifying the impact of individual groups by forging connections and offering support to diverse community organisations. Their work extends beyond providing resources; it develops a more vibrant and effective voluntary sector throughout the city.

At its core, true leadership springs from a deep connection with reality and an understanding of our place within the collective consciousness. It involves embracing our unique perspectives and using them to envision a positive future. This vision, both powerful and inspiring, naturally engages others who share our values, leading to collaborative creation of a better world.

As we navigate this landscape of positive impact, we discover the incredible power each of us holds. By recognising our innate leadership qualities, connecting deeply with our communities, and aligning our actions with broader goals, we can create ripples of change that cascade far beyond our immediate circles. In doing so, we not only enrich our own lives but also contribute to a more connected, compassionate, and resilient world.

The journey to positive impact is often a quiet one. It's about consistent, thoughtful actions that align with our values and resonate with others. It's about seeing the interconnectedness of all things and understanding that even our smallest choices can contribute to a larger shift. As we move forward, let's carry this awareness with us, recognising that each interaction, each decision, each moment of connection is an opportunity to shape our shared future for the better.

Practical Applications of Connection

"The most basic and powerful way to connect to another person is to listen. Just listen. Perhaps the most important thing we ever give each other is our attention." – Rachel Naomi Remen

The heart of connection lies in the pure state of being truly present with one another. When we give our full attention, we reveal the potential for deeper, more meaningful relationships. As we explore ways to bring this presence into our daily lives, we'll see how it enriches our interactions and strengthens our communities.

In Sheffield, connection comes to life in unexpected places. Church halls double as community kitchens, where people from all walks of life cook and share meals together. These aren't just about filling stomachs; they're catalysts for genuine interaction, melting away social barriers to reveal our shared humanity.

The digital world offers its own challenges and opportunities. While technology keeps us in touch, it often lacks the depth of face-to-face encounters. Love Sheffield's digital community has found a balance, using online platforms to build bridges to in-person engagement. It's a reminder that virtual connections can complement, but shouldn't replace, the richness of in-person interactions.

Vulnerability plays a crucial role in deepening our bonds. The "Man-Up" campaign in Sheffield encourages men to open up about mental health, demonstrating how embracing our softer sides can actually strengthen our communities. It's a powerful example of how sharing our struggles can create ripples that cascade into broader wellbeing throughout our city.

Small, daily actions can enrich our relationships. A word of gratitude, a shared meal, or joining a community activity – these simple gestures weave a stronger social fabric. The "Random Acts of Kindness Sheffield" initiative taps into this power, encouraging small but meaningful gestures that spread positivity across the city.

Several thinkers offer us frameworks for authentic connection. Don Miguel Ruiz's *The Four Agreements* provides a deep, practical philosophy for honest interaction. Brené Brown's work, particularly in *Daring Greatly*, shows how vulnerability leads to deeper trust and connection. Marshall Rosenberg's *Nonviolent Communication* offers tools for empathetic listening and clear self-expression. Jon Kabat-Zinn's mindfulness teachings help us to be fully present in all our interactions.

Emerging technologies are opening new frontiers for connection. Virtual and augmented reality promise shared experiences that transcend physical limitations. While exciting, these developments raise questions about maintaining authenticity in virtual spaces.

As we put these ideas into practice, it's worth remembering that building relationships is a skill we can develop over time. It requires patience, practice, and a willingness to step beyond our comfort zones. Whether we're volunteering at a local food bank, chatting with a neighbour, or simply being more present in our daily interactions, each small step towards authentic connection contributes to a more compassionate community.

In Sheffield and beyond, opportunities for deeper connection surround us. By embracing these practical strategies and remaining open to connection in our daily lives, we create ripples of positive change that cascade far beyond our immediate circles. As we move forward, let's carry these insights with us, using them to enrich our relationships, strengthen our communities, and contribute to a more connected world.

Conclusion: Revealing the Landscape of Connection

"The world is full of magic things, patiently waiting for our senses to grow sharper." – W.B. Yeats

The wonders of life often remain hidden until we sharpen our awareness. As we conclude this chapter, we can see that our journey into connection is only just beginning. We've started to glimpse the intricate web that links us all – individuals, communities, and the world at large. This newfound perspective shifts us from passive participants to active creators of our shared future, revealing the true magic that Yeats described – a living reality that we are now about to embrace.

Our journey began with a simple truth: connection is the pulse of human existence. We've seen how our brains are wired for social engagement, how our very sense of self is shaped by our interactions with others. The concept of relationalism challenged us to see the world not as separate entities, but as a vibrant interplay of relationships.

We confronted the challenges of our modern 'toxic fishtank', where digital overwhelm and cultural pressures often cloud our connections. Yet, in recognising these challenges, we've uncovered opportunities for renewal.

From ancient philosophies to cutting-edge science, we've unearthed a wealth of wisdom on connection. We've seen how true influence stems not from domination, but from creating positive ripples that cascade far beyond our immediate circles.

The idea of distributed intelligence showed us how communities, like starlings in flight, can achieve remarkable feats through interconnected efforts. We've traced connection's thread through history and culture, discovering a universal yearning for belonging.

Symbols emerged as powerful connectors, bridging time and space, shaping our collective understanding. And in our everyday lives, we found that seeking connection is a quiet, consistent, mindful effort to create spaces of trust and shared purpose.

As we move forward on this journey, remember that every bond we form, every authentic interaction we engage in, strengthens not just our own life but the entire fabric of our shared world. We can embrace this responsibility with an open heart, knowing that our relationships are the key to a life of purpose, impact, and legacy.

3. Level 1 – Personal Connection

"To be yourself in a world that is constantly trying to make you something else is the greatest accomplishment." – Ralph Waldo Emerson

---

In a world constantly urging us to conform, staying true to ourselves is not only an act of courage but a powerful foundation for building authentic relationships. Embracing our true selves is the first step on the path to a fulfilling life of genuine relationships and personal growth.

This struggle to maintain our individuality is deeply ingrained in the character of Sheffielders, giving rise to a special blend of determination and compassion. It's this authenticity and friendliness that form the ideal foundation for a new movement of connection, as we begin to explore the journey of personal connection and its transformative impact on our lives.

When I first began what would become the Love Sheffield Community, it felt like making the first ascent of a new rock-climbing route. I was guided mainly by instinct and the wisdom gathered over my first half-century of life. At first, I wasn't even sure I was growing a community. My focus was clear: genuine, person-to-person connection.

I didn't want an audience; I was opening a beautiful secret garden, to help make it easier for people to connect more deeply for themselves. I learned that the strength of a community begins with the authenticity and depth of our personal connections.

I designed the virtual space to create a peaceful, personal sense of one-to-one connection, quite different from the typical social media noise. I was trying to craft something genuine from a platform that, to my mind, wasn't built for true connection. As our space blossomed, welcoming thousands of new friends, I realised that my ability to guide and inspire others was deeply tied to my own journey of self-discovery and connection.

This realisation humbled and enlightened me. To truly inspire connection in others, I needed to deepen my understanding of myself – my values, my driving forces, and even my flaws. This led me to explore a wealth of wisdom. Ryan Holiday's *Ego Is the Enemy* encouraged me to find strength in humility and service. Don Miguel Ruiz's *The Four Agreements* offered a framework for powerful connection in our complex human world. Johann Hari's *Lost Connections* reinforced my gut feeling that disconnection lies at the root of much of the world's pain, and highlighted the basic impact of genuine human bonds on our wellbeing.

These insights, among many others, shaped my view of personal connection as the foundation of all meaningful relationships. Think of it as a tree's root system. A tree's strength comes from its hidden, intricate root network, vital for growth. In the same way, our ability to connect with others depends on the often-unseen work of connecting with ourselves. A tree with shallow roots struggles in storms and can't reach great heights. Similarly, without a deep connection to ourselves, our relationships with others stay fragile and surface-level.

To help navigate your journey of self-discovery and connection, we'll use the Personal Connection Compass. This tool will guide you through the key aspects of personal connection, offering balance and direction as you deepen your understanding of yourself and your relationships.

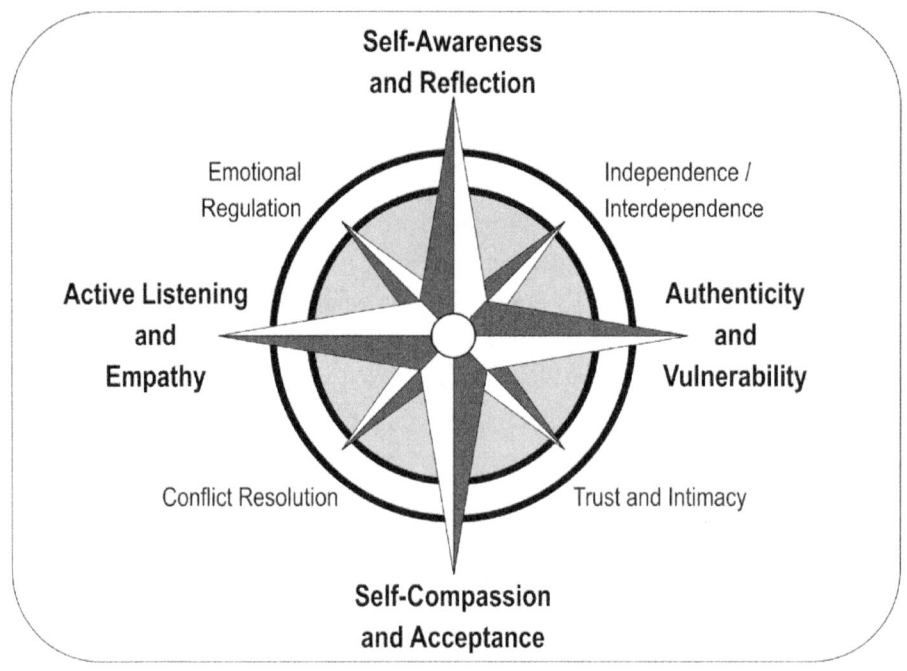

Figure 2. Personal Connection Compass

Through my journey, I've come to recognise several key aspects of personal connection:

1. Self-Awareness and Reflection

2. Self-Compassion and Acceptance

3. Authenticity and Vulnerability

4. Emotional Regulation and Expression

5. Active Listening and Empathy

6. Building Trust and Intimacy

7. Balancing Independence and Interdependence

8. Navigating Conflict and Resolution

Each of these elements has played a major role in developing my own sense of personal connection. As we explore these topics together, please approach them with an open heart and mind. We're just exploring what makes sense, this is your own journey of connection. Some ideas might resonate strongly with you, while others might not feel quite right – and that's perfectly fine. The idea is to find what works for you and helps you to grow.

Let's begin this journey together, with kindness, compassion, and creativity as our sword, shield and torch – these are the core values we've aligned ourselves with over the last 7 years, and now everything I do is living these values. I'll share my experiences and the lessons I've learned along the way, in the hope that they might make sense and help you along your own path towards deeper connection.

Self-Awareness and Reflection

"The unexamined life is not worth living." – Socrates

Living a life without reflection can leave us disconnected from our true selves. Many of us discover personal development at different points in our lives. Without realising we're actually on a journey of connection, we start to become more self-aware.

Self-awareness is more than just an inner exploration – it's the key to transforming our interactions with the world. By understanding our thoughts, emotions, and behaviors, we can begin to reshape our relationships and, ultimately, our entire lives. This journey often begins with simple curiosity about our cognitive processes, but it can lead to transformative insights about our core values, strengths, and areas for growth.

In my experience, true self-awareness goes beyond mere introspection. It's about realising what it means to be a human being, and the human being at the centre of our existence. I'm reminded of the shortest poem, written by one of my heroes, Muhammed Ali "Me We". This shift in perspective brings with it a deep sense of responsibility and interconnectedness. We begin to see how our actions and behaviours ripple out, cascading to affect not only ourselves but others and the world around us.

This holistic approach to self-awareness encourages us to live in harmony with ourselves and our communities. It's about aligning our actions with our values, understanding our impact on others, and continually striving for personal growth.

Over the years, I've found several practices particularly powerful in developing self-awareness:

1. **Mindful Journaling**: More than just recording events, this involves reflecting deeply on our thoughts, feelings, and reactions. It's a dialogue with our inner selves, helping us uncover patterns and insights we might otherwise miss.

2. **Meditation and Mindfulness**: These practices help us observe our thoughts and emotions without judgement, creating space between stimulus and response. This space is where self-awareness flourishes.

3. **Seeking Diverse Perspectives**: Actively seeking feedback from trusted friends, colleagues, or mentors can provide invaluable external perspectives on our behaviour. This multi-faceted view of ourselves can reveal blind spots and areas for growth.

4. **Regular Self-Reflection**: Setting aside time for deliberate self-reflection allows us to examine our actions, decisions, and their consequences. This practice supports continuous personal growth and helps us align our behaviour with our values.

5. **Engaged Learning**: Approach diverse sources of information – from academic texts to social media – as mirrors for self-reflection. Each encounter becomes an opportunity to deepen our understanding of ourselves and our place in the world.

By integrating these practices into our daily lives, we enable a deeper understanding of ourselves. It's crucial to approach this process with kindness and curiosity, rather than harsh self-judgement. As we become more aware of our thoughts, feelings, and behaviours, we open the door to personal growth and create the foundation for deeper, more authentic relationships with others.

Self-awareness is not a destination but a continual journey. Each insight brings us closer to our authentic selves and enhances our capacity for meaningful connection. In the next section, we'll explore how self-compassion and acceptance build upon this foundation, further strengthening our ability to connect deeply with ourselves and others.

Self-Compassion and Acceptance

"You yourself, as much as anybody in the entire universe, deserve your love and affection." – Buddha

As we deepen our self-awareness, or connect with ancient wisdom, it may become apparent that we are not our thoughts. The internal dialogue we've long mistaken for our true selves is, in fact, a competing mix of inherited voices – echoes of parents, teachers, friends, and countless others who've shaped our worldview. Many of these voices, in their attempts to guide or protect us, sadly form a collective of harsh inner critics.

Practicing self-compassion is not just an act of kindness towards ourselves; it's the foundation for all meaningful relationships. When we learn to treat ourselves with the same understanding and forgiveness we would offer a dear friend, we open the door to better relationships with others.

The journey towards self-compassion often begins with a simple yet powerful shift: becoming the observer of our thoughts rather than their captive. This shift allows us to witness our inner dialogue without being swept away by it. We can choose to listen to a more compassionate voice, one that acknowledges our efforts and inherent worth.

Michael A. Singer's *The Untethered Soul* offers valuable insights into this process. Singer emphasises the liberating effect of observing our thoughts without judgement. By creating a gentle distance between our awareness and our mental chatter, we open up space for a more compassionate self-relationship.

Mindfulness serves as a potent tool in this effort. By practicing present-moment awareness, we learn to experience our thoughts and emotions without immediately reacting to them. This practice allows us to respond to life's challenges with greater poise and kindness. It's about truly feeling our way through experiences rather than merely thinking about them.

Self-affirmation, when approached mindfully, can be transformative. Rather than engaging in empty positive thinking, effective self-affirmation involves recognising and appreciating our genuine qualities and efforts. It's about acknowledging our inherent worth as human beings, separate from our achievements or failures.

As we exercise self-compassion, something wonderful often unfolds: the kindness we extend to ourselves naturally begins to radiate outward. Our capacity for empathy expands, and our relationships with others improve. This cascading effect underscores the powerful link between self-care and how we naturally touch the lives of those around us.

To grow self-compassion and acceptance, let's consider these practices:

1. **Compassionate self-dialogue**: Develop the habit of speaking to ourselves as we would to a cherished friend facing a challenge. Notice the tone and content of our inner dialogue and consciously shift towards kindness.

2. **Mindful self-awareness**: Practise observing our thoughts and emotions without judgement. Notice patterns without attaching to them, creating space for new, more compassionate perspectives.

3. **Gratitude and appreciation**: Regularly acknowledge our efforts, strengths, and positive qualities. This will help us to recognise our intrinsic worth.

4. **Embracing imperfection**: Develop an understanding that mistakes and setbacks are part of the human experience. Use these moments as opportunities for growth rather than self-criticism.

It's important to recognise that growing self-compassion may take careful, conscious effort in the beginning but is a worthwhile habit we can achieve through practise. The aim is to gradually shift towards a kinder, more accepting relationship with ourselves. This process requires patience and persistent gentle effort.

As we deepen our practise of self-compassion, we lay the groundwork for more authentic and vulnerable relationships with others. In the next section, we'll explore how this internal work translates into richer, more meaningful relationships, further enhancing our capacity for deep, heartfelt connection.

Authenticity and Vulnerability

"One does not become enlightened by imagining figures of light, but by making the darkness conscious." – Carl Jung

What does it mean to be truly authentic? In our search for connection, it's not enough to show only our best sides. Real growth and understanding grow when we recognise and accept all parts of ourselves – even those we'd rather keep hidden. This sounds simple but presents a daily challenge in our world.

We often feel pressure to put on a mask, especially at work or in social situations. Our society, which values profit and productivity, can make genuine expressions feel risky. We might hide our true selves, thinking it's the only way to succeed. We start to see relationships as transactions, often wondering, "What's in it for me?"

But this approach comes at a cost. When we're not true to ourselves, we miss out on deep, genuine connections. We trade authenticity for a false sense of security, and vulnerability for a hollow version of success.

Embracing authenticity is a deeply rewarding journey. By shedding societal pressures and embracing our true selves, we not only forge stronger, more genuine relationships but also unlock greater creativity and resilience in our lives.

The journey to authenticity involves several key steps:

1. **Spotting societal pressures**: We need to recognise how our surroundings shape how we act and express ourselves.

2. **Questioning transactional thinking**: We should challenge the idea that every interaction needs to have a clear 'return on investment'.

3. **Redefining success**: It's crucial to look beyond material measures and value personal growth, sincere connections, and how we contribute to others.

4. **Creating spaces for authenticity**: We need to build and seek out environments where we can be our true selves, free from excessive expectations.

5. **Embracing vulnerability as strength:** We must recognise that opening up about our struggles can lead to deeper, more meaningful bonds.

This path isn't always smooth. We might worry that being authentic could put our jobs or social standing at risk. We might struggle when we step away from society's measure of success.

Yet, the potential rewards are life changing :
- A sense of freedom from the constant pressure to 'perform' or 'prove our worth'
- More genuine and supportive relationships, both personal and professional
- Increased creativity, as we allow our true selves to flourish
- A stronger link to our personal values and sense of purpose
- Greater resilience in the face of life's challenges

Embracing authenticity in a world that often values transaction over relation is a bold move. It's a way of reclaiming our humanity in a system that often reduces us to our productive capacity. Each step towards genuine self-expression and connection is an act of leadership, creating ripples that can cascade into gradual transformation in our communities and workplaces.

As we move forward, we'll explore how managing and expressing our emotions ties into these ideas, further enhancing our ability to form genuine connections in a world that often prioritises the superficial over the substantial.

Emotional Regulation and Expression

"The curious paradox is that when I accept myself just as I am, then I can change." – Carl Rogers

At the heart of our journey towards deeper connection lies a fundamental relationship – the one we have with our own emotions. In a world that often encourages disconnection and the projection of curated personas, the act of turning inward and truly feeling our emotions becomes a radical form of self-care and authenticity.

Emotional regulation isn't about controlling or suppressing our feelings. Rather, it's about developing a compassionate awareness of our emotional landscape. This awareness is crucial for making deep, authentic connections, as it allows us to engage with reality from a place of emotional clarity and stability.

It involves:

1. **Acknowledging our emotions**: Recognising and naming what we feel without judgement.

2. **Accepting our emotional experiences**: Allowing ourselves to feel fully, even when emotions are uncomfortable or inconvenient.

3. **Observing with curiosity**: Approaching our feelings with an attitude of interest rather than criticism.

4. **Honouring the wisdom of our emotions**: Understanding that each emotion, pleasant or unpleasant, carries valuable information about our needs and values.

This internal work forms the foundation for how we express ourselves and connect with others. When we're attuned to our own emotional world, we're better equipped to navigate the complexities of our social environment.

Practical strategies for deepening our emotional connection might include:

1. **Daily emotional check-ins**: Taking time each day to ask ourselves, "What am I feeling right now?" and sitting with whatever arises.

2. **Embodied emotional awareness**: Noticing how emotions emerge in our bodies, whether as tension, warmth, or other physical sensations.

3. **Expressive arts**: Using drawing, movement, or music to explore and express our emotions beyond words.

4. **Mindfulness meditation**: Practising non-judgemental awareness of our thoughts and feelings as they come and go.

5. **Journaling**: Writing freely about our emotional experiences without censorship or editing.

As we develop this internal emotional awareness and acceptance, we may find that our external world begins to shift. We might become more resilient in the face of social pressures, more discerning about the relationships we develop, and more capable of genuine connection in an often-disconnected world.

Of course, this is a personal journey. There's no 'right' way to feel or express emotions. The goal is to develop a compassionate, curious relationship with our own emotional world, creating a solid foundation from which we can engage authentically with others.

In our next section, we'll explore how this internal emotional work enhances our capacity for active listening and empathy, further improving our relationships with those around us.

Active Listening and Empathy

"The greatest gift you can give another is the purity of your attention." – Richard Moss

At its heart, active listening and empathy are about honouring the person we are with. It's a recognition of their inherent worth, their unique experiences, and their valuable perspective. When we truly listen and empathise, we're saying, without words, "You matter. Your thoughts, feelings, and experiences are important."

In a world that often rushes past individual experiences, taking the time to fully attend to another person is a radical act of connection. We're acknowledging that each person we encounter is a unique, beautiful, and creative human being, often doing their best in tough circumstances.

This approach to listening and empathy involves:

1. **Presence**: Giving our full, undivided attention to the speaker.

2. **Validation**: Acknowledging the legitimacy of their feelings and experiences.

3. **Curiosity**: Seeking to understand their perspective more deeply.

4. **Non-judgement**: Accepting their experience without criticism or immediate problem-solving.

5. **Recognition of humanity**: Seeing the whole person, living through the immediate situation or problem.

When we listen actively and empathise deeply, we create a space where people feel safe to be their authentic selves. This kind of attention can be deeply healing and transformative, both for the listener and the speaker.

Practical ways to grow this honouring attention include:

1. **Mindful listening**: Focusing fully on the speaker, noticing when our mind wanders and gently bringing it back.

2. **Reflective responses**: Paraphrasing what we've heard to ensure understanding and show we're engaged.

3. **Open-ended questions**: Asking questions that invite deeper sharing and reflection.

4. **Acknowledging emotions**: Recognising and naming the emotions we perceive, allowing the speaker to feel truly seen.

5. **Withholding solutions**: Resisting the urge to immediately problem-solve, unless explicitly asked for advice.

By practising active listening and empathy in this way, we're going beyond improving our communication skills. We're contributing to a culture of mutual respect and understanding. We're creating ripples of connection that can cascade into transforming our relationships, our communities, and potentially, our world.

Every interaction is an opportunity to honour another's humanity. Whether it's a brief exchange with a stranger or a deep conversation with a loved one, we have the power to make others feel valued, heard, and understood.

In our next section, we'll explore how this foundation of respectful, attentive listening and empathy contributes to building trust and intimacy in our relationships.

Building Trust and Intimacy

"Trust is the glue of life. It's the most essential ingredient in effective communication. It's the foundational principle that holds all relationships." – Stephen R. Covey

As we progress on our journey of connection, we come to understand that trust and intimacy are the cornerstones of deep, meaningful relationships. Trust is characterised by confidence in the honesty, integrity, and reliability of another person. Intimacy involves a deep sense of closeness and understanding between individuals, built on this foundation of trust. Together, they enable vulnerability, mutual support, and deeper emotional bonds.

In *The Speed of Trust* Stephen R. Covey discusses how trust accelerates relationships and improves their quality. When trust is present, relationships flourish as individuals feel safe to be open and vulnerable. This safety allows intimacy, enabling deeper, more meaningful bonds.

One powerful way to build trust is by living our core values consistently. When we take the time to reflect on what truly matters to us and ensure our actions align with these values, we become more predictable and trustworthy. Others learn that they can depend on us to act in certain ways, which reinforces trust.

For instance, kindness, compassion, and creativity are core values that can significantly enhance our journey towards authentic connection. In my experience with Love Sheffield, these values have been instrumental in creating a sense of community and understanding. Kindness honours an environment of warmth and support, making everyone feel valued and respected. Compassion allows us to empathise with others, understanding their struggles and providing support when needed. Creativity encourages us to express our individuality, bringing a sense of joy and innovation to our interactions.

Building trust and intimacy involves several practical strategies:

1. **Being consistent and reliable**: We follow through on our commitments, no matter how small.

2. **Practising honesty**: We strive to be truthful in our interactions, even when it's difficult.

3. **Respecting boundaries**: We honour each other's needs and limits.

4. **Showing empathy**: We demonstrate that we understand and care about each other's feelings.

5. **Being vulnerable**: We share our own thoughts and feelings, inviting others to do the same.

6. **Communicating openly**: We express our needs and concerns clearly and respectfully.

Again, building trust and intimacy is a journey, not a destination. It requires patience, consistency, and a willingness to be vulnerable. By committing to these practices and living our core values, we not only strengthen our relationships but also contribute to a more connected and compassionate world.

In the next section, we'll explore the delicate balance of independence and interdependence, and how this balance supports healthy, connected relationships.

Balancing Independence and Interdependence

"Interdependence is a higher value than independence."
– Stephen R. Covey

As we deepen our exploration of connection, we come to appreciate the importance of balancing independence and interdependence in our relationships. This delicate balance is vital for maintaining healthy bonds while preserving our individual identity and growth.

Independence, in its essence, is about self-reliance and personal agency. It's the freedom to chart our own course, pursue our passions, and expand our distinct talents. This autonomy is vital for personal growth and self-actualisation. Interdependence, conversely, recognises our inherent social nature. It embraces the power of mutual support and collaboration, acknowledging that our greatest achievements and deepest fulfilment often arise from meaningful relationships with others.

Stephen R. Covey, in his influential work *The 7 Habits of Highly Effective People*, suggests interdependence as a higher evolutionary stage than mere independence. While self-reliance is crucial, Covey argues that true effectiveness and fulfilment come from synergistic relationships where the whole is greater than the sum of its parts.

Striking this balance is an ongoing process, requiring mindfulness and intentional effort.

It involves:

1. **Seeking Individual Growth**: Dedicating time and energy to personal pursuits, hobbies, and self-improvement. This individual development enriches our relationships, bringing diverse perspectives and experiences to our interactions.

2. **Growing Interdependent Capabilities**: Developing skills like empathy, active listening, and collaborative problem-solving. These abilities enable us to create and maintain deeper, more fulfilling relationships.

3. **Practicing Open Communication**: Expressing our needs, desires, and boundaries clearly and compassionately. This transparency allows understanding and respect for both individual and shared needs within relationships.

4. **Supporting Others' Autonomy**: Encouraging and celebrating the individual pursuits of our partners, friends, and family members. This support demonstrates that our relationships enhance rather than constrain personal growth.

5. **Embracing Flexible Boundaries**: Recognising that the balance between independence and interdependence is dynamic, shifting with circumstances and personal needs. Flexibility allows relationships to adapt and thrive through various life stages.

6. **Supporting Mutual Growth**: Creating shared goals and experiences that allow for both individual and collective development. This synergy can lead to achievements and insights beyond what we could accomplish alone.

It's important to understand that there's no universal 'correct' balance between independence and interdependence. This varies among individuals and relationships, and even within the same relationship over time. The key lies in maintaining awareness of both aspects and striving for a harmony that allows both personal growth and deep connection.

By integrating these principles into our relationships, we create a dynamic that honours individual autonomy while celebrating the power of connection. We learn to stand confidently in our own identities while embracing the beauty and strength of mutual support and shared experiences.

As we navigate this balance, we inevitably encounter conflicts and disagreements. In our next section, we'll explore how to approach these challenges in ways that strengthen, rather than undermine, our relationships. We'll see how the very tensions that arise from balancing independence and interdependence can become catalysts for deeper understanding and more resilient relationships.

Navigating Conflict and Resolution

"In the middle of difficulty lies opportunity." – Albert Einstein

Conflict, an inevitable aspect of human interaction, need not be destructive. When approached with wisdom and compassion, it can serve as a powerful catalyst for personal growth, deeper understanding, and stronger relationships.

Understanding the Nature of Conflict

To navigate conflicts, we must first grasp their fundamental nature:

1. **Diverse Mental Models**: Each party in a conflict operates from a unique perspective shaped by their experiences, beliefs, and expectations.

2. **The Role of Ego**: Our ego often emerges as the primary obstacle to effective conflict resolution.

3. **Emotional Triggers**: Conflicts frequently arise when we're off-balance, disconnected from reality and compassion, and struggling to manage our emotions in the moment.

Foundational Principles for Conflict Resolution

Don Miguel Ruiz's *The Four Agreements* offers a solid foundation for approaching conflicts:

1. **Be Impeccable with Your Word**: Employ clear, honest communication to prevent misunderstandings. Be kind.

2. **Don't Take Anything Personally**: Recognise that others' actions often reflect their own struggles. Be compassionate.

3. **Don't Make Assumptions**: Avoid creating conflict by presuming to know others' thoughts or feelings. Seek to understand.

4. **Always Do Your Best**: Approach each conflict with the intention of giving your fullest effort. Be creative.

Taming the Ego

Our ego often impedes effective conflict resolution by prioritising being right over finding a solution. By embracing humility, we acknowledge the potential limitations of our perspective. This shift allows us to focus on addressing the issue at hand rather than protecting our self-image. Viewing each conflict as a learning opportunity transforms us into perpetual students, open to new understandings and perspectives.

Mindful Approaches to Conflict Resolution

With our ego in check, we can approach conflicts with greater clarity and compassion. Feeling genuine curiosity about the other person's perspective opens doors to deeper understanding. By practising calm compassion, we create a safe space for honest dialogue. Prioritising understanding over being understood shifts the conversation's dynamic, often leading to more collaborative outcomes.

The 'Steel Man' Approach

Dan Dennett's concept of the 'steel man' argument enhances our conflict resolution skills. This approach involves:

1. Charitably interpreting the other party's argument

2. Articulating it in a way they would agree is fair and accurate

3. Seeking confirmation before offering counterpoints

This method not only demonstrates respect but often reveals common ground previously obscured by misunderstanding.

Practical Strategies for Resolution

Effective conflict resolution relies on:
*   **Active listening**: Truly hearing to understand, not merely to respond
*   **Inclusive language**: Inviting collaboration
*   **Perspective-taking exercises**: Helping articulate the other person's position fairly
*   **Patience**: Allowing time to explore different mental models
*   **Flexibility**: Remaining open to unexpected solutions

The goal of conflict resolution extends beyond solving immediate issues. It's about strengthening relationships and building a foundation for better future cooperation. By focusing on others' needs and remaining open to different perspectives, we often find our own needs met in unexpected ways. This approach embodies kindness, compassion, and creativity, creating better relationships and more harmonious communities.

In essence, each conflict becomes an opportunity to practise humility, expand our understanding, and contribute to a more connected and empathetic world. By embracing these principles and strategies, we transform potential division into a catalyst for growth and deeper human connection.

Conclusion: The Journey of Personal Connection

"We cannot live only for ourselves. A thousand fibers connect us with our fellow men." – Herman Melville

Our lives are intertwined with those around us, and the connections we cherish are vital to our shared existence. Throughout this chapter, we've considered the core elements that help us to create deeper, more meaningful relationships with both ourselves and others. From growing self-awareness and compassion to embracing authenticity, vulnerability, and effective conflict resolution, each aspect enhances our ability to connect genuinely.

We've learned that personal connection begins with understanding ourselves – our thoughts, emotions, and behaviours. By strengthening self-awareness and practising self-compassion, we create a solid foundation from which to engage with others. We've seen how embracing authenticity and vulnerability, despite the challenges they present, opens doors to more powerful and fulfilling relationships.

The skills of active listening and empathy have shown us how to truly hear and understand others, creating spaces where people feel valued and understood. We've explored the delicate balance between independence and interdependence, recognising that healthy relationships allow for both individual growth and mutual support.

Finally, we've looked into the complex terrain of conflict resolution, discovering how disagreements, when approached with wisdom and compassion, can become opportunities for deeper understanding and better relationships.

Developing personal connection is a lifelong journey that requires patience, practise, and a willingness to continually learn and grow. As we move forward, let's carry these insights with us, applying them in our daily lives to create more meaningful connections and contribute to a more compassionate, understanding world. In the chapters that follow, we'll build upon this foundation to explore how we can extend these principles to our broader relationships and communities.

4. Level 2 – Relationships

"Relationships are the fertile soil from which all advancement, all success, all achievement in real life grows." – Ben Stein

Relationships profoundly impact the quality of our connections. If connection is the dance of life, relationships provide the rhythm and melody that guide our movements. They shape our perspectives as we navigate the world, influencing our experiences and our very sense of being. By nurturing good relationships, we unlock the potential for deeper connections and a more fulfilling existence.

Relationships are fundamental to our existence, some would say they represent the sum total of our reality. They extend beyond the bounds of family and friends, encompassing every transformative connection that alters our state of being or deepens our wisdom,

Connection is how life energy flows through us. It's the way our inner selves are brought to engage with the world around us. In my work with Love Sheffield, I've lived and seen this engagement transform people and communities in inspiring, surprising and lasting ways.

Our relationships with people, nature, and ideas all create opportunities for life energy to flow. They help us to become more connected to reality or truth, and to transform ourselves into more conscious beings. These relationships challenge and inspire us, shaping how we see the world and our place in it.

Throughout this chapter, reflect on your own relationships. Consider how they allow life energy to flow through you, help you engage with reality, and contribute to flourishing communities. We'll explore the interplay of love, trust, and intimacy, offering practical ways to strengthen your connections. By the end, you'll have new tools to develop more meaningful relationships, laying the groundwork for a richer, more connected life.

The Relationships Compass will guide us through the essential elements of building and nurturing relationships. This tool will help us find balance and direction in our interactions, ensuring that every relationship we establish contributes to our personal development and emotional well-being.

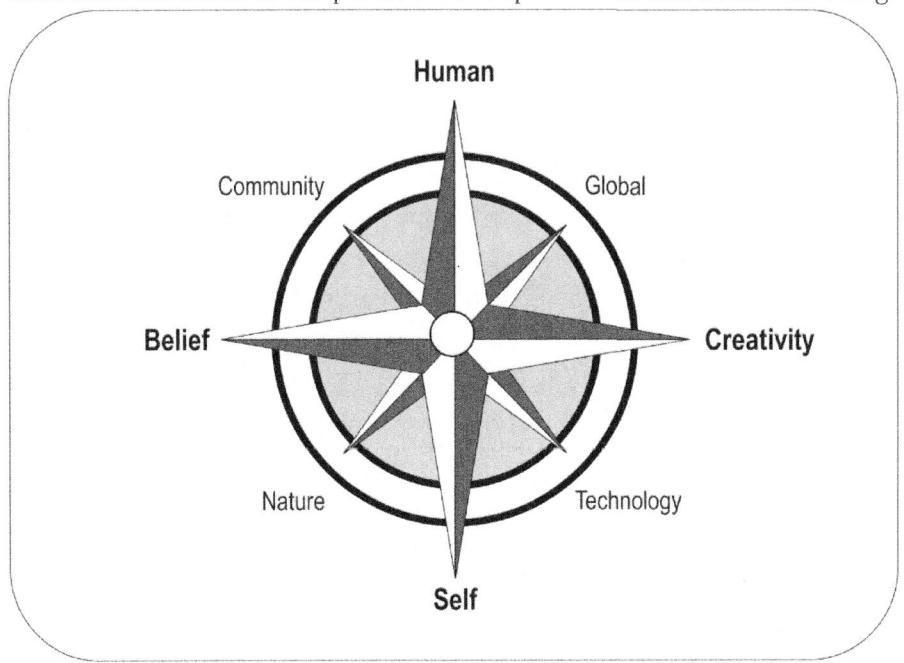

Figure 3. Relationships Compass

Self-Relationship and Personal Growth

"To love oneself is the beginning of a lifelong romance."
– Oscar Wilde

Our relationship with ourselves is the foundation of all our connections. It's a journey of honest engagement with our inner world. When we connect authentically with ourselves, we allow life energy to flow more freely, which we experience as love. This opens the door to deep personal growth and transformation and for our relationships with others to flourish from a place of genuine self-understanding and love.

Self-love is nothing to do with vanity or ego, instead it's about stepping out of the cage we've made for ourselves from years of conditioning and judgement. It's about extending the same kindness to ourselves that we'd offer a dear friend. By embracing our personal qualities – even those we might consider flaws – we create space for authentic connections with others.

Our inner dialogue shapes our reality, either constricting or amplifying the flow of life energy. As we realise we're not our thoughts, but the observer of often conflicting mental echoes, we can choose a more compassionate inner voice. This loving friend stays with us always, much as we become aspects of that inner voice for our children as they grow.

Attachment theory, developed by John Bowlby and Mary Ainsworth, offers valuable insights into this process. Our early relationships with caregivers deeply shape our self-concept and approach to personal growth. These formative bonds influence our capacity for connection throughout life, helping explain why we each connect differently.

Mindfulness and reflection serve as powerful tools for deepening our self-connection. They help us engage fully with our experiences, seeing ourselves more clearly. Through consistent practise, we uncover layers of inner wisdom, expanding our consciousness through lived experience.

Daniel Siegel's research in interpersonal neurobiology uncovers how self-reflection and mindfulness can physically reshape our brain. As we create a deeper relationship with ourselves through these practices, we're not merely shifting our thoughts – we're transforming the very architecture of our minds.

As we strengthen our self-bond, our ability to connect with others naturally grows. Self-understanding breeds empathy, while self-acceptance allows us to embrace others more fully. Consider how your relationship with yourself influences your other connections. How might deepening this self-connection help you engage more authentically with the world around you?

"The present moment is filled with joy and happiness. If you are attentive, you will see it." – Thich Nhat Hanh

Mindfulness and reflection are potent practices for deepening our connection with ourselves. Far from fleeting trends, they offer robust methods for maintaining a healthy inner world.

Mindfulness invites us to be fully present, without judgement. It quiets the mind's constant chatter, creating space for self-awareness to emerge. As we practise mindfulness, we allow life energy to flow more freely, untethered by past worries or future anxieties. This simple yet powerful shift can dramatically reduce stress and enhance our overall sense of wellbeing.

Stephen Porges' Polyvagal Theory provides a fascinating biological perspective on this process. It explains how mindfulness practices can help regulate our nervous system, directly influencing our capacity for connection. By engaging in mindful awareness, we can shift our physiological state to one that's more open to social engagement and empathy.

Practising mindfulness needn't be complicated. It can be as simple as focusing on your breath for a few minutes each day. Sit comfortably, close your eyes, and pay attention to the sensation of air moving in and out of your body. When your mind wanders – as it inevitably will – gently guide your focus back to your breath without judgement. This basic exercise can be expanded to mindful walking, eating, or even washing up. The key is to fully engage with whatever you're doing, using your senses to anchor you in the present moment.

Reflection, meanwhile, involves looking inward to make sense of our experiences. It might take the form of journaling, meditation, or simply setting aside time to think deeply about our lives. Through reflection, we can uncover patterns in our behaviour, gain insights into our motivations, and make choices that align with our true selves.

Journaling offers a particularly effective method of reflection. Set aside regular time to write freely about your thoughts, feelings, and experiences. Don't worry about grammar or structure – simply let your thoughts flow onto the page. You might reflect on challenging situations, moments of joy, or patterns you've noticed in your behaviour. Ask yourself probing questions like 'What did I learn from this experience?' or 'How did this situation make me feel, and why?' Over time, patterns and insights will likely emerge, offering a clearer understanding of yourself and your place in the world.

When we combine mindfulness and reflection, we create a potent recipe for self-discovery and growth. We begin to see ourselves more clearly, embracing both our strengths and our challenges. This self-understanding becomes the foundation for all our other relationships. By seeking inner peace, we create a solid base from which all our external connections can flourish.

Consider bringing these practices into your daily life. Experience how mindfulness can anchor you in the present moment, allowing you to engage more deeply with the here and now. Reflection offers a path to a richer understanding of yourself and your connection to the world around you. These practices aren't about striving for perfection, but about developing a gentler, more conscious relationship with yourself.

Human Relationships and Emotional Depth

"The meeting of two personalities is like the contact of two chemical substances: if there is any reaction, both are transformed." – Carl Jung

Human relationships are the heartbeat of our emotional existence, filling our lives with depth, meaning, and belonging. Whether we're seeking support in difficult times or companionship in our daily journey, these connections are the threads that weave the fabric of our emotional world.

Let's explore the particular qualities of different relationship types:

1. **Family Relationships**: Our earliest and often most influ
   bonds, family relationships establish the foundation for
   understanding of love, trust, and belonging. Developme
   psychologist Erik Erikson noted these connections shape the
   core of our social development. In *The Whole-Brain Child*,
   Daniel J. Siegel and Tina Payne Bryson offer practical strategies
   for nurturing children's developing minds, providing invaluable
   insights into family dynamics. These connections can be
   sources of strength and support, but also present distinct
   challenges as we navigate intricate dynamics and shared
   histories.

2. **Romantic Relationships**: These intimate partnerships often
   involve the deepest levels of emotional and physical closeness.
   John Gottman's research, presented in *The Seven Principles for
   Making Marriage Work*, offers evidence-based strategies for
   sustaining these bonds. For a more accessible approach, Sue
   Johnson's *Hold Me Tight* presents revolutionary techniques to
   help couples create stronger, more secure bonds. Both
   underscore the importance of friendship, mutual respect, and
   shared meaning in long-term romantic relationships.

3. **Friendships**: Robin Dunbar's research, detailed in *Friends*,
   highlights the evolutionary significance of friendships. These
   chosen companions provide emotional support, shared
   experiences, and often help to protect us from life's pressures.
   In *Friendship*, Lydia Denworth explores the science behind why
   friendship is critical to our health and happiness. Quality
   friendships correlate with improved mental health and
   longevity.

4. **Professional Relationships**: Often overlooked in discussions of
   emotional connection, workplace relationships significantly
   influence our wellbeing. As we dedicate a substantial portion of
   our lives to work, positive professional relationships can
   enhance job satisfaction, productivity, and overall life
   contentment. *The Power of Positive Leadership* by Jon Gordon
   offers practical insights on developing a positive work
   environment and building strong professional relationships.

The Social Brain Hypothesis, pioneered by Dunbar, suggests our brains evolved specifically to navigate these intricate social landscapes. His research proposes that our neocortex can maintain about 150 meaningful relationships across these categories – a concept known as Dunbar's Number.

At the neurobiological level, hormones like oxytocin and vasopressin play crucial roles in forming and maintaining our bonds across all relationship types. In *Attached*, Amir Levine and Rachel Heller explore how these neurochemical underpinnings shape our attachment styles and relationship patterns.

Trauma can seriously affect our ability to form and maintain healthy relationships of all kinds. Bessel van der Kolk's *The Body Keeps the Score* explores how trauma alters brain chemistry and structure, impacting areas linked to fear, emotion regulation, and social interaction.

Authenticity and vulnerability form the foundations of deep, meaningful connections in all relationship spheres. Brené Brown, in *Daring Greatly*, emphasises that embracing vulnerability builds trust and intimacy, creating space for open communication and emotional connection across all relationship types.

Active listening, as described in Marshall B. Rosenberg's *Nonviolent Communication*, is crucial for deepening all forms of relationships. This approach involves fully engaging with the other person, truly understanding their message, and responding thoughtfully.

"What children need most are the essentials that grandparents provide in abundance. They give unconditional love, kindness, patience, humor, comfort, lessons in life. And, most importantly, cookies." – Rudy Giuliani

As we experience each of these various relationship landscapes, we continually grow and evolve. Each connection offers a unique opportunity for self-discovery and mutual transformation. Indeed, three years ago, we experienced the joy of becoming grandparents and felt one of the most extraordinary bonds – a meeting of pure innocence with a lifetime of wisdom, wrapped in love.

This intergenerational connection is an striking example of life's most amazing human bonds. Grandparents, with their wealth of experience and unconditional love, offer a special form of support and understanding. They often have the time and patience to listen, to share stories, and to impart life lessons in a gentle, unhurried manner.

For children, grandparents can be a source of unconditional love and acceptance, free from the day-to-day pressures of parental responsibility. This relationship allows for a special kind of play and discovery, where the wisdom of age meets the wonder of youth.

In her book *The New Age of Ageing: How Society Needs to Change*, Caroline Lodge explores the changing role of older people in society, including the vital part grandparents play in family life. She highlights the invaluable insights and support that older generations can offer to their grandchildren and the wider community.

This special bond also benefits the older generation. Research has shown that strong relationships with grandchildren can enhance grandparents' cognitive function, reduce depression, and increase their sense of purpose and vitality.

The grandparent-grandchild relationship embodies many qualities we've explored: unconditional love, sharing of wisdom, joy of play, and deep emotional connection spanning generations. It strengthens family bonds and bridges past and future. Recognising and nurturing these special connections enriches individual lives and strengthens our communities.

Community Relationships

"Alone, we can do so little; together, we can do so much."
– Helen Keller

The strength of a community lies in its power to magnify individual agency. When we come together, the resonance of our combined efforts transforms simple acts into powerful forces for change.

A thriving community pulses with the collective energy of its members. It's a space where individual sparks of creativity and kindness ignite, fuelled by shared love and purpose, to create waves of positive transformation. This reveals the true power of community relationships.

At the heart of strong communities lies a potent symbol of transformation: picture a butterfly, representing each unique, beautiful and creative individual; a heart, symbolising the love that binds us and amplifies our creativity; and a tidal wave, illustrating the far-reaching impact of our combined energies. This triptych captures the journey from personal growth to collective change that defines flourishing communities.

Like a butterfly's delicate wings influencing weather patterns continents away, our personal growth creates ripples that touch lives far beyond our immediate circles. The heart, beating steadily, sets the rhythm of shared values and aspirations, synchronising our efforts into a coherent, living system of connection. And like a wave that cascades and gradually reshapes coastlines, our collective actions mould social landscapes, overcoming obstacles with persistent, fluid motion.

In Love Sheffield, we've witnessed this alchemy of connection transform our city. What begins as a single act of kindness or a moment of shared understanding often blossoms into community-wide movements of compassion and creativity. It's a daily reminder of the butterfly effect in action, where the gentle flutter of individual kindness can, through the amplifying power of our connected community, become a force that reshapes our world for the better.

As we try to simplify and clarify the complex interplay of community bonds, we'll uncover the elements that unite us – trust, diversity, shared purpose, and the creative potential of working together. We'll discover how holding spaces where each person's worth is recognised, where love guides our actions, and where individual efforts combine to create significant change, we create communities that go beyond mere survival to true flourishing.

The Love Sheffield Symbology

The Butterfly Effect: Celebrating Individual Uniqueness

"In diversity there is beauty and there is strength." – Maya Angelou

We are all human beings, our differences are not merely to be tolerated, but celebrated as a source of collective power. By embracing the full spectrum of human experience, we unlock a treasure trove of creativity and resilience that can transform our communities.

Each person in our community brings a unique blend of experiences, skills, and perspectives. Like a butterfly's beautiful wings, these individual qualities create a vivid mosaic of shared wisdom and creativity. When we honour this uniqueness, we unlock huge potential for community growth.

nal development plays a crucial role in this process. As
grow and evolve, they contribute new ideas and energies to the
y. This personal growth creates ripples that can cascade far
bey ur immediate circles, much like a butterfly's wingbeats influencing
weather patterns continents away.

Scott E. Page's research, presented in *The Difference*, offers compelling
evidence for the power of diversity in problem-solving and innovation. Page
demonstrates that diverse groups consistently outperform homogeneous
ones in tackling complex challenges. In our communities, this means that
embracing a wide range of viewpoints and experiences doesn't just make us
more inclusive – it makes us more effective and resilient.

The Heart of Community: Growing Love and Compassion

"Love and compassion are necessities, not luxuries. Without them, humanity cannot survive." – Dalai Lama

At the heart of any thriving community are the core elements of love
and compassion, this is the energy we feel when we are authentically
connected. Love and compassion are the heartbeat and expression of our
shared existence, setting the rhythm for all our interactions.

Shared values and aspirations act as this communal pulse,
synchronising our efforts into a coherent, living system of connection. When
we align around common principles – be it kindness, sustainability, or social
justice – we create a shared language that honours individual differences.

However, growing this heart of compassion requires vulnerability.
Brené Brown's research, detailed in *Daring Greatly*, shows how embracing
vulnerability builds trust and deepens relationships. In community terms,
this means creating spaces where people feel safe to be authentic, to share
their struggles, and to celebrate their joys.

Trust, built through these vulnerable exchanges, becomes the lifeblood
of our community. It allows for open dialogue, collaborative problem-solving,
and a deeper sense of belonging. When trust flourishes, our community
becomes a place of growth and transformation for all its members.

The Wave of Change: Amplifying Collective Impact

"The strength of the team is each individual member. The strength of each member is the team." – Phil Jackson

When we align our personal efforts with a shared purpose, we set in motion a wave of transformation that can reshape our entire community.

This wave of change begins with small actions – a kind word, a helping hand, a moment of understanding. But in a connected community, these individual acts don't exist in isolation. They cascade outward, inspiring others and gaining momentum. A single act of caring for our environment can spark a city-wide green initiative. A moment of intercultural understanding can blossom into a movement for social justice.

Robert D. Putnam, in his influential book *Bowling Alone*, warned of the decline in social capital – the connections between individuals – in American society. He observed how people were increasingly "bowling alone" rather than in leagues, symbolising a broader trend of disconnection. However, in Love Sheffield, we've seen a different story unfold. By consciously encouraging connections and shared purposes, we're reversing this trend, creating waves of positive change that strengthen our social fabric.

The power of these collective movements lies in their resilience and adaptability. Like ocean waves that gradually reshape coastlines, our united efforts can overcome seemingly insurmountable obstacles. We might face setbacks, but the persistent, fluid motion of a community working together can, over time, transform our social landscape in meaningful and powerful ways.

This adaptability is crucial in our rapidly changing world. As we face complex challenges – from climate change to social inequality – our ability to come together, learn, and evolve our approaches will determine our success. By developing this collective resilience, we create a community that doesn't just survive change, but harnesses it as a catalyst for positive transformation.

Community as Ecosystem: The Web of Connection

"The greatest delight which the fields and woods minister, is the suggestion of an occult relation between man and the vegetable. I am not alone and unacknowledged. They nod to me, and I to them." – Ralph Waldo Emerson

Just as every element in nature is interconnected, our human communities exist by the complex relationships between their members. These connections create a thriving ecosystem where everyone plays a vital role, contributing to the health and resilience of the whole.

In this human ecosystem, each person plays a vital role, much like different species in a forest. Some might be the towering trees, providing shelter and stability. Others could be the pollinators, spreading ideas and growing connections. Still others might be the decomposers, breaking down old structures to make way for new growth.

This ecological view helps us appreciate the importance of diversity and interdependence. Just as a forest relies on a variety of plant and animal species to maintain health and resilience, our communities grow stronger through a rich variety of perspectives, skills, and experiences.

Moreover, like the hidden fungal networks that connect trees in a forest, our social bonds form an intricate web of support and information exchange. These unseen links allow resources and knowledge to flow where they're needed most, ensuring the wellbeing of the entire community.

By recognising our communities as living, breathing ecosystems, we can work more effectively to create environments where every member can flourish and contribute to the whole.

The Roots of Trust: Building Foundations for Growth

"A community is like a ship; everyone ought to be prepared to take the helm." – Henrik Ibsen

A thriving community is built on shared responsibility and mutual trust, which form the foundation that supports and sustains communal life. Trust is like the root system of a tree, providing the stability and nourishment necessary for growth.

Peter Block, in his important work *Community*, emphasises that trust is built through authentic conversations and shared accountability. He argues that the key to creating a sense of belonging is to shift from a mindset of problems and deficits to one of possibility and gifts. This perspective aligns perfectly with our understanding of trust as a foundation for community growth.

We can think of trust in communities as existing on multiple levels:

1. **Interpersonal trust**: This is the foundation of one-to-one relationships. It's built through honest interactions, kept promises, and mutual respect.

2. **Social trust**: This represents our faith in the goodwill of others in our community. It allows us to engage with strangers, believing in their basic decency and shared values.

3. **Institutional trust**: This is our confidence in community structures and leadership. It enables us to participate in civic life and contribute to collective decision-making.

When we develop trust at all these levels, we create an environment where relationships can flourish and innovation can take root. People feel safe to share ideas, take risks, and work together towards common goals.

However, trust is not a given – it must be earned and maintained. Like tending a garden, building trust requires consistent effort, patience, and care. But the rewards are immense: a community bound by trust is resilient in the face of challenges and quick to seize opportunities for growth.

Community Alchemy: Transforming Individual Contributions

"The next Buddha may take the form of a community, a community practicing understanding and loving kindness, a community practicing mindful living. This may be the most important thing we can do for the survival of the Earth."
– Thich Nhat Hanh

The true power of a community lies in its ability to transform the contributions of its members into something greater than the sum of its parts. This process, like alchemy, allows individual efforts to merge and evolve into collective wisdom and impactful action.

In the crucible of community, individual experiences and ideas undergo a remarkable change. Through the heat of dialogue, the pressure of shared challenges, and the catalyst of collective purpose, these individual elements transmute into something greater – a communal wisdom and capability that far exceeds the sum of its parts.

This alchemy can be seen in action during community problem-solving sessions, where diverse perspectives combine to create innovative solutions. It's evident in collaborative art projects, where individual creative sparks fuse into breathtaking collective expressions. It emerges in grassroots movements, where personal passions coalesce into powerful forces for social change.

The beauty of this process is that it enhances rather than diminishes individual contributions. Each person's personal gifts are recognised and valued, but they're also magnified through their interaction with others. In this way, community alchemy doesn't just solve problems or create beauty – it also helps individuals discover new dimensions of their own potential.

By creating environments that support this alchemical process, we can unlock the true magic of connected communities – their power to transform not only circumstances but also the very individuals who make them up.

Holding Inclusive Spaces: Embracing Diversity and Building Belonging

"Diversity is being invited to the party; inclusion is being asked to dance." – Verna Myers

True inclusivity goes beyond simply acknowledging diversity; it's about actively creating spaces where everyone feels valued, heard, and able to contribute fully. This commitment to inclusion is what transforms diverse communities into thriving, interconnected networks of belonging.

Cultural humility plays a crucial role in this process. Unlike cultural competence, which suggests an endpoint of knowledge, cultural humility recognises that understanding others is an ongoing journey. It involves continual self-reflection, acknowledging our own biases, and remaining open to learning from others' experiences.

Creating inclusive spaces requires active effort. It means amplifying marginalised voices, challenging our assumptions, and redesigning our systems and practices to accommodate diverse needs. This might involve rethinking how we conduct meetings, reimagining our public spaces, or reevaluating our community decision-making processes.

In Love Sheffield, we've seen the power of inclusive practices in action. When we create environments where all voices are valued, we tap into a source of creativity and innovation. Problems are solved more effectively, relationships deepen, and our community becomes more resilient.

The Cascade Effect: Small Acts, Massive Impact

"The smallest act of kindness is worth more than the grandest intention." – Oscar Wilde

It's often the small, everyday actions that truly make a difference. These seemingly minor acts of kindness have the potential to set off a cascade of positive effects, ultimately transforming entire communities.

This cascade flows through our social networks in remarkable ways. Researchers James Fowler and Nicholas Christakis have shown that positive actions can influence not only the immediate recipient but also their friends, and even friends of friends. A single act of kindness can inspire others to pay it forward, triggering a chain reaction of goodwill.

We've witnessed this in our community initiatives. A neighbour helping with a garden sparks a street-wide beautification project. A small gesture of support to a struggling family leads to the creation of a community support network. These are not just feel-good stories; they illustrate how small actions can address complex social issues from the ground up.

By recognising the power of these small acts, we empower every community member to be an agent of positive change. It's a reminder that we don't need to wait for grand solutions or top-down initiatives. The power to transform our community lies in our everyday choices and interactions.

Conclusion: The Love Sheffield Vision

The most basic and powerful way to connect to another person is to listen. Just listen. – Rachel Naomi Remen

As we reflect on community relationships, let's return to the symbology that encapsulates the Love Sheffield vision: the butterfly, the heart, and the wave.

The butterfly reminds us of the unique beauty and potential within each individual. Just as a butterfly's delicate wings can influence weather patterns continents away, our personal growth and actions can create ripples that cascade, touching lives far beyond our immediate circles.

The heart symbolises the love and compassion that bind us together. It's the pulse of our community, setting the rhythm of our shared values and aspirations. This heartbeat synchronises our efforts, creating a coherent, living system of connection which resonates and amplifies our creative potential.

The wave illustrates the far-reaching impact of our combined energies. Like a wave that gradually reshapes coastlines, our collective actions mould our social landscape, overcoming obstacles with persistent, fluid motion.

Together, these symbols capture the essence of our vision: a community where every individual is valued, where love is the guiding and amplifying force, and where our combined efforts create waves of positive transformation.

By embracing our vision of community - where every individual is valued, love guides and amplifies, and combined efforts create waves of transformation - we nurture communities that truly thrive. We create resilient, creative, and compassionate spaces equipped to weather challenges and seize growth opportunities. Connection becomes the lifeblood of our community, with every interaction bringing us closer to a more vibrant, connected reality.

Relationships with Nature and the Physical World

"In every walk with nature one receives far more than he seeks."
– John Muir

Ever since that day I was shocked by the destruction of our street trees, I've grown to understand more and more, the fundamental need we have for connection to nature. It really is a cornerstone of our wellbeing. This connection shapes our mental, emotional, and physical health massively, intertwining our existence with the rhythms of the earth.

The Biophilia Hypothesis, proposed by Edward O. Wilson, suggests that humans possess an innate tendency to seek connections with nature and other forms of life. This concept, rooted in evolutionary psychology, frames our need for natural connections as an adaptive trait crucial to our species' survival and flourishing.

Ecopsychology reveals the intimate link between our mental health and the health of our environment. Time spent in nature is far more than scenic appreciation; it's a healing dialogue with the world around us. Practices like forest bathing, gardening, and wilderness retreats help us reconnect with ourselves and the broader ecosystem we inhabit.

These natural connections can markedly reduce stress, anxiety, and depression while enhancing our mood and cognitive function. Nature soothes our overstimulated minds, allowing life energy to flow freely. Our inner selves engage more authentically with reality through our senses and physiology, creating a multisensory, embodied experience that deeply reconnects us with ourselves and the world.

Environmental stewardship deepens this connection. When we recycle, plant trees, choose locally sourced whole foods, or advocate for environmental policies, we strengthen our sense of purpose and belonging. These actions reinforce our collective responsibility towards future generations and strengthen our bond with the entire ecosystem.

Bessel van der Kolk's work in The Body Keeps the Score illuminates nature's healing power for trauma and stress. Natural settings offer safe spaces for processing emotions and experiences, providing a sense of calm and stability. For trauma survivors, activities like walking in nature, interacting with animals, and gardening can help re-establish a sense of safety and grounding.

Our relationship with nature is reciprocal. As we care for the environment, we care for ourselves. This allows a deeper sense of interconnectedness and responsibility, reminding us that we are not separate from nature, but an integral part of it.

"The things you own end up owning you." – Chuck Palahniuk

Our connections with spaces and objects are equally fundamental to our emotional wellbeing, shaping our mood, comfort, and sense of identity in often overlooked ways.

Evolutionary psychology offers insights into why we form attachments to places and things. These connections likely served our ancestors well, helping them remember safe havens, productive hunting grounds, and useful tools. Today, this built-in tendency shows in our emotional bonds with our surroundings.

We naturally give personal spaces and objects emotional significance, linking them to our internal map of reality. They become tokens of past experiences and associated emotional states, deeply influencing our subsequent feelings. Our environments, filled with personally significant items, contribute to our sense of identity and comfort. These emotional mappings provide stability and security, playing a crucial role in our overall wellbeing.

While many of our emotional connections with spaces and objects are positive, it's important to recognise that negative relationships are equally possible. These might show as clutter that overwhelms us, spaces that evoke anxiety, or objects that trigger painful memories. These negative relationships can significantly impact our emotional wellbeing, often in subtle ways we might not immediately recognise.

We can thoughtfully curate and manage our environment to create constructive, empowering and self-affirming circumstances for connection. This process is a deeply personal and creative act of shaping our environment, by carefully considering how each space and object in our lives affects us. Does it support our goals and values? Does it allow life energy to flow freely? Does it create a sense of peace and possibility?

"The space in which we live should be for the person we are becoming now, not for the person we were in the past."
– Marie Kondo

Configuring our environments to enhance emotional wellbeing involves a thoughtful process of arrangement and personalisation. When we organise our spaces with intention, we can transform a house into a home, or an office into a sanctuary of productivity and calm.

Including elements of nature can significantly boost our connection to the world around us. Plants, natural light, and natural materials can serve as powerful reminders of the broader ecosystem. Even small interactions with nature can improve our mood and overall sense of wellbeing. Scents and sounds can also be subtly yet powerfully evocative.

Personal items that bring back positive memories can create a space that feels welcoming and familiar. Photographs, souvenirs, and cherished objects are physical reminders of our experiences and relationships. By thoughtfully displaying these items, we create an environment that continually reinforces our sense of identity and belonging.

Designing spaces that promote relaxation and mindfulness can be particularly powerful. This might involve creating a quiet nook for reading or meditation, using soothing colours, or arranging furniture to encourage conversation and connection. These intentional choices can help reduce cognitive noise and create circumstances that support deeper, more meaningful interactions.

By paying close attention to how we interact with our spaces and the objects within them, we can create surroundings that not only reflect who we are but also who we aspire to become, authentically supporting our journey of growth and connection.

Relationships with Food and Drink

"One cannot think well, love well, sleep well, if one has not dined well." – Virginia Woolf

Our relationship with food and drink is one of our earliest and most formative connections. It begins with our first moments of life, intimately linking us to our mother and our sense of safety and nurture. This primal bond shapes our emotional landscape, creating lasting associations between sustenance, comfort, and love.

The act of eating and drinking engages all our senses in a rich symphony of experience. The visual appeal of a well-presented dish, the aroma that triggers anticipation, the texture we feel, the complex dance of flavours, and even the associated sounds all contribute to our experience. These sensory cues are integral to our enjoyment and memory of food and drink, often bringing powerful emotions and recollections.

The family home, often centred around the kitchen or dining table, becomes our first culinary universe. The smells, tastes, sounds, and rituals associated with meals give us a great sense of belonging and security. A favourite dish or a special drink becomes a powerful reminder of previous emotional peaks in our lives, perhaps evoking the safety and warmth of home, or the exciting times of our young adult years.

Interpersonal neurobiology, a field pioneered by Daniel Siegel, sheds light on how shared meals can strengthen neural pathways associated with connection. When we eat together, our brains engage in a complex dance of social interaction, sensory processing, and emotion regulation. This shared experience can enhance our sense of bonding and belonging, reinforcing social connections at a neurological level.

As we grow, food and drink continue to be powerful relationships which bring social, cultural, and religious meaning. Family recipes and traditional beverages passed down through generations carry heritage, identity, and often, spiritual significance. Many religions have specific dietary laws, fasting periods, or sacred foods and drinks that play a central role in worship and community life. These traditions often extend beyond the spiritual realm, shaping cultural identities and social bonds.

Socially, food and drink bring people together. The act of sharing a meal or raising a toast is a universal language of connection and care. From intimate family dinners to large community feasts, these shared experiences allow for bonding and understanding. The simple act of breaking bread together can bridge divides and create lasting relationships.

However, in our fast-paced world, we often lose touch with the mindful, sensory experience of eating and drinking. Fast food, eaten on the go without attention or joy, can lead to poor nutrition and a loss of the social aspects of dining. Similarly, when drinking becomes a coping mechanism rather than a social pleasure, it can lead to dependency and health issues.

Disconnection can also show in our relationship with the source of our food and drink. When we're unaware of where our sustenance comes from or how it's produced, we lose an important link to our environment and community. This can lead to choices that are damaging to our health and the health of our planet.

Food and drink offer a canvas for creativity. Preparing meals and beverages are art forms that allow us to express ourselves and innovate. Whether we're experimenting with new flavour combinations or putting a personal twist on a traditional recipe, we're engaging in a creative process that connects us deeply to what we consume.

Our food and drink choices also connect us to broader environmental and ethical concerns. Choosing locally sourced, sustainably produced items creates a link to our local ecosystem and the people who look after it. This mindful approach can deepen our sense of place and our commitment to environmental care.

Our connection to food and drink reflects our connection to life itself. It engages our senses, links us to our earliest experiences, connects us to our culture, sparks creativity, and reminds us of our place in nature. A mindful approach to eating and drinking can enhance our overall sense of connection and wellbeing. Consider how food and drink feature in your connections with others, cultural traditions, and the world around you. How might a more mindful approach enhance your sense of connection?

Relationships with Technology

"We become what we behold. We shape our tools, and thereafter our tools shape us." – Marshall McLuhan

Technology, particularly digital communication, has fundamentally transformed how we connect with one another. It offers both unprecedented opportunities and distinct challenges, dramatically reshaping the landscape of human interaction.

Digital tools allow us to maintain relationships across vast distances and connect with like-minded individuals through instant communication. However, these interactions can often feel superficial, lacking the depth of emotional engagement we experience in face-to-face encounters.

Social Exchange Theory, proposed by George Homans, offers an interesting perspective on how people evaluate their digital relationships. This theory views social behaviour as an exchange of goods, both material and non-material. In the context of digital connections, people may weigh the benefits of convenience and broad reach against the costs of reduced intimacy and potential misunderstandings.

Social media platforms have dramatically altered our social landscape. While they provide spaces for sharing and connecting, they often present curated, idealised projections of people's lives. This can lead to unrealistic comparisons, feelings of inadequacy, and a distorted sense of reality. The constant stream of information and the pressure to maintain an online presence can contribute to anxiety and a sense of disconnection from our authentic selves.

Moreover, the algorithms driving these platforms are designed to keep us engaged, often at the expense of meaningful interaction. They can create echo chambers that reinforce existing views and limit exposure to diverse perspectives, potentially deepening societal divides rather than bridging them.

The key lies in how we approach and use these digital tools. When used mindfully, technology can enhance our real-world connections, allowing us to share experiences, ideas, and support in ways previously impossible. However, excessive screen time can lead to digital fatigue and diminish the quality of our in-person interactions.

Developing healthy digital habits is essential for balancing online and offline relationships. This might involve setting boundaries for screen time, prioritising face-to-face interactions, and being mindful of the quality of our digital communications. James Clear's *Atomic Habits* offers valuable insights into how small, consistent changes can lead to significant outcomes. We can apply this principle to our digital behaviours, gradually replacing habits that disconnect us with ones that enhance our relationships.

> *"The question of whether a computer can think is no more interesting than the question of whether a submarine can swim."*
> *– Edsger W. Dijkstra*

The rise of AI companions and virtual assistants represents a significant shift in human-technology interaction. These AI personas simulate emotional support, companionship, and therapeutic interventions through sophisticated algorithms that mimic human-like conversations. For individuals experiencing loneliness or isolation, AI companions can offer non-judgmental and always-available comfort. However, the psychological risks and long-term impacts of these relationships are unknown, raising questions about the quality of emotional support provided by non-human entities.

The Mirror Neuron System, a neurological finding that helps explain empathy and our ability to understand others' actions and emotions, might offer insights into why we form emotional connections with AI, even when we know they're not human. This system could provide a biological basis for our capacity to connect deeply with artificial entities, as our brains respond to their simulated emotions and behaviours in ways similar to human interactions.

Forming relationships with AI personas presents several ethical considerations. Dependency on AI over human relationships can lead to increased social isolation, while privacy concerns arise from the need for AI companions to access personal data. Ensuring transparency is crucial so that users are fully aware they are interacting with AI, not humans, to prevent deception and maintain informed consent.

As AI technology advances, its integration into social lives is expected to become more pervasive. Future AI systems may become more adept at understanding and responding to human emotions, creating sophisticated interactions. Michio Kaku, in *The Future of Humanity*, speculates that AI could serve as companions, advisors, and even partners, transforming how we form and maintain relationships.

This integration offers new opportunities for connection but also challenges in distinguishing between human and artificial interactions. The future of AI in relationships will hinge on balancing technological innovation with ethical considerations and human values. As we navigate this evolving landscape, it's crucial to approach our relationship with technology mindfully, harnessing its potential to enhance our connections while preserving the irreplaceable value of human-to-human interaction.

Relationships with Belief, Culture and Ideology

"The eye sees only what the mind is prepared to comprehend."
– Robertson Davies

Our beliefs, deeply intertwined with our cultural, spiritual, and ideological backgrounds, shape our identities and relationships with others in powerful ways. They form the lens through which we view the world and interpret our experiences.

Social Identity Theory, developed by Henri Tajfel and John Turner, offers valuable insights into how shared beliefs create strong group bonds. This theory explores how our sense of self is intrinsically linked to our group memberships. When we share beliefs with others, it reinforces our social identity, creating a sense of belonging and shared purpose. This can lead to deep, meaningful relationships within groups, but also potentially to intergroup conflict when beliefs differ.

"Culture is the widening of the mind and of the spirit."
– Jawaharlal Nehru

Cultural backgrounds significantly influence our beliefs and sense of identity. Cultural traditions, rituals, and shared histories provide a foundation for communal bonds, reinforcing our sense of belonging and continuity. These cultural elements create shared experiences and mutual understanding, building strong community ties and a cohesive sense of identity.

"The spiritual life does not remove us from the world but leads us deeper into it." – Henri J.M. Nouwen

Spirituality and religion play fundamental roles in forming a sense of purpose and community. These beliefs often inspire deep connections by providing shared values, moral frameworks, and communal practices that unite individuals and promote collective wellbeing. Participation in religious or spiritual practices can enhance emotional resilience and provide a supportive network, helping individuals navigate life's challenges with a sense of shared purpose.

"The highest activity a human being can attain is learning for understanding, because to understand is to be free."
– Baruch Spinoza

Shared beliefs and values can form a strong foundation for building sympathetic relationships. When individuals align ideologically, it encourages mutual understanding and respect, strengthening relationships across personal, professional, and community contexts. Shared ideologies provide common ground for conversations and collective actions, reinforcing bonds.

However, while ideological alignment can enhance relationships, it can also create echo chambers, stifling growth and understanding if dissenting views are not tolerated. Critical thinking and open-mindedness are vital for maintaining healthy ideological relationships. Engaging in critical thinking involves analysing and evaluating beliefs with an open and questioning mindset, encouraging dialogue and understanding even amidst ideological differences.

Open-mindedness allows individuals to consider alternative perspectives, supporting inclusive and dynamic interactions. Prioritising these qualities makes relationships more resilient and adaptable, enabling growth and mutual respect despite differing beliefs.

In A *New Earth*, Eckhart Tolle discusses the importance of overcoming ego and ideological rigidity to create harmonious relationships. Tolle explains that the ego often clings to rigid ideologies for identity and security, leading to conflict and division. By moving beyond ego-driven stances, individuals can adopt a more flexible and open approach to beliefs, allowing for greater empathy and understanding. This shift enables genuine connection, highlighting the transformative power of letting go of rigid ideologies to inspire more meaningful relationships.

As we navigate our beliefs, cultural backgrounds, and ideological perspectives, we're challenged to strike a balance between honouring our identities and remaining open to diverse viewpoints. This delicate equilibrium allows us to form meaningful relationships based on shared beliefs while also encouraging growth, understanding, and empathy across different belief systems. In doing so, we create a richer, more interconnected world where diversity of thought enhances rather than divides our collective human experience.

Relationships with Art and Creativity

"Every child is an artist. The problem is how to remain an artist once we grow up." – Pablo Picasso

In a world where recognition and reward is so often forced into the commercial or capitalist frame, our relationship with art and creativity are far more important to our human experience. Creation is a fundamental dialogue between our inner selves and reality, offering those who experience our work a chance to discover hidden realms within themselves through reflection and connection.

The Mirror Neuron System, which helps explain our capacity for empathy, also illuminates how art can evoke deep connections. When we observe art or creative expressions, these neurons fire in patterns similar to those of the creator, allowing us to experience a form of emotional resonance. This neurological response underpins art's power to inspire empathy and connection across diverse human experiences.

When we create, we're not merely producing commodities, but engaging in a fundamental dialogue with our deepest unconscious, our soul, and the universe that surrounds us. This view of creativity encompasses all forms of human expression and innovation, from community initiatives to spontaneous acts of kindness. Each creative act becomes an invitation for others to explore their own inner landscapes and forge deeper connections with the world around them.

The emergence of generative AI in art offers an opportunity to reflect on what makes human creativity particularly valuable. It's not about technical perfection or market value, but about our capacity to express and evoke genuine emotion, to share lived experiences, and to connect on a deeply human level.

"Art enables us to find ourselves and lose ourselves at the same time." – Thomas Merton

Creative activities offer a powerful channel for expressing thoughts and emotions that may be difficult to articulate through words alone. This process not only helps us explore and communicate complex feelings but also invites others to connect with these shared human experiences.

"Creativity is contagious. Pass it on." – Albert Einstein

Creativity plays a vital role in strengthening community bonds. Collaborative projects, public art, and shared creative experiences allow a sense of belonging and collective purpose to emerge. These initiatives demonstrate how creativity can unite people around shared goals and values.

"The creative adult is the child who survived." – Ursula K. Le Guin

Engaging in creative processes, whether through traditional art forms or innovative problem-solving, can significantly enhance mental and emotional wellbeing. It offers a means to reduce stress, improve mood, and gain new perspectives on personal challenges.

"Creativity is thinking up new things. Innovation is doing new things." – Theodore Levitt

Creativity is a powerful catalyst for innovation and social transformation. It encourages flexible thinking, resilience, and the ability to envision new possibilities. Through creative expression, individuals and communities can challenge norms, inspire action, and shape the future of society.

"Art is not a mirror held up to reality, but a hammer with which to shape it." – Bertolt Brecht

Art and creativity serve as both a mirror and a shaping force for our collective reality. They provide platforms for commentary, critique, and reimagining of social norms. By engaging creatively with the world around us, we participate in an ongoing dialogue about our shared human experience and our potential futures.

This expanded view of creativity invites us to see the artistic potential in all aspects of life, from community initiatives to personal interactions. It encourages us to value these expressions for their ability to open connection, inspire reflection, and touch the deepest parts of our shared humanity.

By recognising the importance of our relationship with art and creativity beyond commercial frames, we open ourselves to a richer, more connected human experience. This approach invites us to see and value creative potential in all aspects of life. Consider how embracing this view of creativity could transform our relationships with art, each other, and the world around us.

Global Relationships

"The world is becoming a global village, and we are all neighbors. Our challenge is to learn to live together in peace." – Kofi Annan

As our world becomes increasingly interconnected, the challenge lies in forging genuine bonds that transcend borders and cultures. In this rapidly evolving global village, it's not enough to simply see each other across the globe; we must actively build connections that bridge divides and foster understanding. In this section, we'll look into the complexities of global relationships, exploring how to unite people across differences and create a world where peace and harmony can thrive.

Cultural Exchange and Understanding:

"The real voyage of discovery consists not in seeking new landscapes, but in having new eyes." – Marcel Proust

Cultural exchange programmes, like the Fulbright Program, have shown how exposure to diverse cultures enhances our worldview and inspires global connections. Research by Tadmor et al. (2012) in the Journal of Personality and Social Psychology demonstrates that multicultural experiences enhance creativity and reduce intergroup bias.

Digital Connections Across Borders:

"The Internet is becoming the town square for the global village of tomorrow." – Bill Gates

Technology enables unprecedented global connectivity. However, as Sherry Turkle discusses in *Alone Together* we must balance online and offline interactions to maintain authentic connections. The challenge lies in harnessing digital tools to enhance, rather than replace, meaningful global relationships.

Global Citizenship and Shared Responsibility:

"We have to acknowledge that we are all part of a web of life around the world." – Jane Goodall

The concept of global citizenship, explored by Kwame Anthony Appiah in *Cosmopolitanism* emphasises our shared responsibilities in addressing global challenges. Climate change and pandemics have highlighted our interdependence, demonstrating how individual actions can have global impacts.

Economic Interdependence and Fair Trade:

"Every time you spend money, you're casting a vote for the kind of world you want." – Anna Lappé

Global trade connects us in complex ways. Fair trade initiatives, as discussed by Joseph Stiglitz in *Fair Trade for All* show how consumer choices can enable positive global relationships and economic justice.

Diplomacy and International Relations:

"Peace cannot be kept by force; it can only be achieved by understanding." – Albert Einstein

While official diplomacy remains crucial, people-to-people diplomacy, or "citizen diplomacy" plays an increasingly important role. Initiatives like Sister Cities International demonstrate how grassroots connections can complement and enhance official international relations.

Global Arts and Creative Expression:

"Art is the lie that enables us to realize the truth." – Pablo Picasso

Art transcends national boundaries, creating connection through shared human experiences. The World Culture Festival and global artistic movements like Fluxus showcase how creativity can unite people across cultures.

Environmental Stewardship as a Global Connection:

"We are the first generation to feel the effect of climate change and the last generation who can do something about it."
— Barack Obama

Care for the environment connects us globally. The Paris Agreement and initiatives like Earth Day Network demonstrate how individual and collective actions contribute to global environmental efforts.

Education and Global Understanding:

"The soul is healed by being with children." – Fyodor Dostoevsky

Global education initiatives, such as UNESCO's Global Citizenship Education programme, create international connections. Research by Deardorff (2006) in the Journal of Studies in International Education highlights how intercultural competence, developed through such programmes, enhances global understanding.

Challenges and Opportunities in Global Relationships:

"Our ability to reach unity in diversity will be the beauty and the test of our civilization." – Mahatma Gandhi

Navigating cultural differences and political divides remains a challenge in global connections. However, as Yuval Noah Harari argues in *21 Lessons for the 21st Century* our shared challenges also present opportunities for unprecedented global cooperation.

As we grow our global connections, we contribute to a more interconnected and empathetic world. By engaging in cultural exchange, leveraging technology responsibly, embracing global citizenship, and inspiring creativity and education across borders, we can build stronger, more resilient global relationships.

In Love Sheffield, we've seen how local actions can create cascades of global impact. Our community initiatives, when shared globally, inspire similar projects worldwide, demonstrating the power of local action in a global context. As we move forward, let's recognise that each of us has the power to contribute to our global movement of connection, one relationship at a time.

Practical Applications and Exercises

"The art of connection lies not in grand gestures, but in the quiet dedication to daily practice." – Octavia Butler

Developing relationships requires consistent effort, and adopting daily practices can significantly enhance connection and intimacy.

Here are some evidence-based exercises to strengthen our relationships:

1. **Gratitude Journaling**: Emmons and McCullough's (2003) research in the Journal of Personality and Social Psychology demonstrates that gratitude journaling enhances well-being and relationships. Spend a few minutes each day writing down three things you appreciate about your relationships. This practice activates the brain's reward system, reinforcing positive associations with your connections.

2. **Active Listening Exercise**: Based on Carl Rogers' person-centered approach, try the "three-minute listening exercise." One person speaks for three minutes while the other listens without interrupting, then summarises what was heard. This exercise enhances empathy and understanding, key components of strong relationships according to attachment theory (Bowlby, 1969).

3. **"I" Statements**: Rooted in Thomas Gordon's Parent Effectiveness Training, practicing "I" statements allows for constructive expression of feelings and needs. For example, say "I feel upset when..." instead of "You make me upset." This approach, supported by conflict resolution research (Hargie, 2011), promotes respectful dialogue and reduces defensiveness.

4. **Shared Novel Experiences**: Aron et al.'s (2000) self-expansion model suggests that engaging in new activities together enhances relationship satisfaction. Plan regular novel experiences with your partner or friends to create shared memories and strengthen bonds.

5. **Mindfulness Practice**: Jon Kabat-Zinn's Mindfulness-Based Stress Reduction (MBSR) techniques can be applied to relationships. Before important conversations, take a few moments to practise mindfulness. This can improve presence and emotional regulation, enhancing the quality of your interactions.

6. **Emotional Triad Technique**: Introduced in Cloe Madanes and Anthony Robbins' *Relationship Breakthrough* this technique involves altering patterns of focus, language, and physiology to shift emotional states. By consciously changing these elements, you can improve your emotional state and, consequently, your interactions.

7. **Empathy Mapping**: Originating from design thinking, create an empathy map for someone close to you. Write down what they might be thinking, feeling, saying, and doing in a particular situation. This exercise, grounded in perspective-taking theories (Galinsky et al., 2008), deepens understanding and emotional connection.

8. **Love Languages Exercise**: Based on Gary Chapman's *The Five Love Languages* identify your primary love language and that of your partner or close friends. Tailor your expressions of affection to match their preferred language. This personalised approach enhances feelings of being understood and valued.

9. **Relationship Check-ins**: Regular check-ins, supported by John Gottman's research on successful relationships, keep communication lines open. Schedule weekly or monthly conversations to discuss your relationship, addressing concerns and celebrating successes.

10. **Loving-Kindness Meditation**: This Buddhist practice, studied by Fredrickson et al. (2008), involves directing well-wishes towards yourself and others. Regular practise can increase feelings of social connection and positivity towards others.

By adding these practices into our daily lives, we can build deeper, more meaningful connections. With time, they become more natural. As we engage in these exercises, we're not simply improving individual relationships – we're shaping a more connected and empathetic approach to all our interactions.

Conclusion: The Living Reef of Relationships

"Coral reefs are the nursery of the ocean, and if you kill the coral reefs, you'll kill everything else." – Dr . Sylvia Earle

Our exploration of relationships has revealed a world as vibrant and complex as a coral reef. Each connection we form, like a coral polyp, may seem small on its own, but together they create structures of astounding beauty and resilience.

We began by looking inward, recognising that our relationship with ourselves forms the foundation of our personal reef. This continual inner work allows us to create a strong base from which our other relationships can flourish.

As we widened our view, we saw how our bonds with family, friends, and partners form the core of our social ecosystem. These relationships, with all their varieties and challenges, are where we learn the delicate balance of give and take. Like the diverse species inhabiting a reef, each relationship plays its influential role in our lives, contributing to our growth and wellbeing.

Our journey then took us into the realm of community, where we discovered the amplifying power of collective connection. Here, we saw how our individual actions can create waves of change, influencing the broader ecosystem of our society. In community, we find the power to transform our shared world.

Perhaps most strikingly, we uncovered the vast scope of what 'relationship' truly means. Our connections extend beyond people to encompass nature, ideas, and even our relationship with change itself. Like a coral reef influencing ocean currents and global climate, our web of relationships shapes realities far beyond our immediate perception.

As we reflect on these insights, we're reminded that relationships, like living reefs, require care and attention. They can be vulnerable to life's storms, but with nurturing, they demonstrate remarkable resilience and capacity for renewal.

Looking ahead, we're invited to approach our relationships with renewed awareness. Every interaction holds the potential for meaningful connection, for adding new life to our personal reef. By staying open, curious, and compassionate, we contribute to a world that's more interconnected and understanding.

As we close this chapter, let's carry with us the understanding that we're all part of this grand, living structure of relationship. In our daily lives, communities, and world, we have the opportunity to nurture these connections, creating a more vibrant and resilient future for all. Every interaction holds the potential for meaningful connection, for adding new life to our personal reef. By staying open, curious, and compassionate, we actively shape the vast ecosystem of our shared reality.

5. Level 3 – Influence

"You don't need a title to be a leader." – Mark Sanborn

You don't need a title to be a leader because true influence comes from within. It's the quiet power of authentic connection that tilts the floor, guiding others naturally towards positive change. In this chapter, you'll discover how to harness this subtle yet powerful influence to become a beacon of inspiration and transformation in your community.

The Nature of Influence

"True influence doesn't push or pull; it gently tilts the floor, allowing others to move naturally towards positive change."
– Brian Mosley

Influence, at its core is a quiet, natural force that emerges from genuine connections. It's not a skill to master, but a natural outcome of how we relate to ourselves, to others and the world around us.

In Love Sheffield, we've experienced influence work like a gentle current in a river, shaping our community far more effectively than any top-down directive ever could. You can harness this power in your own life, guiding your relationships and initiatives with a gentle hand, allowing natural, positive change to unfold.

This quiet power often emerges in the simplest of ways: an inspiring idea shared with passion and humility, or a consistent example of kindness that opens hearts. These subtle forces, born from authentic connection, can transform individuals and communities alike.

True influence thrives on trust and mutual respect. When we value others as equals, appreciating their wisdom and experiences, we create a space where ideas flow freely and collective wisdom emerges. It's akin to levelling the ground, replacing rigid structures with an open field of collaborative exploration.

Interestingly, our most powerful influence often stems from simply being ourselves – open about our challenges and eager to grow. By sharing our vulnerabilities, we implicitly invite others to do the same. This honesty allows deeper connections and creates an environment ripe for genuine change.

Deep listening is central to this process. When we truly hear others, beyond waiting for our turn to speak, we gain insights that enrich our understanding. This receptive stance allows us to respond more effectively to the needs and aspirations of our community. It's as if by opening our ears, we create channels for influence to flow both ways.

As we deepen our connections and engage more fully with our passions and communities, leadership naturally emerges. We don't set out to lead; we simply respond authentically to what we perceive through our strengthened bonds. This is how influence transforms into leadership – not through force or decree, but by embodying shared values and rallying others around a common purpose. The simple question, "how can I help?" is incredibly powerful to have in mind at all times.

Seth Godin explores this concept in his book *Tribes*, noting how humans naturally form groups connected by shared ideas and values. Within these groups, leaders emerge organically, their influence amplified by the network effect of the community.

This naturally emerging influence, however, comes with responsibility. Ethical influence uplifts and empowers rather than controls or deceives. It respects the autonomy of others while creating conditions for positive change to flourish. By approaching influence with authenticity and integrity, we create environments of trust and mutual respect, where our actions contribute to the greater good and strengthen community bonds.

Ultimately, influence is about creating an environment where positive change occurs naturally. It's not about 'herding cats', but about 'tilting the floor' – creating conditions where movement in a positive direction happens of its own accord. By deepening our connections and living our values authentically, we inadvertently become beacons that others naturally want to follow.

As we explore influence further, we'll discover how deepening our connections leads us to become agents of positive change. We'll see how being true to ourselves and our values can 'tilt the floor' in ways that inspire and uplift those around us. Through our own journey of connection, we become guiding lights for others, gently nudging our shared reality towards greater understanding, compassion, and collective growth.

Personal Agency and Influence

"The most common way people give up their power is by thinking they don't have any." – Alice Walker

At the heart of our ability to influence lies a simple truth: we each possess the power to shape our reality and affect those around us. This power, which we call personal agency, is not granted to us by external forces, but is an intrinsic part of our being that we must recognise and exercise. When we embrace this agency fully, we find that every choice, every interaction becomes an opportunity to create a cascade of positive change.

In Love Sheffield, we've witnessed time and again how individuals who embrace their personal agency become catalysts for positive change. It's not about grand gestures or heroic acts, but about recognising that each choice we make, each interaction we have, carries the potential to create a positive difference in the world.

Daniel Pink, in his book *Drive*, argues that autonomy – the urge to direct our own lives – is one of the key motivators of human behaviour. He writes, "Control leads to compliance; autonomy leads to engagement." When we truly internalise this insight, we begin to see ourselves not as passive recipients of circumstances, but as active co-creators of our environment.

Realising our sense of agency empowers us to influence in several key ways:

1. **It encourages authenticity**: When we recognise our power to act, we're more likely to express our true selves, which as we've seen, is a powerful form of influence.

2. **It encourages initiative**: Understanding our agency prompts us to take action rather than waiting for others to solve problems or initiate change.

3. **It builds resilience**: Knowing we have the power to affect our circumstances helps us bounce back from setbacks, setting an inspiring example for others.

4. **It enhances creativity**: Agency unleashes our innovative potential, allowing us to envision and create new possibilities that can inspire others.

5. **It deepens connections**: When we act from a place of agency, we engage more fully with others, enabling deeper, more meaningful relationships.

However, embracing our personal agency doesn't mean going it alone. As Margaret Wheatley suggests in *Leadership and the New Science*, we're constantly influencing and being influenced by those around us, much like particles in quantum physics. Our agency exists within a web of relationships, each action rippling out to affect the whole.

To develop personal agency as a means of positive influence, we can :

1. **Reflect on our values and align our actions with them**: Ensuring that what we do is consistent with what we believe.

2. **Take responsibility for our choices and their outcomes**: Acknowledging the impact of our decisions.

3. **Seek out opportunities to contribute our exceptional gifts**: Finding ways to share our strengths and talents.

4. **Embrace failures as learning opportunities**: Viewing setbacks as chances to grow and improve.

5. **Celebrate the agency of others and support their initiatives**: Recognising and encouraging the contributions of those around us.

By recognising and cherishing our personal agency, we position ourselves to be powerful, positive influences in our communities. We create an environment where everyone feels empowered to contribute, generating a collective sense of responsibility and engagement.

Anthony Olaseinde's powerful work, *One Knife, Many Lives*, offers a perfect example of how personal agency can be harnessed to create meaningful change. His words resonate deeply with our understanding of influence:

"The sharpest blade isn't the one in your hand; it's the choices you make. Every decision can cut through darkness, leading either to a path of light or into shadows. Choose to carve out a future that honours life, not one that slices it away." – Anthony Olaseine

This potent metaphor illuminates the weight of our daily decisions, reminding us that each choice we make has the power to either strengthen or sever the bonds of our shared humanity.

Anthony's work in Sheffield exemplifies how embracing our personal agency can spark transformative change. His efforts remind us that our influence extends far beyond our immediate circle. When we fully grasp the power of our choices, we can ignite positive change, showing paths forward even in the face of daunting societal challenges. As we continue our journey of connection, let's consider how we can more fully embrace our personal agency and create spaces that encourage the agency of others.

The Power of Alignment with Core Values

"Your beliefs become your thoughts, your thoughts become your words, your words become your actions, your actions become your habits, your habits become your values, your values become your destiny." – Mahatma Gandhi

At the heart of genuine influence lies a pure alignment with our core values. When we live in harmony with our deepest beliefs, we create a magnetic force that naturally draws others towards us. This continual process of alignment is about authenticity and consistency in our thoughts, words, and actions. Reflect on your core values and consider how you can more consistently live in harmony with them to amplify your positive influence.

In Love Sheffield, we've witnessed the transformative power of values-driven connection. Our core values of kindness, compassion, and creativity aren't just words on a page; they're the lifeblood of our community, informing every interaction and initiative. This alignment creates a palpable sense of authenticity that people naturally gravitate towards.

Charles Handy, in his book *The Empty Raincoat*, introduces the concept of the 'psychological contract' – the unwritten expectations and obligations in our relationships. When our actions consistently align with our stated values, we honour this contract, allowing trust and stronger relationships.

Living our values creates a natural attractive force in several ways:

1. **It builds trust**: When our actions consistently reflect our values, people learn they can rely on us, creating a foundation for stronger relationships.

2. **It inspires others**: By embodying our values, we silently encourage others to reflect on and live by their own principles.

3. **It creates clarity**: Clear values serve as a compass, helping us navigate complex decisions with consistency and purpose.

4. **It demonstrates authenticity**: Alignment with our values allows us to show up as our true selves, which is inherently attractive to others.

5. **It generates positive energy**: When we live our values, we often feel more fulfilled and energised, creating a positive atmosphere that draws others in.

To harness the power of value alignment, consider:

1. **Clearly articulate your core values**: Reflect deeply on what truly matters to you and express it clearly.

2. **Embed values in decision-making**: Use your values as a framework for both small daily choices and major life decisions.

3. **Live your values visibly**: Don't just talk about your values; demonstrate them through your actions.

4. **Celebrate values-driven behaviour**: Acknowledge and appreciate when you and others act in alignment with core values.

5. **Regularly reflect and reassess**: As we grow, our understanding of our values may evolve. Regular reflection ensures we stay true to our current authentic selves.

Brené Brown, in *Dare to Lead*, emphasises the importance of operationalising values – moving them from abstract concepts to specific behaviours. For each core value, identify three concrete actions that represent that value in your life.

As we continue our journey of connection, let's consider: What are our true core values? How do these values become real in our daily lives? How can we better align our actions with our stated values?

I know that, when we live in alignment with our values, we don't need to force influence or connection. Like a lighthouse on a stormy night, we naturally guide and attract others simply by shining our authentic light.

Influence in Personal Relationships

"To handle yourself, use your head; to handle others, use your heart." – Eleanor Roosevelt

Our closest relationships offer a perfect opportunity for understanding the subtle power of influence. It's in these intimate relationships that we can see the basic impact of authenticity, empathy, and mutual respect.

In my experience, influence in personal relationships stems from trust. When we consistently show up as our genuine selves, vulnerabilities and all, we create a safe space for others to do the same. This honesty allows for deeper understanding and connection, paving the way for mutual growth and positive change. Reflect on how you can bring more authenticity into your relationships and observe how this deepens the bonds you share with those around you.

Active listening is pivotal in this process. By truly attuning ourselves to the emotions and needs behind our loved ones' words, we open pathways for meaningful influence. This deep, attentive presence often inspires reciprocal listening, creating a dialogue where ideas and feelings can flow freely.

The most powerful influence in personal relationships often comes not from what we say, but from how we live. Our actions, choices, and the way we treat others speak volumes. When we embody the values we believe in – kindness, compassion, creativity – we silently inspire those around us to reflect on their own lives and choices.

In Love Sheffield, I've seen how personal relationships can become catalysts for community-wide change. When individuals experience the transformative power of authentic connection in their close circles, they often feel inspired to extend that approach to their broader community interactions.

Importantly, influence in personal relationships isn't about changing others to fit our vision. Instead, it's about creating an environment where everyone feels empowered to grow into their best selves. By offering unconditional support and acceptance, we influence others to recognise and grow their own potential.

Conflict, when approached with openness and compassion, can also be a powerful avenue for influence. By addressing disagreements with a spirit of curiosity rather than defensiveness, we model a approach that values connection over being right. This can deeply influence how our loved ones handle their own conflicts.

Ultimately, influence in personal relationships is a dance of giving and receiving. As we open ourselves to being influenced by those close to us, we create a reciprocal flow of growth and understanding. This mutual influence forms the foundation of strong, resilient relationships that can weather life's challenges and celebrate its joys.

Influence in Professional Settings

"The highest type of ruler is one of whose existence the people are barely aware." – Lao Tzu

The professional world, often dominated by hierarchies and transactional relationships, might seem an unlikely arena for the gentle, connection-based influence we've been exploring. Yet, it's precisely in these environments that such an approach can be truly transformative.

At the heart of this transformation lies the concept of servant leadership, perfectly aligned with our 'tilting the floor' analogy. Servant leaders, like those who gently tilt the floor, create conditions where positive change occurs naturally. They don't push or pull their teams, but rather create an environment where everyone naturally moves in a positive direction.

In Love Sheffield, we've observed how principles of community building can revolutionise professional environments. When workplaces create a sense of belonging and shared purpose, employees naturally become more engaged and motivated. This sense of community often extends beyond the workplace, influencing how individuals interact with the broader world.

To 'tilt the floor' in professional settings:

1. **Recognise inherent value:** Approach each team member with genuine respect and curiosity, regardless of their position. This creates an atmosphere of trust and openness, yielding far more innovative solutions than top-down directives.

2. **Lead by example**: Embody the values you wish to see in your organisation. By demonstrating integrity, compassion, and commitment to growth, you silently influence others to adopt similar attitudes.

3. **Create spaces for dialogue**: Inspire open communication and collaborative problem-solving. When team members feel truly heard, they're more likely to contribute their best ideas, tapping into the group's collective intelligence.

4. **Align individual and organisational goals**: Help team members see how their strengths and aspirations align with the organisation's mission. When work feels meaningful and growth-oriented, motivation naturally follows.

5. **Navigate challenges with empathy**: Approach conflicts and difficulties with emotional intelligence, focusing on solutions rather than blame. This influences teams to tackle problems with a similar spirit.

6. **Celebrate diverse perspectives**: Value and encourage different viewpoints. This not only leads to better solutions but also creates a more inclusive and connected workplace.

7. **Encourage personal growth**: Support the development of your team members in both their professional and personal lives. This comprehensive approach creates deeper engagement and loyalty.

By adopting these practices, leaders can transform workplaces into thriving ecosystems of creativity, innovation, and fulfilment. Like a skilfully tilted floor, this approach doesn't force or manipulate, but creates a natural flow towards positive outcomes.

Often, the most powerful influence comes from simply creating the right conditions and then stepping back. As Lao Tzu suggests, the best leaders are those whose influence is so subtle, people hardly notice it's there. They don't create followers; they create more leaders.

In essence, influencing in professional settings is about creating an environment where everyone can flourish. By inspiring genuine relationships, valuing diverse perspectives, and encouraging growth, we can 'tilt the floor' of our workplaces, allowing the natural flow of ideas, innovation, and mutual support to carry us all forward.

Influence in Communities

"A small group of thoughtful people could change the world. Indeed, it's the only thing that ever has." – Margaret Mead

The true power of influence unfolds when it extends through communities, generating waves of positive change. In Love Sheffield, we've seen how a thoughtful approach to community building can produce transformative results, reshaping not only individual lives but the very fabric of our city.

Love Sheffield stands as a testament to the power of creating spaces for connection, rather than dictating the form that connection should take. By holding a virtual space and inspiring individuals to pursue their own journeys of connection, we've seen an organic blossoming of community ties across Sheffield.

Our approach is not about managing specific groups or orchestrating campaigns. Instead, it's about being a supportive presence, a sounding board, and a friend to individuals. We focus on helping people recognise their unique, beautiful, and creative value, encouraging them to make a positive difference in their lives and communities.

This gentle method of influence aligns nicely with the concept of 'tilting the floor'. Rather than pushing or pulling people towards connection, we've created an environment where moving towards deeper connections feels natural and effortless.

Key elements of this approach include:

1. **Articulating a compelling shared purpose**: Our core purpose – to make it easier for everyone to become more connected – resonates deeply with people's innate desire for belonging.

2. **Demonstrating a shift in focus**: By encouraging gratitude and embodying our core values of kindness, compassion, and creativity, we influence a positive shift in perspective across the community.

3. **Creating opportunities for deep connection**: While our primary space is virtual, it serves as a springboard for real-world connections, allowing people to recognise kindred spirits and form meaningful relationships.

4. **Celebrating diversity**: We recognise that a strong community is built on diverse perspectives and experiences, encouraging people to bring their whole selves to our shared space.
5. **Encouraging peer support**: By creating an environment of mutual support, we've seen individuals naturally step into roles of helping and learning from each other.
6. **Giving voice to all**: Everyone in Love Sheffield has the opportunity to shape our shared culture and values, creating a sense of ownership and belonging.

The results of this approach have been remarkable. We've seen countless instances of spontaneous collaboration, with individuals initiating projects and support networks that extend far beyond our virtual space. One member might suggest an idea – like creating an art exhibition – and before long, a self-organising group forms around this shared purpose, developing its own values and bringing the vision to life.

This organic growth of community initiatives demonstrates the power of influence when it comes from a place of genuine care and respect for individual agency. By creating the conditions for connection rather than forcing it, we allow for a more authentic and sustainable form of community building.

Etienne Wenger's concept of *Communities of Practice* resonates strongly with our experience. Love Sheffield has become a space where people who share a passion for connection can learn and grow together, enhancing both individual and collective capabilities.

As Margaret Heffernan argues in A *Bigger Prize*, collaboration and strong communities often lead to more sustainable and fulfilling achievements than competition. In Love Sheffield, we've seen this play out as people come together not to outdo each other, but to support and inspire one another towards shared goals.

The influence we wield in communities is not about control or manipulation. It's about creating environments where people feel a powerful sense of belonging and shared purpose. By doing so, we tap into deep human needs for connection and meaning, unleashing a source of creativity, resilience, and positive change.

As we consider our own communities, we might ask: How can we create spaces that encourage organic connection? What shared purpose might unite and inspire us? How can we harness our collective energy and wisdom to drive positive change?

By resonating powerful belonging and shared purpose, we create communities that are more than the sum of their parts. We become forces for good in the world, contributing to a more connected, compassionate, and purposeful society. This is the true power of influence in communities – not to dictate, but to inspire; not to control, but to empower.

The Butterfly Effect of Individual Action

"Each time a man stands up for an ideal, or acts to improve the lot of others, or strikes out against injustice, he sends forth a tiny ripple of hope." – Robert F. Kennedy

The butterfly effect, a concept from chaos theory, suggests that small changes can lead to significant consequences. In the realm of human connection, this principle takes on deep meaning. Each personal journey of connection, each small act of kindness or moment of authentic engagement, has the potential to create cascading ripples that can ultimately shift entire cultures.

In Love Sheffield, we've witnessed this butterfly effect in action countless times. A single individual, inspired by our values of kindness, compassion, and creativity, might start by simply smiling at their neighbours. This small act can lead to conversations, which might evolve into community initiatives, eventually transforming the social fabric of entire neighbourhoods.

The power of these individual journeys lies in their authenticity. When people embark on a path of deeper connection, they're not following a prescribed set of rules, but discovering their own unique way of engaging with the world. This genuine approach resonates with others in a way that top-down directives never could.

Consider the cascade effect of one person's journey:

1. **Personal transformation**: As an individual deepens their capacity for connection, they experience positive changes in their own life.

2. **Immediate circle**: Friends, family, and colleagues notice these changes, inspiring curiosity and often, emulation.

3. **Community impact**: As more people in a community adopt connection-oriented behaviours, local culture begins to shift.

4. **Institutional change**: Connected communities start to influence local institutions, from schools to businesses to government.

5. **Wider cultural shift**: As multiple communities experience this change, broader societal norms begin to evolve.

This process isn't linear or predictable, but organic and emergent – much like the growth of Love Sheffield itself. By creating a space that encourages individual journeys of connection, we've set in motion countless butterfly effects across Sheffield.

The key to this influence is leading by example. As John Wooden wisely noted, "The most powerful leadership tool you have is your own personal example." When we consistently embody our values in everyday interactions, we create a cascade effect. Others, seeing the positive outcomes of these behaviours, are naturally drawn to emulate them.

It's important to note that this form of influence evolves as we grow in our understanding of connection. The more deeply we connect with others and with our shared humanity, the more impactful our influence becomes. This influence isn't measured in traditional metrics of power or control, but in the positive changes we inspire in others and in our communities.

Looking forward, we can see that this form of influence – leading by example and inspiring trust – will play a crucial role in shaping our collective future. In a world facing complex challenges, our ability to model positive behaviours and inspire others to connect more deeply becomes ever more vital.

As we continue our journey of connection, it's clear that each of us holds the power to influence our shared reality through our personal example. Every act of kindness, every moment of genuine understanding, every effort to bridge divides contributes to the world we wish to create. By embracing our capacity to inspire through trusted example, we can play an active role in uniting hearts and igniting change on a scale that extends far beyond our individual reach.

Influence Through Media and Technology

"The power of the Web is in its universality. Access by everyone regardless of disability is an essential aspect." – Tim Berners-Lee

In our digital age, media and technology have become powerful conduits for influence. Yet, their true potential lies in their ability to facilitate authentic human connections – a hidden superpower often overlooked in the clamour of marketing and self-promotion.

Digital platforms offer unprecedented opportunities to bridge distances, connecting people who might never have crossed paths otherwise. In Love Sheffield, we've witnessed how a simple online post can resonate across the city, sparking conversations and collaborations that transcend geographical and social boundaries.

When approached with authenticity and a desire for genuine engagement, these platforms reveal their capacity for positive influence. Social media, at its best, can function as a modern-day public park, where people gather to share gratitude, interests, and passions. This requires thoughtful stewardship, but the rewards are significant: a space where ideas flourish, insights emerge, and collective wisdom takes root.

Imagine social media as a welcoming park, where people come together not to compete or impress, but to connect and share. Like a well-tended green space, this digital commons needs care and attention. It calls for mindful moderation and a culture of mutual respect.

In Love Sheffield, we've created this park-like atmosphere online by focusing on gratitude and shared passions. A post about a local beauty spot might kindle a discussion on conservation, leading to a community clean-up effort. Shared enthusiasm for art or music could blossom into collaborative projects, enriching our city's cultural landscape.

By curating these digital spaces with intention, we create environments where people feel safe to express themselves authentically. This approach allows collective wisdom to emerge organically, as diverse experiences and insights interweave.

When we treat our online platforms as cherished public spaces, we harness their power to grow connections and community spirit. In doing so, we transform our city, one interaction at a time, creating a digital landscape that reflects and enhances our shared humanity.

This approach to digital influence complements our broader vision of leadership rooted in connection. By inspiring genuine online interactions, we set the stage for natural leaders to emerge, guided by shared values and common interests. In this context, technology evolves from being merely a communication tool to a powerful catalyst for community growth and positive change.

Ethical Considerations of Influence

"Ethics is knowing the difference between what you have a right to do and what is right to do." – Potter Stewart

As we harness the power of influence to unite hearts and ignite change, it's crucial that we continually reflect on the ethical implications of our actions. It's clear that influence, when wielded thoughtfully and with compassion, can be a force for tremendous good. However, we must remain vigilant to ensure our methods align with our values.

At the heart of ethical influence lies respect for individual autonomy. When we seek to influence others, we're not aiming to control or manipulate, but to create a culture of inspiration and growth. This means presenting ideas and possibilities to begin a conversation, which will engage and harness the collective intelligence of our community. We fully respect everyone's right to make their own choices. In Love Sheffield, we've found that this approach not only aligns with our values but also leads to more genuine and lasting positive change.

This view of ethical influence as a catalyst for collective wisdom resonates deeply with the principles of community building. By framing our efforts as conversation starters rather than final solutions, we create space for diverse perspectives to emerge and blend. This approach acknowledges that the best ideas often arise from the interplay of many minds, each contributing their unique insights and experiences.

In practice, this might look like hosting community forums where ideas are shared not as fait accompli, but as seeds for discussion. Or it could involve using social media to pose thought-provoking questions that invite varied responses, allowing the community's collective intelligence to surface innovative solutions.

Importantly, this approach to ethical influence creates a sense of shared ownership over community initiatives. When people feel their voices are genuinely heard and valued, they're more likely to invest their energy and creativity into bringing ideas to life. This creates a virtuous cycle where influence becomes a collaborative, empowering force rather than a top-down directive.

By respecting individual autonomy and harnessing collective intelligence, we create an environment where ethical influence can flourish, leading to more resilient, creative, and connected communities.

Practical Applications and Exercises

"Stories have the power to create social change and inspire community." – Terry Tempest Williams

Understanding and harnessing influence responsibly can significantly enhance our ability to create positive change. Here are some practical ways to develop and apply influence in various settings:

1. **Active Listening Practice:** Dedicate a day to focusing intently on truly understanding others. In each conversation, aim to grasp not only the words but also the underlying emotions and needs. Reflect on how this deep listening influences your interactions and enriches your relationships.
2. **Storytelling for Connection:** Craft a personal story that illustrates a value or idea you're passionate about. Share it with a friend or small group, focusing on authenticity rather than persuasion. Notice how sharing your genuine experience influences others.
3. **Empathy Mapping:** When faced with a disagreement, try creating an empathy map for the other person's perspective. Write down what they might be thinking, feeling, saying, and doing. This exercise can broaden your understanding and influence your approach to resolving conflicts.
4. **Community Idea Exchange:** Organise a gathering where people share their ideas for community improvement. Encourage everyone to build on each other's suggestions. This collaborative approach can reveal the power of collective intelligence.

5. **Digital Detox and Reconnect:** Take a brief break from digital media, then re-engage with a focus on creating genuine connections. Pay attention to how this intentional approach changes your online interactions and influence.
6. **Values Clarification:** Spend time reflecting on and articulating your core values. Consider how these values show in your actions and how they might silently influence those around you.
7. **Feedback Loop:** Ask trusted friends or colleagues for honest feedback about how you influence others. Use this insight to refine your approach and ensure it aligns with your intentions.
8. **Random Acts of Kindness:** Commit to performing one unexpected kind act each day for a week. Observe how these small actions influence the mood and behaviour of those around you.
9. **Collaborative Problem-Solving:** When faced with a challenge at work or in your community, invite others to brainstorm solutions together. Notice how this inclusive approach affects the outcome and people's engagement.
10. **Reflection Journal:** Keep a daily journal focusing on your interactions and their impacts. Reflect on moments where you felt you influenced others or were influenced yourself. Consider what made these moments effective or meaningful.

By engaging in these exercises, we can develop our capacity for positive influence while remaining grounded in ethics and genuine connection. Truly, the goal isn't to accumulate power, but to help create a more compassionate and collaborative world.

Stories of Influence

"The purpose of life is not to be happy. It is to be useful, to be honorable, to be compassionate, to have it make some difference that you have lived and lived well." – Ralph Waldo Emerson

Life's true purpose lies in making a meaningful difference, not just for ourselves but for those around us. These stories of influence illustrate how individuals and groups, driven by compassion and purpose, can spark transformative change within their communities. Through these narratives, we witness the transformative power of ethical connections and see how simple, caring actions can blossom into movements that leave a lasting impact.

As we explore these tales, we'll see how the ideas we've talked about work in the real world. They show us that each of us, in our own way, can create a huge positive difference in the world.

Mums United in Sheffield offers a compelling example of how grassroots influence can transform communities. Founded by a group of local mothers in response to rising youth violence, Mums United has become a powerful force for positive change. Their approach, rooted in community connection and understanding, has led to initiatives ranging from youth mentoring programmes to family support services. By tapping into the strength and wisdom of mothers, Mums United demonstrates how influence born from genuine care and local insight can address complex social issues effectively.

Andy's Man Club, which started in Halifax but has spread across the UK, including to Sheffield, showcases the transformative power of creating safe spaces for connection. Founded in response to the high rate of male suicide, Andy's Man Club provides a place for men to talk openly about their mental health. Their motto, "It's Okay to Talk," has influenced societal attitudes towards male mental health. By creating an environment of trust and mutual support, they've started a cascade effect of openness and vulnerability that extends far beyond their weekly meetings.

In Love Sheffield, we've seen how creating spaces for connection can spark numerous initiatives across the city. For instance, one member of the Love Sheffield Artists group proposed the idea of creating an art exhibition. Without top-down management, this spark of an idea blossomed into a self-organising community project. People came together, allocating roles based on their strengths and bringing the vision to life. This organic growth demonstrates how influence, when rooted in connection and shared purpose, can lead to transformative action.

The Incredible Edible movement in Todmorden, West Yorkshire, provides another powerful example of community influence. Started in 2008 by a small group of residents, this initiative transformed public spaces into edible gardens, growing food for anyone to harvest. What began as a local project to promote community resilience and food security has now spread to communities worldwide, showcasing how a simple idea, when aligned with community values, can have far-reaching influence.

These stories highlight different aspects of influence – from addressing urgent social issues to creating spaces for creative expression and community resilience. They remind us that influence isn't about control, but about creating environments where positive change can flourish naturally. By sharing these narratives, we hope to inspire readers to recognise their own potential for influence, whether through starting a support group, initiating a community project, or simply being a supportive presence for others.

Conclusion: From Butterfly Wings to Global Waves

"The true meaning of life is to plant trees, under whose shade you do not expect to sit." – Nelson Henderson

As we reflect on our exploration of influence, we're reminded that true power lies not in control or manipulation, but in our capacity to inspire positive change through authentic connection. The journey we've taken through this chapter has illuminated the powerful impact that each of us can have when we align our actions with our deepest values and engage with others from a place of genuine care and understanding.

We began by examining the nature of influence, recognising it as a natural outgrowth of our connections rather than a skill to be mastered. This perspective shifts our focus from seeking to exert power over others to creating environments where positive change can flourish organically. By embracing our personal agency and living our values consistently, we create a magnetic force that naturally draws others towards shared purpose and collective growth.

Our exploration of influence across various spheres – from personal relationships to professional settings to broader communities – revealed a common thread: the transformative power of leading by example. When we embody the qualities of kindness, compassion, and creativity in our daily interactions, we inspire those around us to do the same. This cascading effect of positive behaviour has the potential to reshape entire communities, as we've witnessed in Love Sheffield.

The butterfly effect of individual action emerged as a powerful metaphor for understanding our sphere of influence. Each small act of connection, each moment of empathy, and each step towards personal growth sends ripples through our social fabric, cascading into waves of change that extend far beyond our immediate circles. This realisation empowers us to see every interaction as an opportunity to contribute to the world we wish to create.

As we've seen, influence in the digital age presents both challenges and opportunities. By approaching our online interactions with mindfulness and intention, we can harness the connective power of technology while maintaining the depth and authenticity that meaningful relationships require. This balanced approach allows us to expand our reach while staying true to the core principles of genuine human connection.

Perhaps most importantly, our journey has underscored the ethical imperative that accompanies influence. As we grow in our capacity to affect others, we must remain vigilant in our commitment to using that influence for the greater good. This requires ongoing self-reflection, a willingness to listen deeply to others, and a steadfast dedication to our shared values.

As we move forward from this chapter, let us carry with us the understanding that true influence is not about accumulating power, but about creating spaces where everyone can thrive. It's about tilting the floor towards connection, compassion, and collective wellbeing. Each of us, in our own unique way, has the power to be a catalyst for positive change.

In Love Sheffield, and indeed in communities around the world, we have the opportunity to put these principles into practice. By embracing our capacity to influence through trusted example, by growing environments where authentic connections can flourish, and by consistently choosing kindness and understanding in our interactions, we actively shape the reality we share.

The path of influence we've explored here is not always easy. It requires vulnerability, patience, and a willingness to grow. Yet, as we've seen, the rewards – in terms of personal fulfilment, community resilience, and collective transformation – are immeasurable.

As we conclude this chapter, consider that our journey of influence is ongoing. Each day presents new opportunities to deepen our connections, to inspire positive change, and to contribute to the web of compassion that binds us all. By embracing this journey with open hearts and minds, we become active co-creators of a more connected, vibrant, and compassionate world.

What steps will you take today to expand your positive influence? How might you create ripples of connection that cascade beyond your immediate circle? These questions invite us to continually engage with the power we each hold to unite hearts and ignite change, one connection at a time.

6. Level 4 – Collective Wisdom

"We are a way for the cosmos to know itself."
– Carl Sagan

Our quest for understanding is part of an ancient, grand continuum that stretches far beyond our individual lives. When we tap into collective wisdom, we're not just accessing a human resource, but participating in a cosmic dance of knowledge that has been unfolding since the dawn of time. This perspective invites us to see our shared insights as part of a larger, interconnected whole.

By embracing this view, we begin to grasp the true depth and breadth of our distributed intelligence. Collective wisdom is far more than the sum of our individual experiences; it's something greater that arises when we come together as a community, resonating with a shared purpose. As we pool our understanding and insights, we're part of a grand dance of knowledge that connects us not only to each other, but to the very fabric of the universe itself.

This cosmic view of collective wisdom challenges us to think beyond our immediate concerns and see our quest for understanding as part of a greater journey of discovery. It reminds us that every insight we share, every connection we make, reverberates through a web of consciousness that extends far beyond our individual lives.

I've come to believe that this collective wisdom emerges naturally as a result of everyone becoming more connected. As we engage with this distributed intelligence, we become part of something far greater than ourselves – we become a living, breathing community of understanding.

This shared consciousness emerges when we create spaces where diverse perspectives can mingle freely, where every voice is valued and heard. In these vibrant environments, a shared understanding begins to take root and flourish. It's as if the very act of coming together in trust and openness creates a catalyst for insights that none of us could have reached alone – insights that reflect our collective human wisdom.

James Surowiecki, in his thought-provoking book *The Wisdom of Crowds*, explores how large groups can often make better decisions than individual experts. While I find truth in this idea, I believe the real magic happens when communities move in harmony to address challenges that only they can fully comprehend. For this natural emergence of collective wisdom to unfold, certain elements must be present: mutual trust, emotional resonance, honesty, and a shared sense of purpose that extends beyond our individual lives to encompass our role in the wider world.

As we explore collective wisdom, we'll examine how our local efforts to seek connection and shared understanding contribute to a larger process of discovery and growth. This journey will take us from the intricacies of human connection to the broader implications of our distributed intelligence, revealing the extraordinary potential within our united hearts and minds.

Historical Perspectives on Collective Wisdom

"The whole is greater than the sum of its parts." – Aristotle

The idea of combined power being magnified is not a modern revelation, but a timeless truth that has guided human societies for millennia. This concept, central to our understanding of collective wisdom, has been a constant companion in our journey as a species, shaping our cultures, governance, and ways of knowing long before we gave it a name.

Indigenous cultures around the world have long recognised the power of collective decision-making. The Haudenosaunee people of North America, for instance, have practised a form of engaged democracy that predates European contact. Their system of governance, known as the Great Law of Peace, emphasises consensus-building and the importance of considering the impact of decisions on seven generations into the future. This approach ensures that diverse perspectives are not only heard but valued, creating a rich body of shared wisdom that has sustained their communities for centuries.

In Africa, the concept of 'Ubuntu' – often translated as "I am because we are" – speaks to a deep understanding of our interconnectedness. This philosophy recognises that our unique identities are closely intertwined with those of our community. It's a beautiful expression of collective wisdom, acknowledging that our knowledge and understanding grow through our relationships with others.

Eastern philosophies offer yet another lens through which to view collective wisdom. The Buddhist concept of 'dependent origination' suggests that all phenomena arise in dependence upon multiple causes and conditions. When applied to human knowledge and decision-making, this idea aligns well with our understanding of how collective wisdom emerges from the intermingling of diverse insights and experiences.

As we move into more recent history, the Age of Enlightenment in Europe saw a surge in recognising the power of collaborative thinking. The coffeehouses of 18th century London and Paris became vibrant hubs of intellectual exchange, where individuals from various backgrounds could freely share and debate ideas. These spaces, much like our community gatherings today, grew the kind of relaxed, authentic connections that seem essential for collective wisdom to flourish.

In our digital age, we've witnessed the emergence of new forms of collective wisdom. Platforms like Wikipedia, Quora and Reddit harness the knowledge of countless contributors to create a vast repository of information. Generative AI has absorbed these sources and created something even more accessible. While these tools are undoubtedly powerful, they often lack the deep, local connections that enable communities to 'dance together' in addressing distinct challenges. It's a reminder that while technology can facilitate knowledge sharing, it's the human element – our ability to connect, empathise, and collaborate – that truly brings collective wisdom to life.

Throughout history, the most effective forms of collective wisdom have always involved a delicate balance. It's a balance between structure and spontaneity, between diverse viewpoints and shared values, between individual contributions and group synergy. As we continue to explore and grow collective wisdom in our modern world, maintaining this equilibrium seems key.

I find myself wondering: How might these historical lessons inform our understanding and cherishing of collective wisdom today? How can we honour the timeless wisdom of ancient cultures while embracing the opportunities presented by our increasingly connected world? These are questions worth deep reflection as we seek to unite hearts and ignite change in our communities.

As we move forward, let's remain open to the wisdom that flows through the ages, recognising that our efforts to grow collective understanding are part of a grand human tradition. By creating spaces for authentic connection and mutual exploration, we engage in a timeless dance of collective discovery that holds the power to transform our world.

Cultural Perspectives on Collective Wisdom

"Wisdom is like a baobab tree; no one individual can embrace it."
– African proverb

The vastness of wisdom cannot be fully grasped by any one individual alone; it is a shared endeavour that spans cultures and communities. Across the world, different traditions have recognised this truth, offering valuable insights into how collective understanding is grown.

Eastern philosophies shine a clear light on this concept. Buddhism's 'Indra's Net' presents a captivating metaphor – a vast cosmic web, each intersection adorned with a jewel reflecting all others. Here, collective wisdom is more than pooled knowledge, it's a recognition of our intrinsic interconnectedness.

Thich Nhat Hanh expands on this idea in *The Heart of Understanding*. He writes, "To be is to inter-be. We cannot just be by ourselves alone." His words invite us to see collective wisdom not as our creation, but as an energy we tap into by acknowledging our connection to all things.

Taoism offers another intriguing perspective through 'Wu Wei' – the wisdom of non-action. In the dance of collective understanding, this principle suggests that sometimes the wisest move is to step back, allowing insights to emerge naturally from the group.

Indigenous cultures have long demonstrated forms of collective wisdom we're only beginning to fully appreciate. Robin Wall Kimmerer's *Braiding Sweetgrass* shares the story of the 'Three Sisters' – corn, beans, and squash growing in harmony, each supporting the others. This agricultural practice serves as a powerful metaphor for community collaboration, where diverse elements contribute their inherent strengths.

The African concept of 'Ubuntu' – often expressed as "I am because we are" – speaks to a deep understanding of our shared humanity. Desmond Tutu describes it as the very essence of being human – a recognition that we are part of a greater whole, diminished when others suffer.

As we weave these perspectives together, we see collective wisdom as more than a sum of individual knowledge. It's a recognition of our interconnectedness, an allowance for natural emergence, an appreciation of diversity, and an understanding that our individual wellbeing is inextricably linked to that of all.

In Love Sheffield, embracing diverse viewpoints enriches our community connection. Creating spaces that honour varied ways of knowing allows us to draw from a deeper well of collective wisdom. As we continue our journey, consider how we might bring these cultural insights into our daily lives and community practices. By creating opportunities for diverse perspectives to mingle, we allow a distinctly Sheffield form of collective wisdom to emerge – one that honours our heritage while embracing our multicultural present.

Everyday Wisdom in Depth of Community

"The true voyage of discovery consists not in seeking new landscapes, but in having new eyes." – Marcel Proust

True discovery often comes from seeing the familiar in a new light. Collective wisdom isn't always found in grand gestures; it often springs from fresh perspectives on the everyday experiences that shape our lives. By uncovering the richness within our daily interactions, we reveal the deep knowledge that exists throughout our communities.

Our journey of connection reveals deep insights in unexpected places. A chat in the street, a shared project to green a neglected space, or neighbours banding together to support the vulnerable – these everyday moments, approached with open hearts and curious minds, become rich sources of collective wisdom.

Peter Block, in *Community*, suggests we already hold the wisdom we seek. "The wisdom resides in us," he writes, "and we need to give form and structure to what we already know but have become hesitant to act on." His words encourage us to explore our existing relationships and networks for answers to shared challenges.

Consider the deep well of knowledge our elders carry. Their lives span decades of change – social, economic, technological. By creating space for their stories, we tap into a stream of wisdom that might otherwise flow unseen.

Equally, our children and young people bring fresh eyes and unbridled creativity to community issues. Their candid observations often cut through complexities that cloud adult vision. By truly hearing our youngest voices, we enrich our collective understanding.

Margaret Wheatley, in *Turning to One Another*, highlights the power of genuine conversation. She suggests that gathering in small groups to discuss what truly matters helps us rediscover our wisdom and mend the fabric of our communities.

This everyday wisdom, bubbling up from the depths of community life, reminds me of an underground stream – ever-present, yet often hidden. Our role is to create conditions for this wisdom to rise and flow freely.

This might mean:

1. Opening spaces for unhurried community dialogue, free from agendas or pressure.

2. Seeking out diverse voices, especially those often overlooked.

3. Listening deeply – beyond the words, to the experiences and emotions that lie beneath.

4. Celebrating small acts of wisdom and kindness that pepper our daily lives.

5. Encouraging curiosity, where each interaction offers a chance to grow and understand.

As we attune ourselves to this everyday wisdom, our communities transform. They become living, breathing entities brimming with untapped insight. We begin to see that solutions to many challenges already exist within our collective knowledge.

By deepening our connections and valuing the wisdom in ordinary moments, we set the stage for extraordinary change. We unlock the shared potential lying dormant in every street, neighbourhood, and town.

What glimpses of everyday wisdom have you seen in your community lately? How might we amplify these insights to spark positive change? Creating regular spaces for community dialogue, where people can share their experiences and insights without agenda or pressure.

The Role of Art and Symbols in Conveying Collective Wisdom

"Art is not what you see, but what you make others see."
– Edgar Degas

Art has an extraordinary ability to reveal truths beyond words. It serves as a universal language, conveying the essence of our shared experiences and collective wisdom. Through symbols and artistic expressions, we connect on a deeper level, allowing ideas and emotions to resonate within us in powerful, transformative ways.

Throughout human history, art has carried the torch of collective knowledge and values. From ancient cave paintings to vibrant street murals, visual expressions capture the essence of human experience and shared understanding. They tell our stories, preserve our memories, and challenge us to see the world anew.

Joseph Campbell, in his seminal work *The Hero with a Thousand Faces*, uncovers a fascinating pattern. Symbols and myths across cultures often carry similar themes, hinting at a collective unconscious that binds humanity. He writes, "The symbols of mythology are not manufactured; they cannot be ordered, invented, or permanently suppressed. They are spontaneous productions of the psyche." This perspective invites us to see art and symbols as natural expressions of our shared wisdom, bubbling up from the depths of our collective experience.

In our communities today, this principle comes to life in many forms. Public murals often unfold the story of a neighbourhood's history or aspirations, serving as visual anchors for collective memory and shared identity. Street art, with its bold imagery and provocative messages, challenges societal norms and sparks crucial conversations about social issues.

Sculptor Antony Gormley, known for his exploration of the human form in public spaces, speaks to art's power to create collective experiences. He says, "Art is the means by which we communicate what it feels like to be alive." His words ring true when we consider how public art installations become gathering points for shared reflection and understanding.

Symbols, too, play a pivotal role in conveying collective wisdom. A simple peace sign or a rainbow flag can instantly communicate complex ideas about harmony and inclusivity. These visual shorthands allow us to tap into shared understandings swiftly and powerfully.

Indigenous cultures have long recognised the potency of art and symbols in preserving and transmitting wisdom. Aboriginal Australian dot paintings, for instance, are not mere decorations but complex maps of knowledge about land, spiritual beliefs, and community laws. Through these paintings, elders pass down crucial information to younger generations, ensuring the continuity of their collective wisdom.

In our digital age, new forms of visual communication emerge and evolve. Memes, for example, have become a powerful way of sharing ideas and critiques across cultural and linguistic barriers. While often humorous, they can carry deep insights about our shared human experience.

As we consider ways to grow connection in our communities, how might we harness the power of art and symbols more effectively? Supporting local artists, creating spaces for public art, and encouraging community art projects can bring people together in the creative process. Visual storytelling could help share community histories and visions for the future.

By embracing art and symbols as carriers of collective wisdom, we open new channels for connection and understanding. As you move through your community, what art or symbols catch your eye? How do they speak to you about the collective wisdom of your neighbours? Perhaps there's an opportunity to create new art or symbols that capture the unique spirit and aspirations of your community.

In the end, art and symbols remind us that our collective wisdom is more than something we think or speak – it's something we feel, see, and experience together. They invite us to engage with our shared knowledge and values in ways that are visceral and immediate, creating lasting imprints on our collective consciousness.

Collective Memory and Its Influence on Present Reality

"The past is never dead. It's not even past." – William Faulkner

The past is always present, subtly shaping our current realities through the lens of collective memory. How societies remember and interpret their shared history deeply influences our understanding of the present and our visions for the future.

Faulkner's words resonate deeply, reminding us that our present is woven from threads of shared history. Collective memory – the way societies remember and interpret their past – shapes our understanding of the now and colours our visions of tomorrow.

Maurice Halbwachs, in his groundbreaking work *On Collective Memory*, argues that our personal recollections are always framed within a collective context. Our memories, he suggests, are influenced by the social groups we belong to, from family to nation. This insight invites us to consider how our communal narratives mould our individual perceptions and actions.

In our communities, collective memory often takes shape in traditions, monuments, and shared stories. These echoes from the past continue to resonate, influencing everything from social norms to policy decisions. A community's experience of past economic hardships, for instance, might instil a culture of resilience and mutual support that endures long after the initial challenges have faded.

Pierre Nora, in his extensive work *Realms of Memory*, introduces us to 'sites of memory' – places, objects, or events that serve as symbolic elements of a community's memorial heritage. These might be physical locations like war memorials, or intangible elements like shared rituals. Nora argues that these memory sites play a huge role in shaping collective identity and understanding.

Yet, it's important to recognise that collective memory isn't always a faithful mirror of historical facts. James W. Loewen, in *Lies My Teacher Told Me*, points out that our shared narratives can sometimes perpetuate myths or overlook uncomfortable truths. This realisation challenges us to approach our collective memories with a critical eye, always seeking a more complete and nuanced understanding of our shared past.

Collective trauma, too, leaves its mark on present reality. Bessel van der Kolk's *The Body Keeps the Score* offers serious insights into how traumatic experiences, even generations old, can continue to influence community behaviours and relationships. Understanding this can help us approach current challenges with greater empathy and awareness.

So, how might we work with collective memory to create positive change in our communities?

Here are a few thoughts:

1. Encourage intergenerational dialogue to keep important memories alive and allow for new interpretations.

2. Create spaces for sharing diverse perspectives on shared histories, especially from voices that have been historically marginalised.

3. Use arts and storytelling to explore collective memories in ways that drive understanding and healing.

4. Critically examine our shared narratives, being open to revising them in light of new information or perspectives.

5. Acknowledge past traumas while focusing on resilience and growth, using collective memory as a source of strength rather than division.

As we navigate our present and shape our future, our collective memories serve as both a guide and a challenge. They provide us with a sense of identity and continuity, but also call us to question, learn, and grow.

In your own community, what collective memories seem to hold the most influence? How do they shape current attitudes and behaviours? Perhaps there's an opportunity to engage with these shared narratives in new ways, using them as a springboard for deeper connection and positive change.

By understanding and thoughtfully engaging with our collective memory, we can create a present that honours our past while remaining open to new possibilities. In doing so, we create a richer, more inclusive narrative that can guide us towards a future of greater understanding and connection.

Distributed Intelligence in the Modern World

"Never doubt that a small group of thoughtful, committed citizens can change the world; indeed, it's the only thing that ever has."
– Margaret Mead

Collective effort has always been a powerful force for change. In our interconnected world, this shared intelligence has evolved, allowing groups to solve problems and create wisdom in ways that were once unimaginable.

James Surowiecki, in *The Wisdom of Crowds*, presents a compelling case. Under the right conditions, he argues, groups can be remarkably intelligent, often surpassing the smartest individuals among them. "Diversity and independence are important," he writes, "because the best collective decisions are the product of disagreement and contest, not consensus or compromise." His insight challenges us to seek out and value diverse perspectives in our communities and decision-making processes.

The internet has become a powerful conduit for this distributed intelligence. Consider Wikipedia, where collective knowledge is gathered and refined by thousands of contributors. While not without flaws, this model shows the potential for creating vast, evolving repositories of shared wisdom.

In problem-solving, we're witnessing fascinating applications of distributed intelligence. Crowdsourcing platforms allow organisations to tap into global pools of talent and ideas. NASA's use of citizen scientists to classify galaxies or identify Martian features demonstrates how complex tasks can be broken down and distributed, leading to breakthroughs that traditional methods might miss.

Yet, it's crucial to remember that technology is merely a tool. The true power of distributed intelligence lies in human connection and collaboration. Etienne Wenger's work on *Communities of Practice* reminds us that it's through shared engagement in meaningful activities that we develop collective knowledge and capabilities.

In our local communities, distributed intelligence might emerge in community gardens, where diverse knowledge about plants, soil, and local climate comes together to create thriving green spaces. Or in neighbourhood watch schemes, where collective vigilance improves community safety.

As we embrace the potential of distributed intelligence, we must also be mindful of its challenges. Cass Sunstein, in *#Republic*, warns of the risk of echo chambers and polarisation in our digital age. His caution reminds us of the importance of creating spaces where diverse viewpoints can genuinely engage with each other.

So, how might we magnify distributed intelligence in our communities?

Here are some ideas:

1. Create platforms for sharing local knowledge and skills, perhaps through community skill-sharing events or online forums.

2. Encourage participatory decision-making processes in local governance, where citizens can contribute their insights and ideas.

3. Create a culture of open collaboration, where ideas are freely shared and built upon.

4. Develop critical thinking skills in our educational systems, enabling people to engage more effectively with diverse information sources.

5. Use technology thoughtfully to connect people with shared interests or complementary skills.

As we navigate the complexities of our modern world, distributed intelligence offers a powerful model for collective problem-solving and wisdom-gathering. It reminds us that every individual has something valuable to contribute, and that our collective potential far exceeds the sum of our individual capabilities. By recognising and engaging distributed intelligence, we open ourselves to new possibilities for innovation, resilience, and shared understanding.

Practical Applications of Collective Wisdom

"The aim of argument, or of discussion, should not be victory, but progress." – Joseph Joubert

When we focus on progress rather than winning, we open the door to genuine collaboration. This simple shift in thinking can transform how we tap into our shared wisdom. When we talk and listen with the goal of making things better for everyone, rather than proving ourselves right, we create a space where new ideas can grow and positive changes can spread far beyond our own circles. It's this approach that allows us to turn our collective knowledge into real, lasting improvements in our communities. Let's see how we might apply this wisdom in three key areas:

Engaging in Community Activities and Decision-Making

Participatory budgeting, first developed in Porto Alegre, Brazil, offers a compelling model for citizen engagement in community decisions. By allowing residents to directly allocate a portion of public funds, this approach harnesses collective knowledge about local needs and priorities. Archon Fung and Erik Olin Wright, in *Deepening Democracy*, argue that such participatory governance can lead to more equitable and effective outcomes.

Tactical urbanism, described by Mike Lydon and Anthony Garcia, provides another avenue for community engagement. This approach involves small-scale, often citizen-led interventions that test ideas for improving city life. From pop-up parks to community gardens, these initiatives allow us to collectively experiment with and refine solutions to local challenges.

In our own communities, we might consider:

1. Organising town hall meetings where diverse voices can contribute to local planning decisions.

2. Creating citizen advisory boards for various aspects of community life, from environmental initiatives to cultural programmes.

3. Implementing digital platforms for ongoing community feedback and idea-sharing.

Creating Collaborative Learning Environments

Sugata Mitra's "Hole in the Wall" experiments, highlighted in his TED talks, demonstrate the power of peer-to-peer learning. These studies show how children can learn complex subjects through collaborative exploration, without formal instruction. This approach challenges traditional top-down educational models and suggests new ways of tapping into collective intelligence in learning environments.

In adult education, the University of the Third Age (U3A) provides an inspiring model of collaborative learning. This international movement brings together older adults to share knowledge and learn from each other, recognising that every individual has valuable skills and experiences to contribute.

To create collaborative learning environments, we might:

1. Establish skill-sharing workshops where community members teach and learn from each other.

2. Develop intergenerational mentorship programmes, allowing for the organic transfer of knowledge and skills.

3. Create community learning spaces, both physical and digital, where people can come together to explore topics of shared interest.

Establishing Structures of True Belonging

Peter Block, in *Community*, emphasises the importance of creating spaces where people feel they truly belong and can contribute meaningfully. He suggests that true belonging arises when we shift from a consumer mindset to one of shared ownership and responsibility for our communities.

Practical ways to establish these structures might include:

1. Creating regular "wisdom circles" where community members can share insights and collaboratively solve local issues.

2. Implementing restorative justice practices in schools and community organisations, creating a sense of shared responsibility and healing.

3. Developing community rituals and celebrations that honour diverse contributions and strengthen social bonds.

Digital platforms can also play a role in creating structures of belonging. However, as Ethan Zuckerman cautions in *Mistrust*, we must be mindful of creating truly inclusive digital spaces that bridge divides rather than reinforce them.

In all these practical applications, it's important to remember James Surowiecki's insights from *The Wisdom of Crowds*. For collective wisdom to flourish, we need to ensure diversity of opinion, independence of thought, and effective mechanisms for aggregating insights.

As we implement these ideas, we might ask ourselves: How can we ensure that all voices in our community are heard and valued? How might we create spaces that not only solve immediate challenges but also build our collective capacity for wisdom and collaboration?

By finding practical ways to tap into our shared knowledge and insights, we can create more resilient, innovative, and connected communities. We move from being passive recipients of change to active co-creators of our shared future. In doing so, we not only address current issues but also establish a culture of collective wisdom that can guide us through future challenges and opportunities.

Stories of Collective Wisdom in Action

"Great stories happen to those who can tell them." – Ira Glass

Storytelling has the power to illuminate and amplify collective wisdom. Let's explore some vivid examples of communities tapping into their shared knowledge to create positive change.

In Todmorden, West Yorkshire, the Incredible Edible movement began in 2008 with a simple idea: transform public spaces into edible gardens, free for all to harvest. What started as a local project to boost community resilience and food security has blossomed into a global phenomenon.

Pam Warhurst, a founder, explains in her TED talk how they used the universal language of food to unite people across age, income, and cultural divides. The project drew on the community's collective gardening wisdom while giving new skills to eager learners. It strikingly illustrates a community self-organising around a shared vision, pooling skills and resources to create tangible change.

Frome, Somerset, offers another inspiring tale. The Compassionate Frome project, launched in 2013 by GP Helen Kingston, aimed to combat loneliness and enhance health through community connection. They created a directory of local groups and services, training "community connectors" to help people find needed support.

This approach recognised the inherent wisdom within the community itself, moving beyond traditional medical interventions. By facilitating connections and empowering residents to support one another, the project achieved remarkable results: a 17% reduction in emergency hospital admissions over three years, while similar towns saw a 29% increase.

The Sikh community's response to the COVID-19 pandemic provides a powerful example of cultural wisdom in action. Drawing on the principles of seva (selfless service) and the tradition of langar (community kitchens), Sikh communities across the UK swiftly mobilised to support vulnerable people during lockdowns.

In Manchester and Birmingham, gurdwaras (Sikh temples) became hubs of community support, with volunteers preparing and delivering thousands of meals daily. This response showcased how deeply rooted cultural wisdom can quickly adapt to meet new challenges, demonstrating the resilience and flexibility inherent in collective wisdom.

These stories highlight key aspects of collective wisdom in action:

1. Simple, unifying ideas can mobilise diverse community members.

2. Recognising and valuing existing community skills and knowledge is crucial.

3. Small, local initiatives can spark wider movements and inspire far-reaching change.

4. Cultural traditions and values shape collective responses to new challenges.

As we reflect on these stories, we might wonder: What untapped wisdom lies dormant in our own communities? How can we create conditions for this wisdom to emerge and flourish?

These examples show that collective wisdom, given the right conditions, becomes a powerful force for positive change. By creating spaces for collaboration, valuing diverse knowledge, and empowering community action, we unlock the tremendous potential within our shared experiences and insights. What stories of collective wisdom in action have you witnessed in your own community? How might these tales inspire and guide our efforts to create more connected, resilient, and vibrant communities?

Conclusion: Exponential Wisdom

"Individually, we are one drop. Together, we are an ocean."
– Ryunosuke Satoro

The essence of collective wisdom lies in its exponential power – when individual knowledge and insights converge, they form a vast, transformative ocean of shared understanding.

Our inquiry has shown collective wisdom to be a living force that grows when we create spaces for genuine connection and open dialogue. Across Love Sheffield's community of 24,000 friends, we sense a quiet transformation. It's not always visible, but there's a subtle shift – a growing current of empathy, compassion, and shared resourcefulness. This collective consciousness emerges through countless small interactions, gradually reshaping how we approach challenges and opportunities.

We began by seeing how collective wisdom springs from diverse perspectives and shared experiences. Looking at history and different cultures, we found timeless ways of building shared knowledge, from ancient tribal practices to modern philosophy. These varied approaches remind us there's no single path to collective wisdom, but many ways to grow our shared understanding.

We discovered the power of symbols and art in sharing collective wisdom. These creative expressions often speak louder than words, touching our shared human experience. This insight challenges us to use more diverse forms of expression in our community dialogues, enriching our collective understanding through different channels.

Our look at collective memory showed how it shapes our present. Shared stories guide how we see the world and act in it. This understanding invites us to approach our collective stories with both respect and fresh eyes, valuing our shared history while staying open to new views.

The idea of distributed intelligence helped us see how wisdom grows through our combined efforts. Like many streams forming a mighty river, our collective actions can achieve more than any of us could alone. This insight shows the importance of creating systems that support working together and sharing ideas freely. As we consider putting collective wisdom into practice, we're reminded that it's more than just an idea – it's something we can actively co-create.

By making space for real talks, welcoming different views, and building a sense of shared purpose, we can tap into the wisdom that exists in our communities.

Looking ahead, the journey of collective wisdom calls for humility and curiosity. It reminds us that no single person or group has all the answers, yet together, we can tackle complex challenges. Communities worldwide have the chance to try new approaches to learning, decision-making, and collaborative creation.

As we conclude this chapter, let's appreciate that collective wisdom is an ongoing process of growth and discovery. Each connection, shared moment, and new understanding contributes to our expanding pool of shared knowledge.

By embracing collective wisdom, we unlock the power of connection. We create communities that function as living systems of shared insight and innovation, guiding us towards a world of greater compassion, creativity, and shared wellbeing.

As we move forward, let's cherish our essential role in this sea of collective wisdom. By remaining open, curious, and committed to genuine connection, we add to a shared intelligence capable of transforming our communities and our world. With every interaction, we expand the horizons of our shared future.

7. Level 5 – Connection in Business

"What Sheffield says today, the world says tomorrow."
– Herbert Asquith

Herbert Asquith touches on our city's pioneering spirit in this statement. Sheffield's story isn't just one of steel and silver, but of the connections forged in the crucible of innovation and social progress. Our industrial giants, from the Jessop family to the visionaries behind our Advanced Manufacturing Research Centre, have shown time and again that when you connect purpose with people, magic happens. This wisdom, forged from Sheffield's history is our gift to the world. As we navigate the complexities of the 21st century, our city's approach to business, valuing community, creativity, and compassion alongside commerce, offers a blueprint for a more connected and resilient global economy.

The Power of Connection in Business

"Coming together is a beginning, staying together is progress, and working together is success." – Henry Ford

This vision of collaborative progress resonates deeply in today's business landscape. In our interconnected world, the transformative power of connection in business has never been more evident or vital.

Conventional business models often cast companies as machines, with staff merely cogs in a profit-driven engine. Yet, this view is swiftly evolving. Progressive organisations are waking up to the realisation that their true strength lies not in unyielding hierarchies or fierce competition, but in the quality of connections they cultivate – both within their teams and with the wider community they serve.

Simon Sinek, in his thought-provoking work *Leaders Eat Last*, presents a compelling case for this new paradigm. He observes, "When we feel safe inside the organisation, we naturally combine our talents and our strengths and work tirelessly to face the dangers outside together." This insight underscores the deep impact that a sense of connection and belonging can have on business success.

Consider the John Lewis Partnership, a bastion of British retail that has reimagined corporate structure through its employee-ownership model. Their unwavering commitment to staff wellbeing, community involvement, and ethical business practices shows that when a company aligns its purpose with broader social values, it can spark a powerful cascade of positive change while also achieving commercial success. The Partnership's constitution, which declares its ultimate purpose as "the happiness of all its members, through their worthwhile and satisfying employment in a successful business", embodies this connected approach.

But what does it truly mean to embrace connection in business? It goes beyond team-building exercises or corporate social responsibility programmes. At its core, it's about recognising the fundamental humanity in our professional relationships. It's about creating environments where individuals feel valued, heard, and empowered to contribute their distinctive gifts.

By embracing connection as a core business principle, we open the door to a new way of working that honours our shared humanity, harnesses our collective potential, and creates value beyond the bottom line. As we explore this concept further, we'll examine key aspects such as shared purpose, values alignment, individual agency, and visionary leadership, seeing how these elements interweave to create businesses that don't just succeed financially, but contribute meaningfully to the wellbeing of their employees, customers, and communities.

We'll use a business connection compass here, to give us a visual sense of balance and direction as we discuss each of these aspects in the following sections.

Figure 4. Business Connection Compass

Purpose: The Core of Business Connection

"The greatest danger for most of us is not that our aim is too high and we miss it, but that it is too low and we reach it."
– Michelangelo

In business, as in life, our true potential is unlocked when we orient ourselves towards a purpose that inspires and challenges us. This purpose isn't a fixed objective, but rather a guiding principle that draws us ever forward, igniting our collective imagination and driving us to explore and innovate. By embracing an aim that extends beyond immediate profits or tangible goals, we create a magnetic force that aligns our efforts, sparks innovation, and inspires continuous growth. This higher calling becomes the heartbeat of the enterprise, infusing every decision and action with meaning, and transforming the very nature of how we connect and create value in the business world.

Simon Sinek, in his thought-provoking work *Start With Why*, observes "People don't buy WHAT you do, they buy WHY you do it." This insight applies to both customers and to employees. When people understand and believe in the 'why' of their work, they're more likely to feel connected to their roles and to each other.

Consider Timpson, the UK shoe repair and key-cutting chain. Their purpose extends beyond providing services; they aim to be a force for social good by actively recruiting ex-offenders and those from disadvantaged backgrounds. This purpose creates a deep sense of meaning for employees and resonates with customers who appreciate the social impact of their patronage.

But how do we create this sense of purpose in business?

Here are a few key considerations:

1. **Align personal and organisational purpose**: Encourage employees to reflect on their own values and how they align with the company's mission. This could involve workshops or one-to-one discussions that help individuals see how their personal goals contribute to the larger purpose.

2. **Communicate purpose consistently**: Ensure that the company's purpose is clearly and regularly conveyed, both through mission statements and in day-to-day operations and decision-making.

3. **Lead by example**: Leaders should embody the company's purpose in their actions and decisions. This authenticity is crucial for building trust and connection.

4. **Create a shared sense of meaning**: Create an environment where employees can see the direct impact of their work on the company's purpose. This might involve sharing customer stories or highlighting how different roles contribute to the larger mission.

5. **Allow for evolution**: Recognise that as the business and its people grow, the articulation of purpose might need to evolve. Create spaces for ongoing dialogue about what the company's purpose means in practice.

It's worth noting that purpose emerges from connection. It need not be about grand, world-changing statements. For some businesses, the purpose might be as simple as providing excellent service that makes customers' lives easier. What matters is that it's authentic and meaningful to those involved.

Charles Handy, in *The Empty Raincoat*, suggests that profit is like oxygen for a company – necessary for its existence but not the reason for its existence. The true purpose of a business, he argues, should be something that contributes positively to society.

As we think about our own businesses or workplaces, we might ask: What is our true purpose beyond making money? How does our work contribute to something larger than ourselves? How can we better align our daily activities with this larger purpose?

By placing purpose at the core of business connection, we create organisations that don't just survive, but thrive. We grow environments where people feel part of something meaningful, where their work has significance beyond a paycheque. In doing so, we tap into a source of motivation, creativity, and loyalty that can transform the very nature of business itself.

What's your experience with purpose in business? How have you seen it create connections and drive success?

Values: The Foundation of Business Connection

"To be successful, you have to have your heart in your business, and your business in your heart." – Thomas J. Watson Sr.

True success in business stems from a deep, heartfelt commitment that goes beyond mere profit-seeking. When a company's values are clearly defined and genuinely lived, they create a powerful foundation for connection – both within the organisation and with the wider world. This alignment between principles and practice creates a sense of belonging and shared purpose that rises above traditional business relationships.

Charles Handy, in his excellent book *The Empty Raincoat*, introduces the concept of the 'psychological contract' – the unwritten expectations and obligations between an employer and employee. He argues that shared values form a crucial part of this contract, creating a sense of belonging and mutual understanding that goes beyond formal job descriptions.

Consider the Co-operative Group, a UK business built on values of self-help, self-responsibility, democracy, equality, equity, and solidarity. These values aren't just words on a wall; they inform every aspect of the business, from its democratic governance structure to its ethical investment policies. This alignment between stated values and actual practice creates a strong sense of connection among members, employees, and customers who share these principles.

But how do we establish and harness values as a foundation for connection in business? Here are some key considerations:

1. **Identify and articulate core values**: This process should involve input from all levels of the organisation to ensure the values truly reflect the collective ethos.

2. **Embed values in decision-making**: Use values as a framework for making both small daily decisions and major strategic choices. This consistency builds trust and reinforces the importance of the values.

3. **Align personal and organisational values**: Encourage employees to reflect on how their personal values align with those of the organisation. This can lead to deeper engagement and a stronger sense of purpose.

4. **Live the values visibly**: Leaders must embody the company's values in their actions and decisions. As management thinker Peter Drucker said, "Management is doing things right; leadership is doing the right things."

5. **Recognise and celebrate values-driven behaviour**: Create systems to acknowledge and reward actions that exemplify the company's values.

It's worth noting that having strong, clearly defined values doesn't mean everyone in the organisation must think alike. In fact, diversity of thought within a shared value framework can lead to more innovation and resilience.

Brené Brown, in her book *Dare to Lead*, emphasises the importance of operationalising values – moving them from abstract concepts to specific behaviours. She suggests that for each core value, a company should be able to identify three specific behaviours that represent that value in action.

As we think about our own businesses or workplaces, we might ask: What are our true core values? How do these values live in our daily operations? How can we better align our actions with our stated values?

By placing values at the foundation of business connections, we create organisations that are both profitable and principled, with a clear sense of purpose. We develop environments where people feel a genuine sense of belonging and shared mission. In doing so, we build businesses that are more resilient, more inspiring, and ultimately more successful in the fullest sense of the word.

What's your experience with values in business? How have you seen them create connections and drive success?

Agency: Recognising Individual Responsibility

"The price of greatness is responsibility." – Winston Churchill

Achieving greatness in any field demands a deep sense of responsibility. This principle holds especially true in business, where individual agency can serve as a powerful driver for connection and collective success. When people within an organisation feel genuinely responsible and empowered to act, it sparks a transformative energy that can elevate the entire enterprise.

Daniel Pink, in his book *Drive*, argues that autonomy – the urge to direct our own lives – is one of the key motivators of human behaviour. He observes, "Control leads to compliance; autonomy leads to engagement." This insight suggests that by recognising and encouraging individual agency, businesses can harness deeper engagement and more authentic connections.

Consider Buurtzorg, a Dutch healthcare organisation that has revolutionised community care. Their model is built on small, self-managing teams of nurses who have the autonomy to make decisions about patient care, scheduling, and even hiring. This high level of individual agency has not only led to better patient outcomes but also to stronger connections among team members and with the communities they serve.

Charles Handy, in *The Age of Unreason*, introduces the concept of the 'portfolio worker' – an individual who takes responsibility for their own career development and brings a diverse set of skills to an organisation. This idea underscores the importance of recognising and valuing individual agency in the modern workplace.

It's worth noting that agency isn't about leaving people to fend for themselves. Rather, it's about creating a supportive environment where individuals feel trusted and empowered to contribute their best work.

Margaret Wheatley, in *Leadership and the New Science*, draws parallels between organisational dynamics and quantum physics. She suggests that just as subatomic particles influence each other through their mere presence, individuals in an organisation are constantly affecting and being affected by those around them. This perspective highlights the powerful impact that individual agency can have on the entire system.

As we think about our own businesses or workplaces, we might ask: How can we encourage a greater sense of individual responsibility? What barriers might be preventing people from fully exercising their agency? How can we better recognise and celebrate individual contributions?

By recognising and encouraging individual agency, we create organisations that are more than the sum of their parts. We create environments where people feel valued, empowered, and deeply connected to their work and to each other. In doing so, we tap into a source of creativity, innovation, and commitment that can transform the very nature of how we do business.

But how do we establish agency as a means of enabling connection in business? The key lies in understanding agency as the core of our identity within the organisation, with empowerment as the vital force that allows this agency to flourish. This process is dynamic and cyclical, with each element reinforcing and enhancing the others.

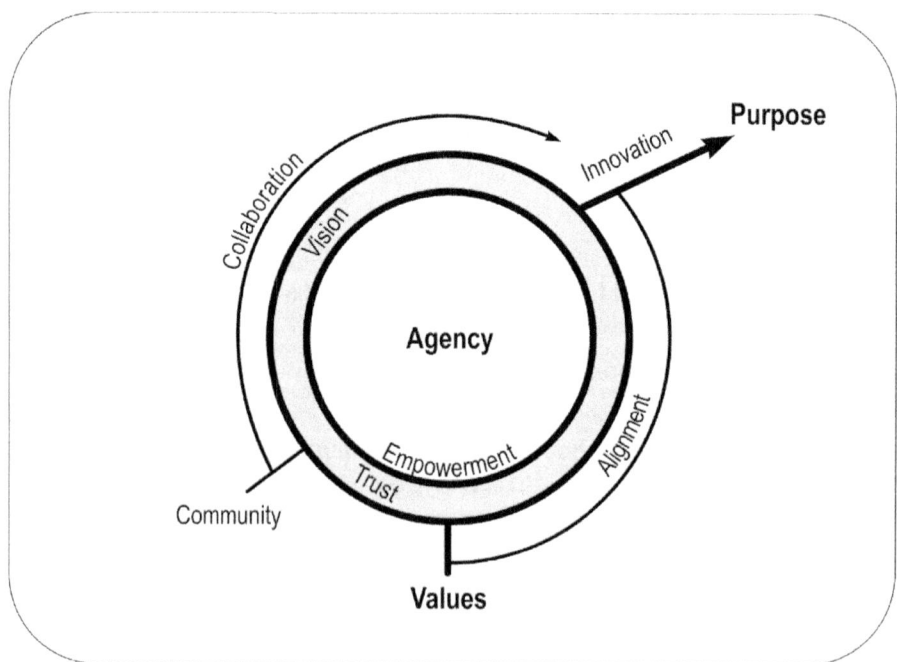

Figure 5. Agency in a Connected Business

Here are some key considerations, based on our model of Agency in Connected Business:

1. **Create a culture of empowerment**: Create an environment where individuals feel genuinely empowered to exercise their agency. This empowerment should be at the heart of the organisation, surrounding and encouraging each person's sense of agency.

2. **Root agency in shared values**: Ensure that the organisation's values are clear and lived daily. Empowered agency relies on a deep, resonating connection to these shared values. Encourage individuals to embody these values in every connection and action they take.

3. **Build trust through community engagement**: Recognise that trust is fundamental to agency. Encourage active, engaged participation in the community. As individuals demonstrate alignment with business values and purpose through their community involvement, trust grows, further strengthening empowerment.

4. **Develop collaborative vision**: Understand that vision emerges from deep connection with the community. Create spaces for collaboration where empowered individuals can use their agency to shape and refine this shared vision.

5. **Encourage innovation towards purpose**: Support individuals in using their agency to innovate, understanding that this is a key pathway to fulfilling the organisation's purpose. Innovation should spring from the empowered individual's connection with the community, collaborative vision, and alignment with values.

6. **Balance individual agency and community interdependence**: While agency is inherently individual, it thrives in an interdependent relationship with the community. Create an environment where individual agency and collective effort harmoniously drive progress towards shared goals.

7. **Facilitate continuous flow**: Recognise the importance of a continuous, cyclical flow in this process. This flow empowers individuals to give their best work as part of an authentic, connected, and passionate community, using their knowledge, skills, and creativity in alignment with values to deliver on the business purpose.

8. **Provide resources for effective agency**: Ensure individuals have the tools, information, and support needed to act autonomously and make informed decisions that align with the organisation's values and purpose.

9. **Embrace learning through action**: Recognise that increased agency may lead to new approaches and occasional missteps. Create a culture that views these as valuable learning experiences and opportunities for growth.

10. **Celebrate diverse expressions of agency**: Acknowledge that agency will materialise differently for each person, based on their individual skills, perspectives, and roles. Recognise and value these diverse contributions to the community and the organisation's purpose.

By developing agency in this holistic, interconnected way, we create a connected business where each individual feels empowered to be an agent of positive change. This not only drives the organisation towards its purpose but also creates a deeply fulfilling work environment where people can thrive, innovate, and grow together. The result is a dynamic, adaptable organisation where personal agency, community collaboration, shared values, and collective purpose align to create exceptional outcomes.

Leadership: Guiding with Connection

"A leader is best when people barely know he exists, when his work is done, his aim fulfilled, they will say: we did it ourselves."
– Lao Tzu

True leadership is about creating a culture of empowered connection. In my experience, leadership that guides with connection is less about wielding authority and more about building relationships, facilitating growth, and developing a shared vision. It's about creating a space where every individual feels valued and understood, and where collective wisdom can flourish.

Simon Sinek, in his book *Leaders Eat Last*, argues that great leaders create environments where people feel safe – both physically and emotionally, as well as psychologically. He writes, "When we feel safe inside the organization, we naturally combine our talents and our strengths and work tirelessly to face the dangers outside together." This sense of safety is fundamental to creating deep connections within a business.

Consider the leadership approach of Julian Richer, founder of Richer Sounds. His commitment to employee wellbeing, fair pay, and shared ownership has created a company culture renowned for its strong relationships and high employee satisfaction. By prioritising his staff's needs and involving them in decision-making, Richer has created a sense of belonging and shared purpose that translates into business success.

But how do we create leadership that guides with connection? Here are some key considerations:

1. **Practise empathetic listening**: Leaders should strive to truly understand the perspectives and experiences of their team members.

2. **Demonstrate transparency**: Open, honest communication builds trust and strengthens relationships.

3. **Empower others**: Delegate both tasks and the authority to make decisions.

4. **Lead by example**: Demonstrate the behaviours and values you wish to see in your organisation.

5. **Encourage a learning mindset**: Show vulnerability by admitting when you don't have all the answers and encourage collective problem-solving.

Mary Parker Follett, a pioneering management consultant in the early 20th century, introduced the concept of "power with" rather than "power over". This idea emphasises collaborative leadership that harnesses the collective intelligence of the group, rather than relying on top-down directives.

It's worth noting that leadership through connection isn't always the easiest path. It requires vulnerability, patience, and a willingness to relinquish control. However, the rewards – in terms of employee engagement, innovation, and overall organisational resilience – can be immense.

Margaret Heffernan, in her book *Wilful Blindness*, highlights the dangers of disconnected leadership. She argues that when leaders become isolated from the realities of their organisation, they risk making decisions that are detrimental to both the business and its people. This underscores the importance of leaders staying deeply connected to all levels of their organisation.

As we think about our own leadership practices or those in our workplaces, we might ask: How can we create more opportunities for meaningful connection? How can we ensure that every voice is heard and valued? How can we balance the need for direction with the importance of collective input?

By embracing leadership that guides with connection, we create organisations that are more than just efficient machines – they become living, breathing communities of purpose. We create environments where people feel seen, heard, and deeply invested in the collective success of the enterprise.

What's your experience with connected leadership? How have you seen it transform relationships and drive success in business? These are questions worth considering as we continue.

Vision: Crafting a Compelling Future

"The very essence of leadership is that you have to have vision. You can't blow an uncertain trumpet." – Theodore Hesburgh

A clear and inspiring vision acts as a beacon, guiding an organisation towards a compelling future. When a business paints a well-defined picture of what it aims to achieve, it creates a powerful rallying point for everyone involved. This shared vision aligns efforts across the organisation, inspiring collective action and creating a deep sense of connection among team members.

Truly effective visions go beyond simple financial targets or market share goals. They lock on to a future that resonates with people's hearts and minds, offering something meaningful to believe in and work towards together. By setting ambitious, long-term goals that might initially seem out of reach, organisations can spark innovation and collaboration, uniting their workforce in pursuit of a shared dream.

Jim Collins and Jerry Porras, in their book on corporate strategy *Built to Last*, introduce the concept of a BHAG – a Big, Hairy, Audacious Goal. They argue that great companies set themselves ambitious, long-term visions that may seem almost impossible at first glance. These visions serve to stretch the organisation, boosting innovation and collaboration in pursuit of a shared dream.

Consider the vision of Marks & Spencer to become the world's most sustainable major retailer. This ambitious goal, part of their Plan A initiative, has driven significant changes in their operations and inspired employees across the organisation to think creatively about sustainability. It's a vision that connects the company's activities to a larger purpose, conveying a sense of shared mission among employees and resonating with environmentally conscious consumers.

But how do we craft a vision that truly connects and inspires? Here are some key considerations:

1. **Make it aspirational yet achievable**: The vision should stretch the organisation without seeming utterly impossible.

2. **Ensure it's values-aligned**: The vision should reflect and reinforce the core values of the business.

3. **Communicate it clearly and consistently**: Everyone in the organisation should be able to articulate the vision.

4. **Connect it to daily activities**: Help employees see how their work contributes to the larger vision.

5. **Allow for co-creation**: Involve employees in shaping and refining the vision to share a sense of ownership.

Peter Senge, in *The Fifth Discipline*, emphasises the importance of shared vision in learning organisations. He argues that when people truly share a vision, they are connected by a common aspiration, which elevates their collective efforts and brings genuine commitment rather than mere compliance.

It's worth noting that a compelling vision is always responsive to the environment. As the business evolves and the external environment changes, the vision may need to be revisited and refined. However, the process of collectively imagining and working towards a better future remains a powerful tool for connection.

Charles Handy, in *The Age of Paradox*, suggests that in a world of constant change, organisations need a vision that provides a sense of continuity and purpose. This underscores the role of vision in creating stability and connection amidst uncertainty.

As we think about our own businesses or workplaces, we might ask: What future are we working towards? How does our vision inspire and connect people? How can we make our vision more compelling and relevant to everyone in the organisation?

By crafting a compelling vision, we create a north star that guides and unites the entire organisation. We develop an environment where people feel part of something larger than themselves, where their work has meaning beyond the immediate tasks at hand. In doing so, we tap into a powerful source of motivation, innovation, and collective effort.

What's your experience with vision in business? How have you seen it create connections and drive success?

Integrity: Building Trust in Business Relationships

"The supreme quality for leadership is unquestionably integrity. Without it, no real success is possible, no matter whether it is on a section gang, a football field, in an army, or in an office."
– Dwight D. Eisenhower

Unwavering commitment to our principles forms the basis of genuine leadership and lasting success. This holds true generally, but perhaps nowhere more so than in business. Integrity serves as the foundation upon which all meaningful business relationships are built. When it's absent, trust crumbles, and relationships risk becoming shallow or purely transactional.

In business, integrity extends far beyond basic honesty. It demands a consistent alignment between words and actions, a steadfast commitment to fulfilling promises, and the courage to uphold ethical standards even in challenging circumstances. True integrity means embodying the same values and behaviour regardless of who is watching.

Stephen M.R. Covey, in his book *The Speed of Trust*, argues that trust is more than just a social virtue; it's a hard-edged economic driver. He writes, "When trust goes up, speed goes up and cost goes down." This insight underscores the tangible business value of integrity – it's both the right thing to do and beneficial for the bottom line.

Consider the example of Timpson, the UK shoe repair and key-cutting chain. Their 'upside down management' approach, where front-line staff are given significant autonomy and trust, is underpinned by a culture of integrity. This trust-based model has not only led to high employee satisfaction but also to strong customer loyalty and business success.

But how do we build and maintain integrity in business relationships? Here are some key considerations:

1. **Be consistent**: Ensure your actions align with your words across all situations.

2. **Communicate openly and honestly**: Be transparent about both successes and challenges.

3. **Take responsibility**: Own your mistakes and focus on solutions rather than blame.

4. **Respect confidentiality**: Handle sensitive information with care.

5. **Make ethical decisions**: Consider the broader impact of your choices; focus on long-term outcomes rather than short-term gains.

Charles Handy, in *The Empty Raincoat*, introduces the concept of the 'psychological contract' – the unwritten expectations in any working relationship. He argues that integrity is crucial in maintaining this contract, as it builds the trust necessary for people to commit fully to their work and their organisation.

It's worth noting that integrity is how we conduct ourselves, and we all have bad days. What matters is how we respond to our mistakes – with honesty, accountability, and a commitment to do better.

Brené Brown, in *Dare to Lead*, emphasises the importance of vulnerability in leadership. She argues that admitting when we don't have all the answers or when we've made a mistake is not a sign of weakness, but of integrity and courage. This vulnerability, paradoxically, builds trust and stronger relationships.

As we think about our own businesses or workplaces, we might ask: How do our actions align with our stated values? How do we handle situations where maintaining integrity is challenging? How can we create a culture where integrity is celebrated and rewarded?

By prioritising integrity, we build businesses that are both profitable and principled. We create environments where people feel safe to be authentic, take risks, and fully engage. This approach develops relationships and connections that can endure challenges and drive long-term success.

What's your experience with integrity in business? How have you seen it create trust and deepen connections?

Community: Powerful Belonging and Shared Purpose

"The greatness of a community is most accurately measured by the compassionate actions of its members." – Coretta Scott King

True community is about how we treat each other and work together towards a common goal. In business, when we create a powerful sense of belonging and common purpose, we unlock an extraordinary force for positive change and success.

Community in business is far more than a nice-to-have; it's a fundamental driver of engagement, innovation, and resilience. When people feel they truly belong and are united by a shared purpose, they bring their whole selves to work. This creates a synergy that can propel a business to new heights.

Etienne Wenger, in his work on *Communities of Practice*, posits that learning and innovation happen best in communities where people share a passion and interact regularly. He writes, "Communities of practice are groups of people who share a concern or a passion for something they do and learn how to do it better as they interact regularly." This insight underscores the power of creating strong communities within businesses.

Consider the approach of Bromford, a social enterprise and housing association based in the Midlands. Their 'neighbourhood coaching' model creates strong communities both within the organisation and in the areas they serve. By providing a sense of belonging and shared purpose among employees and residents alike, they've achieved remarkable outcomes in terms of tenant satisfaction and community development.

But how do we create this powerful sense of belonging and shared purpose? Here are some key considerations:

1. **Articulate a compelling shared purpose**: Ensure everyone understands how their work contributes to a larger, meaningful goal.

2. **Create opportunities for deep connection**: Go beyond surface-level interactions to honour genuine relationships.

3. **Celebrate diversity**: Recognise that a strong community is built on diverse perspectives and experiences.

4. **Encourage peer support**: Create systems where employees can help and learn from each other.

5. **Involve everyone in shaping the community**: Give people a voice in defining and evolving the shared culture and values.

Margaret Heffernan, in her book A *Bigger Prize*, challenges the notion that competition is the primary driver of success. She argues that collaboration and strong communities lead to more sustainable and fulfilling achievements. This perspective invites us to rethink how we structure our organisations to harness cooperation rather than internal competition.

It's worth noting that building a strong sense of community doesn't happen overnight. It requires consistent effort, authentic leadership, and a genuine commitment to putting people first. However, the rewards – in terms of employee satisfaction, customer loyalty, and business performance – can be transformative.

Charles Handy, in *The Second Curve*, suggests that businesses of the future will need to function more like communities of common purpose if they are to attract and retain talented people. This insight highlights the growing importance of creating workplaces where people feel a powerful sense of belonging and shared mission.

As we think about our own businesses or workplaces, we might ask: How can we deepen the sense of belonging for everyone in our organisation? What shared purpose can unite and inspire us? How can we harness the collective energy and wisdom of our community to drive positive change?

By building powerful belonging and shared purpose, we create businesses that are more than just economic entities – they become forces for good in the world. We tap into deep human needs for connection and meaning, creating environments where people can thrive personally and professionally. In doing so, we not only enhance business performance but also contribute to building a more connected and purposeful society.

What's your experience with community in business? How have you seen a sense of belonging and shared purpose transform an organisation? These are questions worth pondering as we continue our exploration of connection in business.

Initiative: Driving Connection Through Action

"The way to get started is to quit talking and begin doing."
– Walt Disney

Action is the lifeblood of innovation and connection in business. When we empower people to take initiative, we create a dynamic environment where relationships naturally flourish and ideas come to life.

In my experience with Love Sheffield, I've seen how individual initiative can spark waves of positive change throughout a community. When people feel empowered to act on their ideas, they naturally connect with others who share their passion, creating networks of support and collaboration that extend far beyond the initial action.

Consider the example of Riverford Organic Farmers. Their 'self-managed teams' approach encourages employees to take initiative in improving processes and solving problems. This has not only led to numerous innovations in their operations but has also created a strong sense of ownership and connection among team members.

But how do we create a culture of initiative that drives connection?

Here are some thoughts:

1. **Create safe spaces for experimentation**: Encourage people to try new ideas without fear of punishment if they don't succeed.

2. **Recognise and celebrate initiative**: Highlight examples of people taking action, regardless of the outcome.

3. **Provide resources for action**: Ensure people have the tools and support they need to turn their ideas into reality.

4. **Allow cross-pollination of ideas**: Create opportunities for people from different parts of the organisation to collaborate.

5. **Lead by example**: Leaders should demonstrate initiative and share both their successes and learnings from failures.

It's worth noting that initiative isn't about reckless action. It's about thoughtful, purposeful steps towards improvement and innovation. As we encourage initiative, we must also exercise the judgement to know when and how to act.

As we think about our own businesses or communities, we might ask: How can we remove barriers to initiative? How can we better support those who step forward with ideas? How can we harness the connective power of shared action?

By encouraging initiative, we create environments where connection and innovation thrive. We tap into the creative potential of every individual, creating a collective force for positive change that can transform our organisations and communities.

What's your experience with initiative in business or community work? How have you seen it drive connection and spark positive change? I'd be keen to hear your thoughts as we continue exploring the power of connection.

Conclusion: Integrating Connection for Business Success

"The most important part of leadership is what happens when you're not there" – Ken Blanchard and Randy Conley.

Great leaders create cultures of empowered, responsible collaboration towards a common purpose. When we truly integrate connection into the fabric of our businesses, we create resilient, thriving organisations that don't rely on constant top-down direction.

As we've journeyed through the various aspects of connection in business – from purpose and values to agency and community – a common thread emerges. Successful, connected businesses aren't built on control and hierarchy, but on trust, shared purpose, and the unleashing of individual potential.

Consider how these elements interweave:
- A clear, compelling purpose provides a north star that guides and unites the entire organisation.
- Strong, lived values create a foundation of trust and mutual understanding.

- Recognising individual agency allows people to bring their full selves to work, driving innovation and engagement.
- Leadership that guides with connection creates environments where people feel safe to take risks and contribute their best.
- A powerful sense of community and belonging taps into our fundamental human needs, creating loyalty and collective strength.

But how do we bring these elements together in a coherent whole? Here are some thoughts:

1. View connection as a strategic priority, not a 'nice-to-have'.

2. Align systems and processes to support connection, from hiring practices to performance reviews.

3. Invest in developing 'connection skills' at all levels of the organisation.

4. Measure and celebrate connection-related outcomes alongside traditional business metrics.

5. Continually seek feedback and evolve your approach to connection.

As we reflect on our own businesses or workplaces, we might ask: How well have we integrated connection into our core operations? Where are the gaps, and how might we address them? What would our business look like if connection truly became our competitive advantage?

By integrating connection into every aspect of our businesses, we create organisations that are more than the sum of their parts. We unlock the full potential of our people, create resilience in the face of challenges, and position ourselves to thrive in an increasingly complex and interconnected world.

What's your vision for a truly connected business? How might you take the first steps towards realising that vision? These questions are worth pondering as we continue our journey of connection.

In the next section, we'll explore some practical tools and exercises to help you enhance connection in your business. However, the most powerful tool is your own commitment to creating environments where people can connect authentically and work together towards shared goals.

Connection Toolkit to Enhance Business Success

"The most powerful person in the world is the story teller. The storyteller sets the vision, values and agenda of an entire generation that is to come." – Steve Jobs

The power of storytelling to shape our perception of reality cannot be overstated. In business, the narratives we create and share can deeply influence how we understand our purpose, our values, and our place in the wider world. These stories can inspire deep connections and drive meaningful change. By viewing our organisations through a 'connection lens', we become storytellers of a new business narrative – one that prioritises human bonds, shared purpose, and collective growth.

Let's consider our 'Connection Compass' for businesses, based on the key elements we've explored.

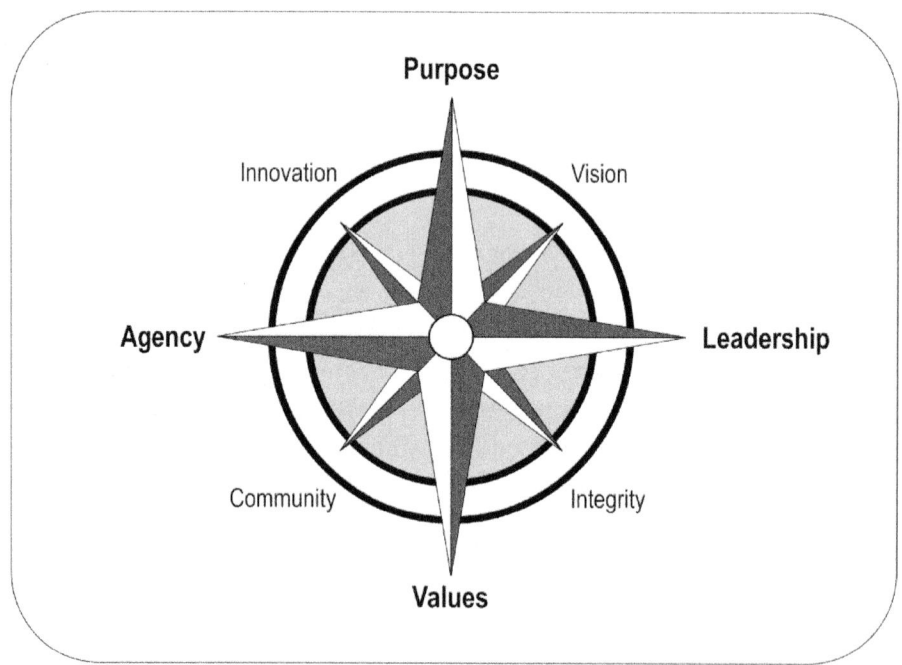

Figure 4. Business Connection Compass

For each point on the compass, we'll consider questions that uncover disconnection and spark ideas for developing stronger bonds:

1. **Purpose:**

   a) Where do our team members feel disconnected from our organisation's mission?

   b) How can we bridge the gap between individual goals and our collective purpose?

   c) Can everyone recount the purpose of the business, inside and out? For example, in Love Sheffield "We help make it easier for everyone to become more connected."

2. **Vision:**

   a) In what ways might our vision be excluding or alienating certain groups?

   b) How can we make our future aspirations more inclusive and connecting?

   c) Every unique, beautiful and creative individual can help deliver our purpose by pursuing their own Journey of Connection.

3. **Leadership:**

   a) Where are leaders failing to connect with their teams on a human level?

   b) How can we create more empathetic and accessible leadership?

   c) Leadership is essential for everyone, good leaders know when to follow.

4. **Integrity:**

   a) Where might our actions be misaligned with our stated values, causing distrust?

   b) How can we create more transparency and consistency in our practices?

c) When we are committed to our purpose, and living our values in every connection. Integrity emerges naturally.

5. **Values:**

   a) Which of our values might be causing division rather than unity?

   b) How can we reframe our values to be more unifying and inclusive?

   c) Human values are surprisingly common – kindness, compassion and creativity appear to be near universal to the connected human.

6. **Community:**

   a) Where are silos or barriers preventing cross-team collaboration?

   b) How might we create more opportunities for meaningful interaction across the organisation?

   c) Community magnifies the creative power of every individual in alignment with our values and purpose.

7. **Agency:**

   a) Where do team members feel powerless or voiceless in decision-making?

   b) How can we empower individuals to take more ownership and initiative?

   c) We need every perspective to be available and engaged, to achieve our purpose. Everyone gets to do the best work of their life.

8. **Innovation:**

   a) How might our innovation processes be excluding diverse perspectives?

b) Where can we create more collaborative spaces for creative problem-solving?

c) Innovation comes from inspired individuals connected to the collective intelligence of the community. They are free to express their creativity towards the purpose and success of the business.

This toolkit encourages businesses to look at challenges through a 'connection lens', identifying areas of disconnection and inspiring creative solutions. It's about seeing the channels of connection that bind us and making sure they are given continuous healthy attention.

To use this toolkit effectively:

1. Engage diverse voices in the process. The richest insights often come from unexpected sources.

2. Create safe spaces for honest answers and collaborative problem-solving.

3. Prioritise action. Choose one or two areas to focus on and create concrete plans for improvement.

4. Regularly revisit and refine. Connection is an ongoing journey, not a destination.

As always, the aim is progress not perfection. Every step towards greater connection can have a cascade effect throughout the organisation.

As you use this toolkit, you might ask: What patterns of disconnection do we see across different areas? How might addressing one area of disconnection positively impact others? What would our business look like if we prioritised connection alongside profit?

By regularly using tools like this Connection Compass, we can create businesses that don't just succeed financially, but also contribute to the wellbeing of their people and communities. We grow organisations that are more resilient, innovative, and ultimately, more human.

What aspects of this toolkit resonate with you? How might you adapt it to your specific context? I'd be keen to hear your thoughts as you begin to apply these ideas in your own work.

Solving The Five Dysfunctions of a Team

"A team is not a group of people who work together. A team is a group of people who trust each other." – Simon Sinek

True teamwork goes beyond mere collaboration to a deeper level of connection. It resonates with the idea that trust is the foundation for overcoming team dysfunctions, aligning with connection and shared purpose. When we focus on building trust, we create an environment where vulnerability, productive conflict, commitment, and accountability can naturally flourish.

Patrick Lencioni's *The Five Dysfunctions of a Team* offers deep insights into the challenges that undermine team performance. An organisation built on deep connection and shared purpose naturally tackles these issues.

Let's examine how:

Absence of Trust

"Trust is the foundation of real teamwork." – Patrick Lencioni

In a connected business, trust isn't forced but emerges organically. As we've seen, "When we are committed to our purpose, and living our values in every connection, integrity emerges naturally." This environment encourages vulnerability and openness, laying the groundwork for deep trust.

Fear of Conflict

"All great relationships, the ones that last over time, require productive conflict in order to grow" – Patrick Lencioni

A culture of connection values diverse perspectives. As our compass reminds us, "Every unique, beautiful and creative individual can help deliver our purpose by pursuing their own Journey of Connection." This approach transforms conflict from a threat to an opportunity for growth and innovation.

Lack of Commitment

"Consensus is horrible. I mean, if everyone really agrees on something and consensus comes about quickly and naturally, well that's terrific. But that isn't how it usually works, and so consensus becomes an attempt to please everyone."
– Patrick Lencioni

When a shared purpose runs through an organisation like a golden thread, commitment follows. "Can everyone recount the purpose of the business, inside and out?" When they can, individual goals align with organisational objectives, producing deep, lasting commitment.

Avoidance of Accountability

"Great teams do not hold back with one another. They are unafraid to air their dirty laundry. They admit their mistakes, their weaknesses, and their concerns without fear of reprisal."
– Patrick Lencioni

In a truly connected business, accountability shifts from a top-down imposition to a shared responsibility. "We need every perspective to be available and engaged, to achieve our purpose. Everyone gets to do the best work of their life." This mindset turns accountability into a form of mutual support and care.

Inattention to Results

"If you could get all the people in an organization rowing in the same direction, you could dominate any industry, in any market, against any competition, at any time." – Patrick Lencioni

A connected organisation recognises that "Community magnifies the creative power of every individual in alignment with our values and purpose." This alignment naturally focuses attention on collective results, as personal and organisational success become inseparable.

By weaving connection into the fabric of an organisation, we create an environment where Lencioni's dysfunctions struggle to take root. Instead, we grow resilient, innovative teams that thrive on collaboration and shared purpose.

As we consider these ideas, we might ask ourselves: How can we deepen connection in our own teams and organisations? What steps can we take to address these dysfunctions through the lens of connection?

By addressing these dysfunctions through the lens of connection, we move towards building businesses that excel not only in performance but also in enhancing the wellbeing and fulfilment of everyone involved. This is the power of connection in action – transforming not only how we work but also how we interact with each other and engage with the world around us.

Conclusion: Forging the Connected Enterprise

"If you hire people just because they can do a job, they'll work for your money. But if you hire people who believe what you believe, they'll work for you with blood, sweat, and tears." – Simon Sinek

When we grow genuine connection in business – rooted in shared purpose and values – we create an environment where people bring their whole selves to work. This is more than merely improving performance; it's about creating a sense of belonging and shared mission that goes beyond traditional notions of employment. It's this deep level of connection that transforms organisations from mere economic entities into vibrant communities capable of creating meaningful change in the world.

We began by recognising that connection in business isn't a superficial add-on, but a fundamental force that shapes every aspect of organisational life. From purpose and values to agency and leadership, we've seen how prioritising human bonds and shared meaning can unlock extraordinary potential within our workplaces.

Our compass of connection guided us through key elements that inspire genuine engagement:

Purpose emerged as the heart of connected business, providing a shared 'why' that aligns individual aspirations with organisational goals. We discovered that when people understand and believe in the deeper meaning of their work, they naturally gravitate towards more authentic and committed engagement.

Values, we found, serve as the basis of trust and mutual understanding in business relationships. By living our stated principles consistently, we create an environment where genuine connections can flourish, leading to deeper engagement and loyalty.

Agency emerged as a crucial factor in empowering individuals to contribute their distinctive gifts. We saw how recognising and encouraging personal responsibility creates a cascade effect of engagement and innovation throughout an organisation.

Leadership, when approached through the lens of connection, transforms into a practice of creating conditions for others to thrive. We explored how leaders who prioritise genuine human bonds develop environments where trust, creativity, and collective wisdom naturally emerge.

Vision stood out as a powerful force for uniting and inspiring people. We saw how a compelling vision of the future can create a focal point for connection, aligning efforts and sparking collective action towards shared goals.

Integrity emerged as the invisible thread that weaves trust through all business relationships. We recognised that consistent alignment between words and actions builds the foundation for meaningful, lasting relationships at all levels of an organisation.

Community, we discovered, is more than a by-product of business activities; it's a powerful force driving organisational success. By creating a sense of belonging and shared purpose, businesses can harness the collective energy and wisdom of their people.

Innovation, we found, flourishes in environments of deep connection. We explored how creating spaces for collaborative problem-solving and diverse perspectives can spark creativity and drive positive change.

As we navigated these interconnected elements, we uncovered a significant truth: businesses that prioritise connection don't just perform better financially; they also contribute to the wellbeing and fulfilment of everyone involved. They become forces for good in the world, creating cascades of positive change that extend far beyond their immediate sphere of influence.

The journey of integrating connection into business is not without its challenges. It asks us to question long-held assumptions about hierarchy, control, and success. It invites vulnerability, deep listening, and a willingness to prioritise long-term relationships over short-term gains. Yet, as we've seen through numerous examples, the potential rewards – in terms of innovation, employee satisfaction, customer loyalty, and sustainable success – are immense.

Looking ahead, we can see that businesses which embrace connection as a core principle are better positioned to navigate the complexities of our rapidly changing world. They achieve the resilience, creativity, and adaptability needed to thrive in uncertain times. More importantly, they contribute to shaping a future where economic activity aligns more closely with human values and societal wellbeing.

As we close this chapter, let's carry forward the understanding that every business interaction, every policy decision, every leadership choice is an opportunity to deepen connection. The toolkit we've explored offers practical ways to 'tilt the floor' towards more connected business practices.

By integrating connection into the very fabric of our business practices, we do more than enhance organisational performance – we contribute to weaving a more compassionate, purposeful, and interconnected world. This is the true power of connection in business: it allows us to create enterprises that make a massive positive difference in the world.

8. Level 6 – World Peace

---

*"If we have no peace, it is because we have forgotten
that we belong to each other." – Mother Teresa*

Peace is rooted in our shared humanity. As we reach this level of connection, we find ourselves with a vision that has moved the hearts of dreamers throughout history. World peace is more than stopping conflicts, it's about creating justice, understanding, and a deep sense of belonging that crosses borders and cultures.

Johan Galtung, often called the father of peace studies, offers a helpful way to understand peace. In his important work *Peace by Peaceful Means*, Galtung talks about two types of peace: 'negative peace' – which is just the absence of violence – and 'positive peace' – which is about integrating human society. This idea of positive peace fits closely with our journey of connection, suggesting that true peace comes from building relationships and systems that help people thrive.

In this section, we'll look at how the principles of connection we've discussed can be used on a global scale. We'll think about historical peace movements, the role of empathy and compassion in international relations, and how small, local efforts can create waves of change that spread far beyond where they started.

We'll also tackle the challenges that stand in the way of world peace – unfair systems, cultural misunderstandings, and the complex web of global politics. But rather than seeing these as impossible obstacles, we'll approach them as chances for growth and transformation.

As we dig into this topic, keep in mind the core values that have guided us so far: kindness, compassion, and creativity. These principles, when applied globally, have the power to dramatically reshape our world.

World peace isn't a distant dream, but a living reality we can create daily through our actions and relationships. Each act of kindness and bridge of understanding contributes to this vision.

Let's begin this final part of our journey with open hearts and curious minds, ready to explore how we can unite hearts and ignite change on a truly global scale.

Historical Movements Towards Peace

"Peace is not an absence of war, it is a virtue, a state of mind, a disposition for benevolence, confidence, justice." – Baruch Spinoza

Peace as an active way of being rather than a passive state. This idea has driven many movements throughout history that have tried to create a more peaceful world.

One of the most powerful examples of peaceful resistance in the pursuit of peace is Mahatma Gandhi's Satyagraha movement. Gandhi's philosophy of nonviolent civil disobedience not only led India to independence but also inspired movements for civil rights and freedom across the world. In his autobiography, *The Story of My Experiments with Truth*, Gandhi writes, "Non-violence is the greatest force at mankind's disposal. It is mightier than the mightiest weapon of destruction devised by human ingenuity."

The Women's International League for Peace and Freedom, started in 1915 during World War I, offers another inspiring example. These women, crossing national and ideological lines, came together to advocate for peace at a time when such ideas were seen as radical. Their work laid the groundwork for women's involvement in peace processes, which has been shown to significantly increase how long peace agreements last.

In more recent history, the end of the Cold War and the fall of the Berlin Wall in 1989 marked a turning point in the movement towards global peace. This period saw a shift from a world divided in two to one with the potential for greater international cooperation. Mikhail Gorbachev, in his book *The New Russia*, reflects on this time: "We had a unique opportunity to change the world... to build a new world order based on genuine partnership."

However, it's important to recognise that these movements, while groundbreaking, have not created a perfect world. They've laid important foundations, but the work continues. As we look at these historical movements, we must ask ourselves: What lessons can we draw from them? How can we build upon their successes and learn from their shortcomings?

Moreover, how do these big historical movements connect to our daily lives and local communities? The answer lies in understanding that global peace starts with individual actions and local relationships. Every time we choose understanding over judgement, cooperation over competition, we're contributing to these historical movements in our own way.

These historical movements remind us that peace is an achievable reality, shaped by our choices and interactions. Let's draw inspiration from their courage as we continue our exploration of world peace.

Philosophical and Ethical Foundations of Peace

"To be at peace with ourselves is the surest way to begin the task of being at peace with others." – Jawaharlal Nehru

Peace starts within us. This idea echoes through different cultures and times, suggesting that the path to world peace is closely tied to our own inner journeys of self-understanding and ethical growth.

In *Perpetual Peace*, Immanuel Kant outlined a vision for lasting peace through free governments, a coalition of free states, and universal hospitality. He argued that peace is more than simply the absence of war; it must be actively created and maintained through intentional actions and ethical principles. As he noted, "The state of peace among men living side by side is not the natural state; the natural state is one of war."

Eastern philosophy offers similar ideas. The Buddhist concept of "ahimsa" or non-violence, as explained by the Dalai Lama, goes beyond physical actions to include thoughts and words. In *Ethics for the New Millennium*, the Dalai Lama writes, "My call for a spiritual revolution is not a call for a religious revolution. It's not about a way of life that is otherworldly or magical. Rather, it's a call for a big shift away from our usual focus on ourselves."

The African philosophy of Ubuntu, meaning "I am because we are", provides a powerful ethical base for peace. Archbishop Desmond Tutu, in his book *No Future Without Forgiveness*, explains, "Ubuntu speaks particularly about the fact that you can't exist as a human being in isolation. It speaks about how we're all connected." This philosophy underlines the idea that our own wellbeing is closely tied to the wellbeing of others, giving a strong ethical argument for peace.

Modern philosopher Peter Singer, in *The Expanding Circle*, argues for an ethics that keeps expanding who we care about. He suggests that as our circle of empathy grows to include more beings, our ethical duties expand, naturally leading to more peaceful interactions. Singer writes, "The circle of altruism has broadened from the family and tribe to the nation and race, and we are beginning to recognize that our obligations extend to all human beings."

These philosophical and ethical foundations raise important questions for our journey of connection. How can we grow inner peace as a foundation for global peace? How might we expand who we empathize with and care about? What role do forgiveness and reconciliation play in building lasting peace?

As we think about these questions, it's clear that the philosophical and ethical foundations of peace are not just abstract ideas, but practical guides for how we live our lives and build our communities. They challenge us to see peace not as a far-off goal, but as a way of being that we can practise in our daily interactions.

These philosophical insights can inspire communities worldwide, including Love Sheffield, to create spaces for inner exploration, empathy growth, and meaningful dialogue about our shared ethical responsibilities. This lays the groundwork for peace that extends beyond our immediate circles.

The Role of Empathy and Compassion in Allowing Peace

"If you want others to be happy, practice compassion. If you want to be happy, practice compassion." – Dalai Lama

Compassion isn't just a good quality to have, but a practical way to create happiness for ourselves and others. As we think about how empathy and compassion help create peace, we start to see how these qualities form the foundation of meaningful connection and global harmony.

Roman Krznaric, in his book *Empathy*, says that empathy is not just a personal trait, but a powerful social and political tool. He writes, "Empathy is the art of stepping imaginatively into the shoes of another person, understanding their feelings and perspectives, and using that understanding to guide your actions." This ability to understand and share others' feelings is crucial in bridging divides and solving conflicts that stand in the way of peace.

Marshall Rosenberg's work on Nonviolent Communication gives us a practical way to use empathy and compassion in our daily lives. Rosenberg suggests that by focusing on universal human needs and feelings, we can overcome cultural and ideological differences. He says, "What I want in my life is compassion, a flow between myself and others based on a mutual giving from the heart."

Research in brain science and psychology supports the transformative power of empathy and compassion. Dr. James Doty, in his book *Into the Magic Shop*, explains how practising compassion can actually alter brain structure, enhancing our capacity for kindness and diminishing our tendencies towards aggression. This indicates that developing compassion is both a moral choice and a biological pathway to peace.

In international relations, we see powerful examples of empathy and compassion creating breakthroughs in seemingly unsolvable conflicts. The Truth and Reconciliation Commission in post-apartheid South Africa, led by Archbishop Desmond Tutu, showed how empathy and compassion could heal deep societal wounds. Tutu writes in *No Future Without Forgiveness*, "True reconciliation exposes the awfulness, the abuse, the hurt, the truth... because in the end only an honest confrontation with reality can bring real healing."

These insights raise important questions for our journey of connection. How can we grow empathy and compassion in our daily lives? How might we create spaces in our communities where people can practise deep listening and understanding across differences? What would our world look like if empathy and compassion were at the heart of our schools, our businesses, our political processes?

In Love Sheffield, and in communities around the world, we have the chance to be testing grounds for empathy and compassion. By creating environments where people feel safe to be vulnerable, to share their stories, and to truly listen to others, we allow the seeds of peace to take root and flourish.

As we progress, each act of empathy and compassion contributes to our collective peace consciousness. These are practical, powerful tools for change that everyone can incorporate into their daily lives.

The Impact of Education and Cultural Exchange

"Education is the most powerful weapon which you can use to change the world." – Nelson Mandela

The transformative power of education in shaping our world cannot be overstated. Mandela's insight, born from the struggles for justice and reconciliation, highlights how learning and cross-cultural understanding can be potent forces for change. Education, when coupled with meaningful cultural exchange, has the capacity to bridge divides, challenge preconceptions, and inspire a deeper sense of our shared humanity. It equips us with the tools to not only understand our complex world but also to actively participate in its improvement.

Paulo Freire, in his groundbreaking work *Pedagogy of the Oppressed*, argues that education should be a practice of freedom, enabling people to deal critically with reality and discover how to participate in the transformation of their world. He writes, "Education either functions as an instrument which is used to facilitate integration of the younger generation into the logic of the present system and bring about conformity or it becomes the practice of freedom, the means by which men and women deal critically and creatively with reality and discover how to participate in the transformation of their world." This perspective illuminates how education can be a catalyst for peace by empowering individuals to become active participants in shaping a more just and harmonious society.

Cultural exchange programmes have long been recognised as powerful tools for building international understanding and peace. The Fulbright Program, established in 1946, stands as a testament to this idea. Senator J. William Fulbright, the programme's founder, believed that by sharing leadership, learning, and empathy between cultures, we could generate the human understanding necessary for a peaceful world. He stated, "Educational exchange can turn nations into people, contributing as no other form of communication can to the humanizing of international relations."

In her book *The Force of Kindness*, Sharon Salzberg explores how education in emotional intelligence and mindfulness can contribute to a more peaceful world. She argues that by teaching people to understand and manage their emotions, and to approach others with kindness and curiosity, we can create a cascade effect of positive change. Salzberg writes, "The cultivation of kindness is a powerful form of peacemaking. Peace can't be only external; it must be born in the human heart."

The work of organisations like Seeds of Peace, which brings together young people from conflict regions for dialogue and leadership development, demonstrates the practical impact of education and cultural exchange on peacebuilding. By creating spaces for young people to engage with 'the other', challenge their assumptions, and develop empathy, these programmes lay the groundwork for future peace.

These insights prompt crucial questions for our journey of connection. How can we integrate peace education into our schools and communities? What opportunities can we create for meaningful cultural exchange, both globally and within our diverse local areas? How can we utilise education to challenge prejudices and build bridges of understanding?

In communities around the world, we have the opportunity to bring our own vision to life through peace education and cultural exchange. By creating spaces for dialogue, shared learning, and cross-cultural experiences, we can raise a generation of peace builders who see diversity as a strength and conflict as an opportunity for growth.

Moving forward, we can take heart that each educational initiative and cultural exchange builds our collective peace consciousness. These are not mere academic exercises, but powerful tools for transformation that benefit us all.

Economic and Social Justice as Pillars of Peace

"Peace is not just the absence of conflict; it's the presence of justice." – Martin Luther King Jr.

True peace is intrinsically linked to fairness and equality. This understanding, rooted in the ongoing struggle for civil rights, reveals the deep dependence of lasting peace on social justice.

Amartya Sen, in his book *Development as Freedom*, argues that economic growth and personal freedom support each other. He says that freedom is both the goal and the main way to achieve development. Sen writes, "Development means removing the big barriers to freedom: poverty, lack of opportunities, social unfairness, poor public services, and oppressive governments." This view shows us that economic and social justice aren't just morally right, but necessary for creating peaceful societies.

Muhammad Yunus, who started Grameen Bank and pioneered microfinance, gives us a powerful example of how economic fairness can lead to peace. In his book *Banker to the Poor*, Yunus says that poverty isn't created by poor people, but by the systems we've built. He imagines a future where "we'll need to build museums to show the horrors of poverty to future generations. They'll wonder why poverty lasted so long – how a few people could live in luxury while billions lived in misery." Yunus's work shows how helping people economically can create more stable, peaceful communities.

Kate Raworth's *Doughnut Economics* offers a fresh look at how we might reshape our economic systems to promote both social justice and environmental care. Raworth argues for an economy that meets everyone's needs within what the planet can provide. She writes, "Our 21st century challenge is to meet the needs of all without putting too much pressure on Earth's life-supporting systems." This balanced approach to economics gives us a map for creating societies that are both fair and peaceful.

The idea of restorative justice, as explored by Howard Zehr in *The Little Book of Restorative Justice*, offers a powerful way to address harm and build peace in communities. Zehr argues that justice should focus on healing relationships rather than punishment. He writes, "Restorative justice is a process to involve those affected by an offence to collectively address harms, needs, and obligations, to heal and make things as right as possible." This approach to justice could transform conflicts and build stronger, more peaceful communities.

These ideas raise important questions for our journey of connection. How can we create economic systems that put human wellbeing and environmental care first? What role can local communities play in promoting economic and social justice? How might we use principles of restorative justice in our everyday interactions and institutions?

In communities around the world, we have the chance to try new models of economic and social organisation that promote justice and peace. By creating local economies that prioritise fairness and sustainability, by addressing inequalities in our communities, and by using restorative approaches to conflict, we can build the foundations for lasting peace.

Every effort towards economic and social justice, no matter how small, contributes to a more peaceful world. These are practical tools for change that each of us can use to make a positive impact.

Environmental Sustainability and Peace

"The environment and the economy are really both two sides of the same coin. If we cannot sustain the environment, we cannot sustain ourselves." – Wangari Maathai

The link between the environment and our survival is a truth we are only beginning to fully grasp. Our planet isn't merely a resource to be exhausted, but a living system of which we are a part, and one that we have a responsibility to preserve for future generations.

E.F. Schumacher, in his eye-opening book *Small Is Beautiful*, challenged us to rethink our relationship with nature. He pointed out the folly of seeing ourselves at war with the natural world. After all, if we 'win' that battle, we'd only be defeating ourselves. His words ring even truer today as we face the realities of climate change.

The environmental crises we're grappling with – from vanishing species to polluted air and water – are pushing us to see our deep connection to the Earth in a new light. It's no longer just about saving trees or recycling plastics. It's about recognising that our fate is tied to the health of our planet.

Here in Sheffield, we've seen something remarkable unfold. Our community gardens and local food projects aren't just about growing vegetables. They're cultivating relationships among people. As hands dig in the soil together, stories are shared, friendships form, and a sense of shared purpose blooms. Caring for the Earth, it turns out, helps us care for each other too.

Joanna Macy, in her book *World as Lover, World as Self*, invites us to go even further. She suggests seeing ourselves not as separate from nature, but as part of its vast, intricate web. When we feel the Earth's pain as our own, she argues, we tap into a deep well of wisdom and strength. This view fits perfectly with our belief in compassion and creativity. It encourages us to face environmental challenges not with fear, but with a sense of connection and shared purpose.

As we look to the future, it's clear that clever gadgets alone won't solve our environmental problems. We need a fundamental shift in how we see our place in the world. By deepening our bond with nature and each other, we can spark collective action for a more sustainable future.

Every time we plant a tree, reduce waste, or advocate for Earth-friendly policies, we're contributing to more than just environmental well-being. We're part of a broader shift in our collective mindset and actions. We're creating a world where caring for our planet isn't a chore, but a natural expression of our love for the Earth and each other.

By embracing this view that intertwines environmental care with human connection, we open doors to fresh, community-driven solutions to our ecological challenges. In doing so, beyond working towards a greener world, we're strengthening the ties that bind us as a global family, recognising that our wellbeing – both as individuals and as a species – is inseparable from the health of our beautiful, blue planet.

A Personal Mission for World Peace: Cascading Connection

"If we are to teach real peace in this world, and if we are to carry on a real war against war, we shall have to begin with the children." – Mahatma Gandhi

True peace in the world begins with nurturing the next generation. Every child enters this world as a natural messenger of peace and love. As we grow, societal expectations and experiences can dim this innate light. Yet, the journey of connection offers us a path to rekindle that childlike spirit of peace and to amplify its message throughout our lives.

Imagine if we could preserve and nurture the peacemaker within each child, providing them with the tools to bring their message of harmony to fruition as they grow. This is the essence of *The Journey of Connection* - a means to rediscover and express our authentic selves, fostering peace from the individual to the global level.

As adults, we have the opportunity to reconnect with our inner child - that wellspring of creativity, love, and peace. By embracing this connection, we can become living examples of the change we wish to see in the world. Our lives become a canvas upon which we paint a masterpiece of peace, inspiring others to do the same.

"My life is my message." – Mahatma Gandhi

Imagine if your life were a message to the world - what would you want that message to be? This question invites us to consider our legacy, not in terms of grand achievements, but in the way we live each day and touch the lives of those around us.

By embracing the principle of cascading connection, you can make world peace your personal mission. It's about consciously shaping your life to reflect the change you wish to see in the world.

Here's how you might begin:

1. **Cultivate Inner Peace**: Start with yourself. Practise daily meditation or mindfulness to build inner calm. Reflect on your values and actions to ensure they align. As you develop self-compassion, you'll naturally extend it to others, creating a ripple of empathy in your interactions.

2. **Radiate Positivity in Your Immediate Circle**: Focus on your closest relationships. Choose kindness in your daily interactions with family, friends, and colleagues. Listen deeply, especially to those with different views. Share your personal growth journey, inspiring others to explore their own paths to peace.

3. **Engage Your Local Community**: Extend your influence beyond your immediate circle. Join or start community dialogues on local issues. Volunteer for peacebuilding initiatives or create your own. Bring diverse groups together, building connections that strengthen your community's social fabric.

4. **Leverage Your Skills and Passions**: Use your particular talents to promote peace. Whether you're an artist, teacher, or business owner, find ways to integrate peacebuilding into your work. Address root causes of conflict or promote understanding through your professional skills and personal interests.

5. **Connect Globally, Act Locally:** Think globally, act locally. Learn about international issues and their local impact. Support global peacebuilding organisations. Share stories of successful peace initiatives from around the world to inspire local action. Be part of the worldwide network of peacebuilders.

6. **Embrace Technology for Peace:** Use digital tools mindfully to spread peace. Share positive stories on social media. Join online forums dedicated to peaceful dialogue. Explore apps designed to promote understanding and resolve conflicts. Extend your peaceful influence beyond geographical boundaries.

7. **Commit to Lifelong Learning:** See peace as a journey of continuous growth. Keep learning about conflict resolution and cultural understanding. Seek diverse perspectives on global issues. Reflect on your progress, adapt your approach, and stay open to new ideas. Your commitment to growth keeps your mission vibrant and effective.

As you align with this personal mission, remember that every action, no matter how small, has the potential to create a cascade of positive change.

Here's how the ripple effect might unfold:

1. Your commitment to inner peace influences your immediate relationships, creating a more harmonious environment.

2. Your positive interactions inspire others to reflect on their own behaviour and values.

3. As more individuals in your community embrace these principles, local initiatives gain momentum.

4. Successful local projects catch the attention of other communities, spreading innovative ideas.

5. A network of peaceful communities begins to influence regional and national policies.

6. Collectively, these efforts contribute to a global culture of peace and understanding.

Embracing this personal mission is not a one-time decision, but an ongoing commitment to growth and positive action.

Here are some strategies to sustain your efforts:
- Regularly reconnect with your 'why' - the core reasons behind your commitment to peace.
- Celebrate small victories and learn from setbacks.
- Connect with like-minded individuals for support and inspiration.
- Practice self-care to avoid burnout and maintain your positive impact.
- Continuously seek new ways to expand your influence and create connections.

Remember, the journey of connection is not about perfection, but about consistent, heartfelt effort. Each step you take towards peace, each connection you make, contributes to the collective wisdom of a peaceful world.

As you move forward, consider: What unique gifts can you bring to this mission? How might you adapt these ideas to resonate deeply with your personal values and the specific needs of your community? Your journey of cascading connection starts now, with your next thought, your next word, your next action. What message will you send today?

Practical Applications and Initiatives for World Peace

"Peace cannot be kept by force; it can only be achieved by understanding." – Albert Einstein

Creating lasting peace goes beyond merely stopping conflicts; it requires a deep understanding of one another. This principle is evident in real-world examples of peace-building across the globe. From small local initiatives to large-scale social enterprises, these efforts demonstrate that by developing understanding, empathy, and shared goals, we can build enduring peace from the ground up, one connection at a time.

Take the **Grameen Bank Model**, started by Muhammad Yunus. It all began with a simple question: Why can't we lend to the poor? The answer changed communities. By giving women the power to earn money and build trust through group lending, Grameen Bank showed that trust can be as valuable as money. This led to more stable economies and, in turn, more peaceful communities.

Then there's **Dialogue in the Dark**, a special experience where people who can see are guided through pitch-black rooms by blind people. It does more than just raise awareness. It challenges what we think about disability, builds empathy by sharing vulnerability, and creates jobs for visually impaired people. By changing how we see things, it helps create a society that's more inclusive and understanding.

The Peace Parks Foundation turns areas of conflict into nature reserves, showing how shared concern for the environment can bring former enemies together. Eco-friendly tourism gives people ways to make money without fighting, while wildlife corridors become paths for people to work together too. Here, peace grows naturally, sustained by taking care of nature together.

The International Cities of Peace network doesn't wait for peace treaties to be signed from above. Instead, cities decide for themselves to commit to peace, share what works in creating peaceful cultures, and get support and recognition from around the world for their local efforts. It shows that peace can be built one city at a time, starting from the ground up.

The Consciousness Quotient Institute is developing ways to measure how aware and connected a community is, showing how we can put numbers to things like empathy and awareness that we can't see or touch. Communities can track how they're doing in growing peace, and this information can inspire and guide peace-building efforts. By making the invisible visible, they're changing how we approach peace.

These projects show that peace isn't some distant ideal, but something we can work on every day. They tell us that small actions can have big impacts around the world, that different approaches can tackle different aspects of peace, and that new ideas and creativity are powerful tools for change.

As we in Love Sheffield continue our journey, we might ask ourselves how we can use these ideas in our own city. What innovative peace projects might grow from Sheffield's soil? How can we connect what we do locally to this global movement?

Each of us, in our own unique way, holds a piece of the peace puzzle. By connecting these pieces, we create a picture of hope that spans the globe.

Stories of Peacebuilding

"There is no way to peace. Peace is the way." – A.J. Muste

Peace is not a destination but a journey we undertake daily. Let's explore some inspiring stories that illustrate this concept in action.

In Northern Ireland, peace is painted on walls and spoken in conversations. The Falls-Shankill Intercommunity Forum, born in Belfast's most divided areas, shows how peace can grow from the ground up. Here, people who were once enemies now work together, turning walls that used to divide into canvases of hope. Through community projects, youth exchanges, and shared businesses, they're writing a new story of working together. Their work shows us that peace isn't just about stopping violence; it's about creating a shared vision for the future.

Across the world in Colombia, we find the story of Juanes, a musician who swapped his guitar for guns as a teenager, only to return to music as a voice for peace. His Peace Without Borders concerts have brought together hundreds of thousands of people, crossing political lines. In 2008, he held a concert on the Colombia-Venezuela border, turning a place of tension into a celebration of shared culture. Juanes' story shows how art can build bridges and create spaces for peace where politics can't.

In the busy streets of Kigali, Rwanda, we find the Women's Bakery. Born after the genocide, this business empowers women by giving them jobs and teaching them about nutrition. It's more than just a bakery – it's a place where women from different backgrounds work together, baking bread and breaking down barriers. Their story teaches us that giving people economic opportunities and a shared goal can be powerful tools for bringing people together after conflict.

Closer to home, in Birmingham, we have the story of Tariq Jahan. During the 2011 riots, when his son was killed, Jahan called for calm and unity. This stopped more violence and brought communities together. He said, "I lost my son. Step forward if you want to lose your sons. Otherwise, calm down and go home." His words touched people across the country. Jahan's story shows us how personal tragedy can be turned into a force for peace and understanding.

These stories, from Belfast to Birmingham, from Colombia to Kigali, show the many ways peace can grow and flourish. They show us that building peace isn't just for diplomats and world leaders, but something we can all do.

I know that in Love Sheffield, we're writing our own story of peace. Every time we bring people together across divides, every time we choose understanding over judgement, we're adding a page to this story. Our challenge is to keep writing, to keep connecting, to keep building bridges where others see only walls.

As we think about these stories, we might ask ourselves: What page are we adding to the global story of peace? How can we in our own community create inspiring tales of connection and understanding?

Conclusion: Growing Peace Through Connection

"The day the power of love overrules the love of power, the world will know peace." – Mahatma Gandhi

True peace emerges not from exerting control but from fundamentally changing how we relate to each other and to power itself. This perspective aligns perfectly with the idea of pursuing world peace through deep, meaningful connections and embracing it as a personal mission.

Our journey through peacebuilding has shown us many insights. We've explored historical movements, philosophical ideas, the role of empathy, education, justice, and care for the environment. We've also discovered how each of us can make world peace our personal mission through the principle of cascading connection. Each part adds to our understanding of what peace really means in our interconnected world.

We've seen that peace isn't a fixed state to achieve, but an ongoing process we must keep nurturing. It's a practice that starts in each person's heart and spreads outward, touching every part of human life. From cultivating inner peace and radiating positivity in our immediate circles to engaging our local communities and leveraging our unique skills, the principles of connection we've explored have the power to transform.

Think about how the African idea of Ubuntu – "I am because we are" – could reshape how countries relate to each other if it were embraced worldwide. Or imagine the big changes if schools everywhere taught empathy and cultural understanding as core subjects, like we've seen in programmes such as Seeds of Peace. These ideas align beautifully with our understanding of peace as a personal mission that begins with reconnecting to our inner child - that source of creativity, love, and peace.

The path to world peace, we've found, isn't about erasing differences, but about creating spaces where we celebrate diversity and find common ground. It's about creative talks that cross borders, cultures, and ways of thinking. In this light, every community – including Love Sheffield – becomes a small version of global peace-building efforts, and every individual becomes an agent of change.

As we move forward, we face both big challenges and new opportunities. Climate change, economic unfairness, and technological changes test our ability to work together globally. Yet these same challenges give us strong reasons to come together, to create new solutions, and to reimagine our shared future. By embracing technology mindfully and committing to lifelong learning, we can turn these challenges into opportunities for growth and connection.

The journey towards world peace asks us to hold contradictions: to think globally while acting locally, to stand firm in our values while staying open to different views, to address current conflicts while working towards long-term system-wide change. It requires us to be both dreamers and doers, recognising that our lives themselves are powerful messages of peace.

At its heart, growing world peace is about deepening our connections – with ourselves, each other, and the living world around us. It's about recognising that the effects of our actions spread far beyond our immediate circles, contributing to a global culture of understanding and compassion. Each small action we take, guided by kindness and compassion, has the potential to create a cascade of positive change.

As we finish this exploration, let's carry with us a sense of both responsibility and possibility. Each of us, in our unique way, has the power to be a peacemaker. Every interaction, every choice, every moment of understanding plants a seed of peace that can grow in unexpected ways. By consciously shaping our lives as messages of peace, we become living examples of the change we wish to see in the world.

The road ahead may be complex and sometimes challenging, but it's a journey full of meaning and potential. By embracing this journey, we not only work towards a more harmonious world, but we also uncover the depths of our own humanity and the endless possibilities of our connections. Let's commit to this ongoing process of growth and positive action, celebrating small victories and learning from setbacks along the way.

Let's move forward with curiosity and courage, confident in our shared capacity for change. We shape the future of peace through our moment-by-moment choices and connections. United in heart and purpose, we can create a world where peace is a lived reality for all. As Gandhi wisely said, "My life is my message." What message do you want your life to be?

9. Level 7 – The Future of Humanity

"The future belongs to those who believe in the beauty of their dreams." – Eleanor Roosevelt

As we stand at the threshold of tomorrow, it's essential to recognise that each of us, with our personal gifts, holds the power to shape both our own lives and the world we share. This journey inspires hope for humanity's future, highlighting the impact of our collective dreams and actions.

David Bohm, a deep thinker in physics and philosophy, suggested in his book *Wholeness and the Implicate Order* that reality isn't made up of separate bits, but is one whole, always changing. He wrote, "The idea that all these pieces exist on their own is clearly an illusion, and this illusion can only lead to endless conflict and confusion." This view fits well with our understanding of connection as a key force in shaping our shared reality.

The journey of connection goes beyond personal growth; it's a big shift in how we perceive and engage with the world. It reveals that by deepening our connections – with ourselves, others, and our environment – we're not only enriching our own lives but also contributing to the creation of a better shared world.

In Love Sheffield, we've seen this idea come to life. Our community has shown that when people embrace their natural ability to connect, they become sparks for change, reshaping our city in inspiring and surprising ways.

As we look to the future in this chapter, we'll think about how new technologies and global challenges might change our world. But our main focus will be on understanding how each of us, through mindful connection, can truly change how we create our personal reality and that of our world.

You've never been just watching the future unfold – you're actively helping to create it. Your connections, your awareness, your very being adds to the collective consciousness that shapes our shared reality. By embracing your journey of connection, you're part of a worldwide shift towards a more aware, caring future.

Let's explore with open hearts and minds, recognising our power to shape our shared reality. Together, we can create a future that embodies our highest aspirations for connection and harmony.

Technological Advancements and Human Connection

"The most important thing in communication is hearing what isn't said." – Peter Drucker

True connection extends beyond the capabilities of technology. As new tools emerge at a rapid pace, it's important to consider how they can be used to strengthen, rather than weaken, our human bonds.

Jaron Lanier, who helped create virtual reality, worries that the internet, instead of bringing different views together, often pushes people into isolated groups. In his book *You Are Not a Gadget*, he writes, "It is the decay of genuine intellectual challenge that worries me. The internet should be an opportunity for people to bridge between different viewpoints, but people tend to congregate in ever-more-isolated bubbles." This highlights a strange truth: we're more connected than ever, yet we risk becoming more alone.

The digital age has changed how we talk and connect. It's opened up new ways to work together across the world and share information. But it's also brought new problems: we can become too dependent on our devices, our privacy is at risk, and we might talk face-to-face less often. To handle these issues, we need to understand both the good and bad sides of digital connection.

New technologies like virtual reality and artificial intelligence promise to change how we interact even more. They could create experiences that feel real and personal, even when we're far apart. But we need to think carefully about what this means for being genuine, fair, and truly connected.

In Love Sheffield, we've seen how technology, used wisely, can help build community. Our online spaces have helped us reach more people and create connections that might not have happened otherwise. But we always stress that online talks should add to, not replace, meeting in person.

It's important to realise that many new technologies are driven by the desire to make money. This can sometimes overshadow what's best for people and real connection. But by showing how important connection is to being human, we can influence how these technologies develop.

Marshall McLuhan, who thought deeply about media, said "The medium is the message" in his book *Understanding Media*. In today's super-connected world, this takes on new meaning. Every online post or interaction can spread far and wide, shaping how people think around the world. This 'butterfly effect' gives us new chances to make positive change.

Moving forward, we must guide emerging technologies to enhance genuine human connection, focusing on kindness, compassion, and creativity. This approach can create a future where technology fosters understanding and collaboration, harmonising our online and offline lives and steering technology towards more human-friendly ends.

The Evolution of Community in a Digital Age

"The Internet is the first thing that humanity has built that humanity doesn't understand, the largest experiment in anarchy that we have ever had." – Eric Schmidt

Our digital world is both new and complex, significantly altering the way we interact. As we navigate this evolving landscape, it's essential to understand how it is reshaping our concept of community.

Benedict Anderson, in his book *Imagined Communities*, suggested that communities exist in the minds of their members. He wrote, "It is imagined because the members of even the smallest nation will never know most of their fellow-members, meet them, or even hear of them, yet in the minds of each lives the image of their communion." In our digital age, this idea takes on new meaning as we can now form connections and communities that reach far beyond our local areas.

The rise of digital platforms has drastically changed how communities form and interact. Social media, online forums, and virtual worlds have created new spaces for people to connect based on shared interests or experiences, rather than just where they live. These digital communities can offer support and a sense of belonging to people who might otherwise feel alone.

However, the move towards digital communities also brings challenges. It's easy to find people who think like us online, which can lead to 'echo chambers' where we don't hear different views. Also, the lack of face-to-face interaction in many digital spaces can sometimes lead to misunderstandings or make it harder to feel empathy for others.

In Love Sheffield, we've seen the power of mixing digital and physical community-building. Our online platforms help create real-world connections, setting up meetups, events, and shared projects. This mixed approach lets us use the reach of digital tools while keeping the depth of in-person interactions.

Ethan Zuckerman, in his book *Rewire*, argues for the importance of bridging digital divides and creating more diverse online communities. He suggests we need to build tools that help us see from other perspectives and hear voices we wouldn't otherwise hear. This fits with our values of kindness, compassion, and creativity, encouraging us to use digital tools to broaden our understanding and connections.

As we move forward, the evolution of community in the digital age offers both chances and responsibilities. We have the opportunity to create more inclusive, diverse, and supportive communities that span the globe. At the same time, we must be careful to keep our connections deep and genuine, making sure our digital interactions add to, rather than replace, our real-world relationships.

By thoughtfully building communities, we can create digital spaces that embody our highest values. This contributes to a global shift towards more connected, caring communities that bridge digital and physical worlds, weaving a global web of human connection.

Growing Global Empathy and Understanding

"To understand the world, you must first understand a place like Mississippi." – William Faulkner

The journey to global understanding often starts with our own surroundings. It's within the familiar that we can discover the seeds of universal truths.

Our world has shrunk. With a few taps on a screen, we can peek into lives halfway across the globe. But true understanding? That's trickier. Peter Singer, in *The Expanding Circle*, suggests we're naturally wired to care about our immediate circle – family, friends, neighbours. Yet over time, he notes, we've stretched this circle wider. Now, we're grappling with the idea that our care should extend to all of humanity.

The internet has thrown open doors to new worlds. We can chat with a student in Tokyo, watch a livestream from Cairo, or join an online class taught in Mumbai. It's a dizzying buffet of cultures and viewpoints. But here's the rub – having access to this feast doesn't mean we're actually tasting it all. Too often, we stick to familiar flavours, creating echo chambers that reflect our own views back at us.

In Love Sheffield, we've seen the power of local action to spark global understanding. When we work on community projects with people from different backgrounds, something magical happens. Stereotypes crumble. Empathy grows. Suddenly, news from a far-off place isn't about strangers – it's about people we know and care about.

Kwame Anthony Appiah, in his book *Cosmopolitanism*, offers a balanced view. He suggests we should be curious about other cultures not to agree on everything, but simply to get comfortable with our differences. It's like learning to appreciate different types of music – you don't have to love everything, but understanding the beauty in various styles enriches your world.

As our planet faces challenges that don't stop at borders – climate change, pandemics, economic inequalities – growing our capacity for global empathy isn't just nice, it's necessary. It's about seeing the humanity in a face halfway around the world. It's about understanding that their struggles and joys are not so different from our own.

By embracing diverse voices, engaging in cross-cultural dialogue, and approaching differences with curiosity, we weave a new global fabric - one strong enough to hold our differences yet flexible enough for our shared hopes. In this interconnected dance, we're co-authors of a future where our shared humanity outshines our differences.

Caring for Our Earth, Caring for Each Other

"We do not inherit the Earth from our ancestors; we borrow it from our children." – Native American Proverb

Our planet is not something we own; it's a living system we're entrusted to look after for those who come after us.

James Lovelock's Gaia hypothesis offers a fresh way to understand how deeply we're connected to our world. He suggests that Earth works like a living being, with all its parts – including us – working together to keep things in balance. This idea invites us to rethink our place in nature – not as its rulers, but as a vital part of a larger, intricate system.

The environmental challenges we face today – from the loss of plant and animal species to the changing climate – remind us how closely our fate is tied to the Earth's. These issues push us to do more than just save what's left; they ask us to completely rethink how we live with nature.

Here in Sheffield, we're seeing this new way of thinking come to life. Our community gardens and local food projects are growing more than just vegetables. As neighbours come together to work the soil, they're also growing friendships and a sense of shared purpose. These projects show us that when we care for our environment, we naturally start caring more for each other too.

Philosopher Joanna Macy talks about this idea in her work on 'The Great Turning'. She sees our society shifting from one that's always trying to grow and produce more, to one that focuses on supporting life in all its forms. This change, she says, needs more than just new technologies – it needs a whole new way of seeing ourselves as part of the world around us.

Looking ahead, it's clear that solving our environmental problems will take more than new technologies. We need to fundamentally change how we think about our place in the world – to truly feel our connection to the Earth and to each other. As more of us start to see things this way, we'll be able to work together to make real, lasting changes.

Every time we do something to help the environment, no matter how small it seems, we're part of this bigger change. Planting trees, cutting down on waste, or speaking up for Earth-friendly policies – all these actions help create a world where looking after our planet feels as natural as looking after each other.

Viewing environmental care and human connection as inseparable opens doors to community-driven solutions. This approach strengthens our bonds while benefiting the planet, recognising our interconnectedness. It's an opportunity to create a future where love for Earth and each other are unified.

Learning for a Connected World

"The mind is not a vessel to be filled, but a fire to be kindled."
– Plutarch

Learning isn't about cramming facts into our heads; it's about igniting our curiosity. This approach to education remains as relevant today as it has been throughout history.

Ivan Illich, in his thought-provoking book *Deschooling Society*, argued that we learn best not from formal lessons, but from taking part in meaningful activities. His ideas push us to think beyond classrooms and see learning opportunities all around us.

In our increasingly interconnected world, education must extend beyond mere facts. It should instil essential skills such as empathy, critical thinking, and collaboration across diverse backgrounds. By integrating these elements into the learning process, we can nurture individuals who are not only knowledgeable but also deeply attuned to themselves and others.

Sugata Mitra's "Hole in the Wall" project showed something remarkable. When he gave children in poor areas access to computers without any instructions, they taught themselves and each other in amazing ways. This tells us that learning can happen naturally when we create the right conditions.

As we think about the future of education, we need to find ways to use technology that bring us together, while still valuing face-to-face connections. Mixing online and in-person learning could help create rich experiences that work for people no matter where they are.

We're also realising that learning doesn't stop when we leave school. Our world changes so quickly that we need to keep growing and adapting throughout our lives. This means we need to create flexible ways for people to learn that fit with their different needs and life stages.

By viewing education as a lifelong journey of discovery and connection, we pave the way for a future where learning continually enhances our understanding of ourselves, each other, and the world around us. This perspective encourages individuals who are not only well-informed but also deeply engaged and motivated to drive positive change.

Every time we learn something new – whether it's in a classroom, a community garden, or online – we have the chance to spark a change in thinking that could spread far and wide. By encouraging curiosity and connection in education, we're helping to create a more understanding and caring world.

Navigating the Digital Maze with Heart and Mind

"The more elaborate our means of communication, the less we communicate." – Joseph Priestley

Even as our means of communication become more advanced, the challenge remains: how do we use these tools to truly connect, rather than drift apart? This question is more relevant than ever in our increasingly digital world.

Sherry Turkle, in her book *Reclaiming Conversation*, points out a curious paradox of our digital lives. We're often 'alone together' – physically present but mentally elsewhere, tethered to our devices. It's like being at a party but spending the whole time texting friends who aren't there. Turkle reminds us that while digital interactions are valuable, they shouldn't replace the richness of face-to-face chats.

In our connected world, a careless tweet or post can snowball, touching lives far beyond our social circle. It's a stark reminder that in the digital realm, our words can echo far and wide, for better or worse.

Privacy is another thorny issue. Companies hoover up our personal data, often without us fully grasping the implications. Tristan Harris, once a Google insider, now warns that many tech products are designed to hook us, like digital candy we can't stop eating. It's a wake-up call: we need ethical guardrails to protect our personal info and mental health.

As we navigate this new digital landscape, we need to rethink our understanding of right and wrong online. It's about grasping how our online actions impact and shape our shared world, rather than just adhering to a set of dos and don'ts.

Digital literacy – knowing how to use tech tools wisely and critically – is crucial. But it goes beyond just knowing which buttons to click. We need to grasp how these tools affect us and society at large. It means questioning the info we consume and share, and considering how our online behaviour touches others.

By wrestling with these ethical questions, we can craft a digital world that brings out our best selves. We have a chance to create online spaces that mirror our highest values, supporting understanding and growth.

As we move forward, let's realise: our digital choices aren't just personal. They're brushstrokes in the bigger picture we're painting together. By approaching our online lives thoughtfully and with integrity, we can build a future where technology deepens our connections with each other and the world around us, rather than eroding them.

Maven: A New Paradigm for Digital Connection

"The greatest achievements become possible when we venture off the charted path and wander into the unknown."
– Kenneth O. Stanley

Kenneth O. Stanley's insight, from his visionary work, particularly in *Why Greatness Cannot Be Planned*, resonates deeply with the future of digital connection. As we explore Maven, a platform that embraces serendipity and unexpected discoveries, we see how technology can be harnessed to support meaningful connections and unleash human potential.

As we swim with the tide of new technology, it's essential that we seek out tools that align with our values and support genuine human connection. One such innovative platform is Maven, a 'serendipity network' that represents a dramatic departure from traditional social media models.

Unlike conventional platforms that operate on a popularity contest model, Maven is built around shared interests rather than followers or likes. This fundamental shift in approach creates an environment where authentic connection can flourish, free from the pressures of performance or the distortions of algorithmic manipulation.

At its core, Maven employs artificial intelligence as a matchmaker, connecting users based on their shared interests and curiosities. This clever use of technology serves to broaden our horizons, introducing us to diverse perspectives and ideas we might not encounter in our usual digital bubbles. It's a practical embodiment of the principles we've explored throughout this book – using technology to convey kindness, compassion, and creativity in our online interactions.

For communities like Love Sheffield, Maven offers a powerful tool for expanding human connections online and sparking collective action. Imagine a platform where every Sheffielder has the opportunity to initiate meaningful conversations about the issues that matter to them, reaching others who share their concerns and passions. Whether it's addressing local challenges, sharing skills and knowledge, or simply exploring shared interests, Maven provides a space for these interactions to form and flourish.

Moreover, Maven's design inherently counters the isolating effects often associated with social media use. By encouraging genuine dialogue and collaboration, it helps bridge the gap between our online and offline lives, potentially stimulating real-world meetings and initiatives.

As we look to the future, platforms like Maven offer a glimpse of how we might reshape our digital interactions to better serve our human needs for connection and understanding. They challenge us to reconsider what social media could be - not a space for passive consumption or performative sharing, but a tool for active engagement, learning, and community building.

In embracing Maven and similar innovations, we take a step towards realising the vision of a more connected, compassionate world. We move closer to a future where technology serves to unite hearts and ignite positive change, starting right here in Sheffield and rippling out across the globe.

The Future of Work and Connection

"The empires of the future are the empires of the mind."
– Winston Churchill

The workplace of tomorrow will be shaped by our ability to connect, create, and collaborate. As we move rapidly into an era of unprecedented technological change, these capacities will significantly influence not only our livelihoods but also the very fabric of human interaction.

Lynda Gratton, in her book *The Shift*, points out that work is becoming more flexible and networked. "Work is no longer a place you go, but a thing you do," she says. This idea turns traditional notions of the office on their head and opens up new ways to connect across distances.

The recent surge in remote work has shown both the promise and the problems of spread-out teams. While technology lets us chat easily across miles, it also raises questions. How do we balance work and home life? How do we avoid digital burnout? And how do we keep those spontaneous, face-to-face chats that often spark new ideas?

Artificial Intelligence and automation are changing the job market, getting rid of some jobs while creating new ones. This shift means we need to rethink how we learn and what skills we need. The World Economic Forum says skills like critical thinking, problem-solving, and emotional intelligence – things that make us particularly human – are becoming more important.

The idea of having one job for life is fading. Instead, we're seeing people build portfolio careers or join the gig economy. While this offers flexibility and variety, it also brings challenges. How do we keep job security and a sense of community when work is less stable?

As traditional workplaces change, we need to think about creating new spaces for meaningful human interaction. Co-working spaces, community hubs, and online platforms that help local connections could play big roles in keeping our social fabric strong in an increasingly digital world.

There's also a growing interest in work that has a purpose beyond just making money. People want to feel they're making a difference. This fits with our need for connection, suggesting that the most successful future workplaces will be those that create a sense of belonging and shared purpose.

As we navigate these changes, it's crucial to make sure everyone benefits. The gap between those who have access to digital tools and skills and those who don't could make existing inequalities worse if we're not careful.

By embracing a vision of work that prioritises human connection and wellbeing, we can shape a future where technology enhances rather than replaces our essential humanity. In this future, work evolves from merely a means to earn a living into a way to contribute to a more connected and compassionate world.

Growing Resilience in Connected Communities

"I am because we are." – Ubuntu philosophy

This African wisdom cuts to the heart of community strength. In our interconnected world, our power comes from our bonds and shared stories.

Rebecca Solnit, in her eye-opening book A *Paradise Built in Hell*, shows how tough times often bring out the best in communities. She suggests that the seeds of a better world are already within us, just waiting for the right conditions to sprout. It's a hopeful reminder of the hidden potential for connection and support that lies in every neighbourhood.

Connected communities have a knack for bouncing back from hard times. Whether it's a natural disaster, money troubles, or social upheaval, tight-knit groups often recover quicker. This resilience comes from strong friendships, shared resources, and a common sense of purpose.

Technology plays a mixed role in community strength. Online tools can be great for organising help and spreading important news during emergencies. But if we rely on them too much, we risk weakening the face-to-face connections that are the real backbone of strong communities.

Local food systems show community resilience in action. City gardens, farmers' markets, and food-sharing schemes don't just put food on the table – they build relationships between neighbours. These projects weave a web of support that can stand up to outside pressures.

Shared spaces are vital for growing community bonds. Parks, community centres, and voluntary groups give us chances to bump into each other and share experiences. As more of our lives move online, it's more important than ever to protect and improve these physical meeting places.

When different generations mix regularly, it makes communities stronger. Young people learn from their elders, while older folks stay connected to new ideas and energy. Programs that bring different age groups together help keep the community fabric strong and flexible.

Storytelling plays a big part in building resilient communities. Sharing local histories and personal tales creates a sense of shared identity and helps communities make sense of challenges. Understanding their collective story helps communities face the future with more confidence.

Schools can help lay the groundwork for stronger communities by teaching cooperation and problem-solving. When schools engage with local issues and encourage community service, young people start to see themselves as active contributors to their community's wellbeing.

As we look ahead, growing resilience in our communities will be key to facing global challenges. By strengthening our connections and building our shared ability to adapt and thrive, we create a foundation for a more stable and caring world.

At its heart, resilient communities are those that recognise how deeply we're all connected. By strengthening these bonds, we're going beyond preparing for future challenges – we're making our daily lives richer with deeper meaning and shared purpose.

Conclusion: Our Role in Shaping the Future

"The best way to predict the future is to create it." – Peter Drucker

We are not passive observers of the future but active architects of it. Our journey through this book has highlighted both the challenges and opportunities that await us.

We've seen how new technologies are changing how we talk, work, and live. These tools offer amazing chances to work together across the world, but they also risk pulling us apart. Our job is to use these new gadgets to bring us closer, not push us away from each other.

The way we work is changing too. We might have more freedom in our jobs, but we need to make sure everyone gets a fair chance to succeed and feel valued.

Taking care of our planet has become a big concern. It's a tough task, but as we realise how connected we are to nature, we find new ways to work together and look after our world.

Learning will be crucial to our future. We need to impart more than just facts; we must also teach how to understand others, think critically, and adapt to change. This approach will better equip us to face whatever challenges come our way

Above all, we've learned how important it is to be strong together. By building caring communities and helping each other, we can handle even the toughest problems.

In Love Sheffield, we've seen how small actions can make big changes. A chat between neighbours might start a project that helps the whole city. These local efforts often grow into much bigger movements.

As we move forward, staying connected is more important than ever. We face big problems that cross borders and affect us all. By working together – person to person, community to community, country to country – we weave a strong web of support that covers the whole world.

The future may be uncertain, but it's full of possibilities. As we understand how connected we all are, we find new ways to organise our societies, our work, and how we live with nature. This understanding unlocks our power to create positive change.

Let's move forward with hope, knowing our collective strength. We shape the future through daily choices to connect, understand, and show kindness. By doing so, we create a world where everyone thrives and contributes to our shared story.

The future beckons. Let's respond with open hearts, curious minds, and faith in connection's power. Together, we can create a tomorrow surpassing our boldest dreams.

10. Conclusion: The Ever-Evolving Journey

"To be human is to need others, and this is no flaw or weakness." – David Whyte

Our need for connection isn't a shortcoming, but the very essence of our humanity. Our exploration began with a moment of awakening in Sheffield, showing how our personal experiences intertwine with the world around us. This set us on a path to uncover the significance and power of connection, revealing its crucial role in our wellbeing.

We've seen how self-love and honest dialogue can help us overcome the fears that often hinder genuine connection. Through thoughtful reflection and real-life stories, we've illuminated ways to deepen our bonds with ourselves and others.

Our view then widened to encompass the intricacies of relationships and the subtle power of influence. We've seen how connection enhances our ability to create positive change, from personal interactions to community leadership.

As we broadened our perspective, we tapped into collective wisdom and its global reach. We've examined how history, culture, and technology have shaped our societies and continue to guide us towards harmony.

Each step of our journey has built upon the last, revealing connection not as a fixed state, but as a living force that continually reshapes our lives and communities.

The insights we've gained aren't endpoints, but springboards for further exploration. They invite us to keep growing, learning, and connecting in ever more meaningful ways. Each step forward offers fresh opportunities for personal and collective growth.

In essence, we're all part of an ongoing story of connection. We contribute to this story with every interaction, every moment of understanding, and every act of kindness. By embracing this journey, we become active creators of a more connected, compassionate world.

Moving forward, let's explore how to practically apply these insights to unite hearts and spark change in our communities and beyond.

Embracing Change and Growth

"The measure of intelligence is the ability to change."
– Albert Einstein

Growth and adaptation are key to a rich life. This idea of change as a path to growth has been a constant companion in our exploration of connection.

Our journey began with a personal tale of transformation – my shift from chasing profit to making a difference through connection. This change sparked a voyage of personal growth, setting the stage for our shared exploration.

We've discovered that change isn't just an occasional visitor, but a constant companion on our path to deeper understanding. From the intricate steps of personal relationships to the complex rhythm of collective wisdom, each part of our journey has shown that growth is both a personal and shared adventure.

Inspiring thinkers like Viktor Frankl and Don Miguel Ruiz have long recognised how change shapes personal growth. Their insights show how embracing change, even when it's uncomfortable, can lead to extraordinary self-transformation. We've seen these ideas come to life in the stories we've encountered, each showing how challenges, met with openness, can become gateways to deeper understanding and connection.

As we look ahead, embracing change takes on new dimensions. The swift progress of technology, especially in areas like artificial intelligence, offers both challenges and opportunities for human connection. By approaching these changes thoughtfully, we can use their potential to enhance our relationships rather than diminish them.

Our journey has revealed that embracing change isn't just about personal resilience, but about our ability to grow together as interconnected individuals and communities. When we approach change with curiosity and compassion, we create chances for deeper understanding and more meaningful connections.

Our journey of connection is intrinsically linked to our willingness to embrace change and grow. Each new understanding and step outside our comfort zone strengthens our relationships and expands our impact. Embracing change is a powerful tool for creating the connected world we envision, allowing us to adapt, seize opportunities, and evolve. Let's explore how this openness can create cascades of positive transformation in our communities and beyond.

The Power of Influence Revisited

"The most powerful leadership tool you have is your own personal example." – John Wooden

Our actions, more than words, inspire others and shape the world around us. When we live our values, others naturally follow.

We've seen throughout our journey how influence, wielded with care and kindness, can transform lives and knit communities together. True influence isn't about grand gestures or wielding power. It's about our daily choices, small but meaningful.

In Love Sheffield, this idea has blossomed. By consistently embodying kindness, compassion, and creativity, we've inspired others to do the same. It's like a gentle current, carrying these positive behaviours through our community.

As our understanding of connection has deepened, so too has our influence. The more we listen and truly see the humanity in others, the deeper our impact becomes. This kind of influence isn't about control or achieving set goals. It's about the cascades of positive change we create, often without realising it.

Looking ahead, this way of leading by example will be crucial in tackling the complex challenges we face. In a world that can feel divided and uncertain, our ability to model connection and understanding becomes even more vital.

Let's be clear that each of us holds this power. Every time we choose kindness, seek to understand, or work to bring people together, we're shaping our shared world. These seemingly small actions can create waves of change that reach far beyond what we might imagine.

By advancing on this path, we contribute to a more connected, compassionate, and creative world - a truly meaningful endeavour.

Empathy and Compassion: The Heart of Connection

"Compassion is the wish to see others free from suffering."
– Dalai Lama

Compassion lies at the core of human connection, embodying a deep and transformative power. True compassion goes beyond mere sympathy; it is an active desire to alleviate the suffering of others, forming the foundation of genuine human bonds.

Throughout our journey, we've seen empathy and compassion emerge as drivers of connection. These twin forces of understanding and care drive personal growth, strengthen communities, and spark global change.

In our personal relationships, growing empathy and compassion transforms our interactions. As we truly listen and understand others, wishing for their wellbeing, we create spaces where trust and openness flourish.

Viktor Frankl's insights on finding meaning through hardship, and Bessel van der Kolk's work on healing trauma, show how our personal growth ripples outward. As we tend to our own emotional wounds and develop self-compassion, we naturally extend this understanding to others.

Thich Nhat Hanh's teachings on mindful living reveal how daily compassion can be a powerful force for peace and connection. His concept of "interbeing" – our interconnectedness – echoes our understanding of compassion as a bridge between individuals and communities.

On a broader scale, empathy and compassion play crucial roles in addressing complex societal issues. Jeremy Rifkin's concept of an empathic civilisation highlights how these qualities can inspire cooperation and innovation globally. They're essential for tackling challenges like environmental degradation and social inequality, building the collective action needed for positive change.

In the workplace, empathetic and compassionate leadership transforms environments. Simon Sinek's work shows how leaders who prioritise understanding create cultures of trust and collaboration, extending beyond the office walls.

Education, too, benefits from breathing empathy and compassion into learning. Programmes that instil these qualities equip young people with the emotional intelligence needed to build resilient, connected communities.

Looking at social justice movements, we see empathy and compassion as driving forces for change. Leaders like Martin Luther King Jr. and Nelson Mandela showed how these qualities can inspire collective action and bring about fundamental societal shifts.

In Love Sheffield, we've witnessed how creating spaces for empathy and compassion can transform a community. By encouraging story-sharing, deep listening, and kind responses, we've seen our community grow more connected, resilient, and vibrant.

As we continue, remember that empathy and compassion grow stronger with use, creating a positive cycle of connection and collective wellbeing. We'll explore practical ways to grow these qualities in our lives and communities, sparking the change we wish to see in the world.

The Impact of Education and Cultural Exchange

"Cultural differences should not separate us from each other, but rather cultural diversity brings a collective strength that can benefit all of humanity." – Robert Alan Aurthur

Cultural exchange plays a vital role in realising connection by turning our diverse backgrounds and perspectives into strengths. Rather than viewing these differences as barriers, we should embrace them as rich resources that enhance our collective experience and understanding.

Throughout our journey, we've seen how education and cultural exchange build bridges between diverse individuals and communities. These bridges aren't just metaphorical; they're pathways for empathy to flow, stereotypes to crumble, and mutual understanding to flourish.

In the UK, programmes like Roots of Empathy in schools show how bringing cultural understanding into education can reduce bullying and unite diverse communities. The Erasmus+ programme (and its successor, the Turing Scheme) has opened doors for students to immerse themselves in different cultures, challenging preconceptions and supporting global citizenship.

Paulo Freire's concept of education as a practice of freedom sheds light on this approach. In *Pedagogy of the Oppressed*, he argues that true education empowers people to critically engage with their reality and actively shape a more just world. This view shows how education, paired with cultural exchange, can spark positive change.

In Sheffield, local initiatives celebrate our city's diversity. The Migration Matters Festival showcases different cultures' rich contributions to our community, encouraging understanding through art, music, and shared experiences. These events remind us that cultural exchange can happen right here in our neighbourhoods, enriching our local experience of humanity.

Cultural institutions and digital platforms have expanded the reach of cultural exchange. The British Museum's community programmes and the British Council's Connecting Classrooms initiative make cultural exchange more accessible, deepening appreciation for diversity and facilitating global understanding.

As we reflect on these insights, we're reminded of the transformative potential in our own lives and communities. How might we create more opportunities for meaningful cultural exchange within our diverse local communities? How can we weave cultural awareness into our schools and community programmes?

In Love Sheffield and beyond, we can encourage cultural exchange by creating spaces for dialogue and shared learning. Every initiative contributes to our collective strength, offering practical tools for transformation. In the pages ahead, we'll explore how to apply these principles, creating cascades of understanding that unite hearts and ignite global change.

Economic and Social Justice: Foundations for Connection

"Injustice anywhere is a threat to justice everywhere."
– Martin Luther King Jr.

Justice and equality are the foundations of our shared humanity. As we've explored, economic and social justice create the ground on which genuine, lasting relationships can grow.

Unfair systems and social injustices often block the path to meaningful connection. When basic needs go unmet, opportunities are unevenly distributed, and voices are silenced, disconnection spreads like a disease. By addressing these core issues, we prepare the soil for deeper, more authentic connection to grow.

In the UK, initiatives like the Living Wage Foundation have shown how fair pay can allow the growth of more stable, united communities. By advocating for wages that truly reflect living costs, this movement has eased financial pressures and allowed people to engage more fully in community life. Similarly, the Equality Act 2010 has established guidelines to combat discrimination and develop a more inclusive society, creating spaces where diverse voices can be heard and valued.

Fair education and healthcare play pivotal roles in social justice. The Pupil Premium in UK schools, aimed at supporting disadvantaged students, recognises that equal learning opportunities are crucial for breaking cycles of inequality. Meanwhile, our treasured National Health Service (NHS) embodies the principle that healthcare is a fundamental right, not a privilege. These institutions, while imperfect, demonstrate that a just society is one that cares for all its members.

Housing projects and grassroots movements have emerged as powerful forces for addressing deep-rooted issues. Community land trusts offer innovative solutions to the housing crisis, providing affordable homes and creating a sense of shared ownership. Organisations like Shelter not only assist those facing homelessness but also advocate for policy changes to address the root causes of housing insecurity.

The Joseph Rowntree Foundation's work has been instrumental in illuminating the links between economic policies and social outcomes. Their research and advocacy remind us that poverty isn't just a financial issue, but a social one with far-reaching effects on community cohesion and individual wellbeing.

In Love Sheffield, we've witnessed firsthand how tackling economic and social justice issues can strengthen community bonds. Projects that unite diverse groups to address local challenges – be it food poverty, social isolation, or environmental concerns – have shown us that working towards a common goal can bridge divides and create lasting relationships.

As we continue our journey, it's clear that the pursuit of economic and social justice isn't separate from our quest for connection – it's at its very heart. By supporting fair wage initiatives, advocating for inclusive policies, and participating in community efforts to address inequality, we help create a more just society where meaningful relationships can flourish.

It's clear that every step towards greater economic and social justice, no matter how small, cascades out to affect our entire community. When we strive to ensure that everyone's basic needs are met and their dignity respected, we create the conditions for deeper, more authentic relationships to thrive.

In the next sections, we'll explore practical ways to bring these principles into our daily lives and community practices. We'll uncover how, through our dedication to economic and social justice, we can actively craft a world where meaningful relationships flourish naturally. This commitment has the power to transform our society, creating an environment where deep, authentic bonds become an integral part of our shared experience.

The Future of Connection in a Technological World

"We are all now connected by the Internet, like neurons in a giant brain." – Stephen Hawking

Our interconnected digital age presents a vivid picture of how technology is reshaping human interaction and collective consciousness. As we approach unprecedented technological advancements, it's crucial to reflect on how these vast networks will influence our shared experiences and connections.

Throughout this book, we've seen how technology has transformed the landscape of human relationships. The digital revolution has rewritten the rules of communication, information access, and community building. Looking ahead, it's clear that technology will continue to play a central role in how we connect with each other and the world around us.

Yuval Noah Harari offers a thought-provoking view in his book *Homo Deus* :

> *"In the 21st century, the human condition might be transformed more than in all of human history."*

His words remind us that technological progress is a double-edged sword – it has the potential to enhance our interactions and understanding, but also to fundamentally alter what it means to be human.

The rise of artificial intelligence and machine learning brings a mix of promise and challenge. AI may help us bridge language barriers, personalise learning experiences, and tackle complex global issues. Yet it also raises serious questions about privilege, privacy, freedom, and the nature of human interaction.

Virtual and augmented reality technologies offer new horizons for interaction, allowing us to transcend physical boundaries in unprecedented ways. These immersive technologies could revolutionise education, healthcare, and social interaction. However, they also challenge us to reconsider what makes a 'real' connection and how we maintain authenticity in virtual spaces.

In Love Sheffield, we've witnessed technology's power to strengthen community bonds. Digital platforms have expanded our reach, improved collaboration, and helped with resource sharing. Yet, we've also recognised the irreplaceable value of face-to-face meetings, understanding that true connection often requires physical presence and shared experiences.

As we chart this new territory, it's crucial that we approach emerging technologies with a critical and ethical mindset. Sherry Turkle offers a poignant warning in *Reclaiming Conversation* :

> *"Technology can create a sense of constant connection that paradoxically leaves us feeling more isolated."*

She advocates for creating spaces for deep, meaningful conversation in our increasingly digital world.

Looking forward, the integration of technology into our lives presents both opportunities and responsibilities. We have the chance to forge more inclusive, diverse, and supportive global communities. At the same time, we must be mindful to preserve the depth and authenticity of our bonds, ensuring that our digital interactions enhance rather than replace our real-world relationships.

By embracing technological advancements with a focus on ethics and human-centred design, we can shape a future where technology deepens our relationships rather than dilutes them. This approach ensures that as we navigate the changing landscape of human relationships, we remain true to the core values of kindness, compassion, and creativity that have guided us throughout our journey.

As we continue to explore the future of connection in a technological world, be sure that we are not passive recipients of these changes, but active shapers of our digital future. By approaching technology with intention and awareness, we can harness its power to unite hearts and ignite positive change on a global scale.

In the pages ahead, we'll consider practical ways to navigate this digital frontier, exploring how we can use technology to enrich our interactions while honouring our fundamental human need for authentic, meaningful relationships.

Practical Applications and Next Steps

"Do not wait for leaders; do it alone, person to person."
– Mother Teresa

Meaningful transformation often begins with individual initiative. Our journey through this book has given us deep insights into human connection and its power to reshape our lives and communities. Now, it's time to turn these insights into tangible actions that can create cascades of positive change in our world.

The essence of this approach aligns perfectly with the idea that connection grows from the ground up. It's about each of us taking responsibility for creating the relationships and communities we envision, rather than waiting for top-down directives.

In Love Sheffield, we've witnessed how small actions can snowball into community-wide transformations. Simple acts of kindness, efforts to bring neighbours together, or reaching out to isolated individuals have often blossomed into larger movements of compassion and connection.

Here are some practical ways to apply what we've learned:

1. Champion fair wages by supporting businesses that pay a living wage.

2. Dive into local projects, from litter picking to neighbourhood watches.

3. Practise active listening in daily interactions, creating spaces where people feel truly heard.

4. Encourage empathy and cultural awareness through programmes in schools, workplaces, and community centres.

5. Bridge generational gaps by creating opportunities for skill and story sharing.

6. Use technology thoughtfully to enhance authentic relationships.

7. Spread kindness through small, everyday acts that inspire others and encourage a compassionate culture.

These are just starting points. The key is to begin where we are, with what we have. As Margaret Mead wisely noted:

"Never doubt that a small group of thoughtful, committed citizens can change the world; indeed, it's the only thing that ever has."

Consider creating personal and community action plans. Set specific goals for building connection, such as volunteering locally, joining cultural exchange programmes, or advocating for policies that promote social justice.

As always, the journey of connection is ongoing. Each step opens new possibilities and challenges. By staying open, flexible, and committed to growth, we can continually deepen our relationships and expand our impact.

As we move forward, let's see every interaction as a chance to strengthen the web of connection that binds us all. Whether it's a chat with a neighbour, collaborating with colleagues, or launching a community-wide project, we have the power to create positive change through our relationships.

In our final reflections, we'll explore how these practical steps contribute to our vision of a more connected, compassionate world, and how each of us can play a part in bringing that vision to life.

The Cascade Effect: Your Role in Shaping Connected Communities

"I alone cannot change the world, but I can cast a stone across the waters to create many ripples." – Mother Teresa

The power of individual action in creating far-reaching change is immense. Just as a stone cast into water sets off a cascade of ripples, small actions can lead to significant changes in our communities and beyond. This imagery perfectly captures how each of us can contribute to building a more connected world.

Throughout our journey, we've seen how our actions can deeply affect those around us. In Love Sheffield, this cascade effect has played out countless times. A simple act of kindness between neighbours might inspire others to reach out. A community garden project might spark conversations about sustainability, leading to broader initiatives. A storytelling event bringing together diverse community members might kindle new friendships that bridge cultural divides.

Each of us, in our unique way, has the power to be that stone cast into the waters – to start a cascade of connection that can transform our communities. This power lies not in grand gestures, but in the consistent, authentic way we embody kindness, compassion, and creativity in our daily lives.

Consider how you might create cascades in your own surroundings:

8. **In close relationships**: Practise deep listening and empathy, modelling these behaviours and creating safe spaces for genuine connection.

9. **At work**: create a culture of teamwork and mutual support, changing how colleagues interact and tackle challenges.

10. **In your neighbourhood**: Start or join community projects, creating opportunities for diverse individuals to form lasting bonds.

11. **In the wider community**: Advocate for inclusive policies or support local initiatives, helping create a more connected and compassionate society.

Keep in mind, the cascade effect works both ways. Just as positive actions can create expanding circles of connection, negativity can spread too. This underscores our responsibility to be mindful of the energy we bring to our interactions and communities.

The beauty of the cascade effect is that it doesn't require us to have all the answers or single-handedly solve complex issues. It simply asks us to start where we are, with what we have, and take that first step in creating connection. As we do so, we often find that others are inspired to join us, amplifying our impact and creating new possibilities for change.

In Love Sheffield, we've witnessed how this cascade effect can transform a city. What began as a small group committed to creating connection has grown into a movement that touches lives across our community. Each person who joins us contributes their own cascades, forming a vast network of connection that continues to grow and evolve.

As we move forward, let's carry with us the understanding that our actions matter. Every conversation, every act of kindness, every effort to bridge divides contributes to the world we wish to create. By embracing our role in creating connected communities, we become active participants in a global movement towards greater understanding, compassion, and collective wellbeing.

In our final reflections, we'll consider how these cascades of connection can contribute to our vision of a more peaceful, just, and compassionate world, and how each of us can continue to play a vital role in this ongoing journey of connection.

An Invitation to Continue the Journey

"The journey of a thousand miles begins with a single step."
– Lao Tzu

The essence of our next step in the journey of connection lies in understanding that great transformations often begin with small actions. Just as we've witnessed in Love Sheffield, where individual acts of kindness have blossomed into community-wide change, this idea encourages us to take that initial step, no matter how modest it may seem.

As we close this book, we find ourselves not at an ending, but at a fresh start. The insights we've shared are not the final word on connection, but the opening lines of an ongoing dialogue – one that extends far beyond these pages and into the fabric of our daily lives.

Our exploration has taken us on a winding path through the landscape of human connection. We've delved into the depths of personal relationships, examined the bridges built by empathy and compassion, and scaled the heights of collective wisdom. We've faced the challenges of our modern, often disconnected world, and glimpsed the potential of a future where technology enhances rather than replaces human connection.

See this moment not as the end of a book, but as the beginning of a new chapter in your journey of connection. The ideas we've explored are more than just knowledge; they are active tools for transformation – seeds of change ready to be planted in the fertile soil of your life and community.

In Love Sheffield, we've witnessed how individuals embracing this journey can create cascades of change that transform entire communities. We've seen how small acts of kindness can blossom into movements of compassion, how bridging cultural divides can lead to rich collaborations, and how inspiring a sense of belonging can build resilient, vibrant communities.

As you move forward, I encourage you to:

1. Reflect on your own journey of connection. How has your understanding evolved?

2. Consider your own gifts and how you might use them to grow connection in your sphere of influence.

3. Seek out opportunities to put these ideas into practice. Every action counts.

4. Stay curious and open to learning. There's always more to discover about ourselves and others.

5. Share your experiences and insights with others. By doing so, you extend the conversation and inspire others.

Wonderfully, the journey of connection is not a solitary one. We're all in this together, each playing our part in growing the seeds of human connection. As we move forward, let's carry with us the understanding that our individual actions, however small they may seem, contribute to a larger movement towards a more connected, compassionate world.

In Love Sheffield, and indeed in communities around the world, the seeds of deeper connection are waiting to be nourished. By embracing this journey with open hearts and minds, we become active co-creators of the future we wish to see – a future where every individual feels valued, connected, and empowered to contribute their personal gifts to the world.

Take the next step, trusting in your ability to create a cascade effect of positive change through connection. As we move forward into a future of deeper understanding and stronger communities, remember that every individual has the power to make a difference. Your journey is just beginning.

11. Summary of Quotes

Introduction: The Essence of Connection

Connection allows life energy, experienced as love, to bring our inner selves to engage with reality.
— Brian Mosley

The Journey of Connection

The most powerful agent of growth and transformation is something much more basic than any technique: a change of heart. — John Welwood

John Welwood: A psychotherapist and pioneer in integrating Eastern and Western approaches to personal growth. Welwood's work bridges Buddhist psychology, Western therapy, and relationship studies, offering a holistic view of human transformation.

The Interconnected Web of Life

In nature we never see anything isolated, but everything in connection with something else which is before it, beside it, under it and over it. — Johann Wolfgang von Goethe

Johann Wolfgang von Goethe: An 18th-century German polymath whose work spanned literature, science, and philosophy. Goethe's keen observations of nature informed his understanding of human interconnectedness, reflected in both his scientific and literary works.

Historical and Cultural Perspectives

The threads of human connection weave a tapestry far richer than any one culture can produce alone. – Zora Neale Hurston

Zora Neale Hurston: An influential African American author and anthropologist of the early 20th century. Hurston's work celebrates the richness of Black culture and explores the complexities of human connections across diverse communities.

Modern-Day Relevance: Bridging the Gap in a Disconnected World

We are all living in cages with the door wide open.– George Lucas

George Lucas: A renowned American filmmaker best known for creating the Star Wars and Indiana Jones franchises. Beyond his cinematic achievements, Lucas often explores themes of human potential and the invisible forces that connect us all.

The Magic of Community

We are like islands in the sea, separate on the surface but connected in the deep. – William James

William James: A late 19th-century American philosopher and psychologist, often called the "Father of American psychology". James's work on consciousness and the nature of experience deeply influenced modern understanding of human interconnectedness.

Conclusion: A Call to Connection

The greatest thing in this world is not so much where we stand as in what direction we are moving. – Johann Wolfgang von Goethe

Level 0 – Understanding Connection

The quality of your life is the quality of your relationships. – Anthony Robbins

Anthony Robbins: An American author and life coach known for his work on personal development and self-empowerment. Robbins' approach emphasises the importance of relationships in shaping our overall quality of life.

The way we talk to our children becomes their inner voice. – Peggy O'Mara

Peggy O'Mara: An American writer and activist, best known as the former publisher of Mothering Magazine. O'Mara's work focuses on conscious parenting and the lasting impact of our words on children's development.

We don't see things as they are, we see them as we are. – Anaïs Nin

Anaïs Nin: A French-Cuban American writer known for her deeply personal and introspective works. Nin's writing often explores the subjective nature of perception and experience.

The journey to connection is not a path we find, but one we create with every authentic step. – Maya Angelou

Maya Angelou: An American poet, memoirist, and civil rights activist whose work celebrates the resilience of the human spirit and the power of authentic self-expression.

The Neuroscience of Connection

The brain is wider than the sky, For, put them side by side, The one the other will include With ease, and you beside. – Emily Dickinson

Emily Dickinson: A 19th-century American poet whose work, often dealing with themes of nature and the human psyche, has had a lasting impact on literature.

Relationalism and Connection

The world is not a collection of things, it is a collection of events.
– Carlo Rovelli

Carlo Rovelli: An Italian theoretical physicist and writer who has made significant contributions to the field of quantum gravity. Rovelli's work often explores the philosophical implications of modern physics.

The Toxic Fishtank

The real problem of humanity is the following: we have Paleolithic emotions, medieval institutions, and god-like technology.
– E.O. Wilson

E.O. Wilson: An American biologist and naturalist, known as the "father of sociobiology". Wilson's work examines the complex relationships between biology, human nature, and society.

The Crisis of Purpose

Those who have a 'why' to live, can bear with almost any 'how'.
– Viktor E. Frankl

Viktor E. Frankl: An Austrian neurologist, psychiatrist, and Holocaust survivor. Frankl's work, particularly his concept of logotherapy, emphasises the importance of finding meaning in all forms of existence.

The two most important days in your life are the day you are born and the day you find out why. – Mark Twain

Mark Twain: An American writer and humorist of the late 19th century, known for his keen wit and social commentary. Twain's work often explores the complexities of human nature and society.

Philosophical Foundations

Everything we hear is an opinion, not a fact. Everything we see is a perspective, not the truth. – Marcus Aurelius

Marcus Aurelius: A Roman emperor and Stoic philosopher whose personal writings, known as *Meditations*, offer insights into the nature of perception and reality.

Agency and Influence

The only way to deal with an unfree world is to become so absolutely free that your very existence is an act of rebellion.
– Albert Camus

Albert Camus: A French philosopher, author, and journalist known for his work in absurdism. Camus' writing often explores themes of freedom and rebellion against societal constraints.

Distributed Intelligence

None of us is as smart as all of us. – Ken Blanchard

Ken Blanchard: An American author and management expert known for his work on leadership and organisational behaviour. Blanchard emphasises the power of collaborative intelligence in problem-solving.

Historical and Cultural Perspectives

If you want to go quickly, go alone. If you want to go far, go together. – African Proverb

Interpreting Symbols in Present Reality

Symbols are the imaginative signposts of life. – Margot Asquit

Margot Asquith: A British author and socialite of the early 20th century, known for her wit and keen observations of society and human nature.

Understanding the Landscape for Positive Impact

If you think you are too small to make a difference,
try sleeping with a mosquito. – Dalai Lama

The Dalai Lama: The spiritual leader of Tibetan Buddhism, known for his teachings on compassion, interconnectedness, and the potential for individual action to create significant change.

Practical Applications of Connection

The most basic and powerful way to connect to another person is to listen. Just listen. Perhaps the most important thing we ever give each other is our attention. – Rachel Naomi Remen

Rachel Naomi Remen: An American author, teacher, and pioneer in the mind-body health field. Remen's work focuses on the importance of human connection in healing and personal growth.

Conclusion: Mapping the Landscape of Connection

The world is full of magic things, patiently waiting for our senses to grow sharper. – W.B. Yeats

W.B. Yeats: An Irish poet and one of the foremost figures of 20th-century literature. Yeats' work often explores mystical and spiritual themes, encouraging a deeper perception of the world around us.

Level 1 – Personal Connection

To be yourself in a world that is constantly trying to make you something else is the greatest accomplishment. – Ralph Waldo Emerson

Ralph Waldo Emerson: A 19th-century American essayist, philosopher, and poet. Emerson was a key figure in the Transcendentalist movement, advocating for individualism and self-reliance.

Self-Awareness and Reflection

The unexamined life is not worth living. – Socrates

Socrates: An ancient Greek philosopher considered one of the founders of Western philosophy. Socrates' method of questioning and self-examination forms the basis of critical thinking.

Self-Compassion and Acceptance

You yourself, as much as anybody in the entire universe, deserve your love and affection. – Buddha

Buddha: The title given to Siddhartha Gautama, the founder of Buddhism. The Buddha's teachings emphasise compassion, mindfulness, and the path to enlightenment.

Authenticity and Vulnerability

One does not become enlightened by imagining figures of light, but by making the darkness conscious. – Carl Jung

Carl Jung: A Swiss psychiatrist and psychoanalyst who founded analytical psychology. Jung's work explores the unconscious mind and the importance of integrating all aspects of the self.

Emotional Regulation and Expression

The curious paradox is that when I accept myself just as I am, then I can change. – Carl Rogers

Carl Rogers: An American psychologist and one of the founders of the humanistic approach to psychology. Rogers developed client-centred therapy, emphasising empathy and unconditional positive regard.

Active Listening and Empathy

The greatest gift you can give another is the purity of your attention. – Richard Moss

Richard Moss: An American physician turned spiritual teacher. Moss's work focuses on consciousness, deep listening, and the transformative power of presence.

Building Trust and Intimacy

Trust is the glue of life. It's the most essential ingredient in effective communication. It's the foundational principle that holds all relationships. – Stephen R. Covey

Stephen R. Covey: An American educator, author, and businessman. Covey is best known for his book *The 7 Habits of Highly Effective People*, which emphasises personal and interpersonal effectiveness.

Balancing Independence and Interdependence

Interdependence is a higher value than independence.
– Stephen R. Covey

Navigating Conflict and Resolution

In the middle of difficulty lies opportunity. – Albert Einstein

Albert Einstein: A renowned theoretical physicist who developed the theory of relativity. Beyond his scientific work, Einstein often shared insights on life, creativity, and human potential.

Conclusion: The Journey of Personal Connection

Relationships are the fertile soil from which all advancement, all success, all achievement in real life grows. – Ben Stein

Ben Stein: An American writer, lawyer, actor, and commentator. While known for various roles, Stein has also written extensively on personal finance and life success.

Level 2 – Relationships

To love oneself is the beginning of a lifelong romance.
– Oscar Wilde

Oscar Wilde: An Irish poet and playwright known for his wit and flamboyance. Wilde's work often explores themes of identity and self-love, challenging societal norms.

Self-Relationship and Personal Growth

The present moment is filled with joy and happiness. If you are attentive, you will see it. – Thich Nhat Hanh

Thich Nhat Hanh: A Vietnamese Buddhist monk and peace activist. His teachings emphasise mindfulness and the importance of living fully in the present moment.

Human Relationships and Emotional Depth

The meeting of two personalities is like the contact of two chemical substances: if there is any reaction, both are transformed. – Carl Jung

What children need most are the essentials that grandparents provide in abundance. They give unconditional love, kindness, patience, humor, comfort, lessons in life. And, most importantly, cookies. – Rudy Giuliani

Rudy Giuliani: Former mayor of New York City, known for his leadership during the 9/11 crisis. While controversial in recent years, this quote reflects on the unique role of grandparents in family life.

Community Relationships

Alone, we can do so little; together, we can do so much.
– Helen Keller

Helen Keller: An American author, political activist and lecturer who was the first deafblind person to earn a Bachelor of Arts degree. Keller's life exemplifies the power of human connection to overcome adversity.

In diversity there is beauty and there is strength. – Maya Angelou

Love and compassion are necessities, not luxuries. Without them, humanity cannot survive. – Dalai Lama

The strength of the team is each individual member. The strength of each member is the team. – Phil Jackson

Phil Jackson: A former American professional basketball player and coach, known for his holistic approach to team building and leadership.

The greatest delight which the fields and woods minister, is the suggestion of an occult relation between man and the vegetable. I am not alone and unacknowledged. They nod to me, and I to them. – Ralph Waldo Emerson

A community is like a ship; everyone ought to be prepared to take the helm. – Henrik Ibsen

Henrik Ibsen: A 19th-century Norwegian playwright and theatre director, often referred to as "the father of realism". His work often critiqued societal norms.

The next Buddha may take the form of a community, a community practicing understanding and loving kindness, a community practicing mindful living. This may be the most important thing we can do for the survival of the Earth. – Thich Nhat Hanh

Diversity is being invited to the party; inclusion is being asked to dance. – Verna Myers

Verna Myers: An American author, cultural change catalyst and diversity advocate who promotes inclusion in the workplace and beyond.

The smallest act of kindness is worth more than the grandest intention. – Oscar Wilde

The most basic and powerful way to connect to another person is to listen. Just listen. – Rachel Naomi Remen

Relationships with Nature and the Physical World

In every walk with nature one receives far more than he seeks. – John Muir

John Muir: A Scottish-American naturalist, author, and early advocate for the preservation of wilderness in the United States.

The things you own end up owning you. – Chuck Palahniuk

Chuck Palahniuk: An American novelist and freelance journalist, known for his transgressive fiction and satirical works that often critique modern consumer culture.

The space in which we live should be for the person we are becoming now, not for the person we were in the past. – Marie Kondo

Marie Kondo: A Japanese organizing consultant and author, known for her KonMari method of organizing and her philosophy that our surroundings affect our inner lives.

Relationships with Food and Drink

One cannot think well, love well, sleep well, if one has not dined well. – Virginia Woolf

Virginia Woolf: A British writer and one of the foremost modernists of the 20th century, known for her pioneering use of stream of consciousness as a narrative device.

Relationships with Technology

The question of whether a computer can think is no more interesting than the question of whether a submarine can swim. –
Edsger W. Dijkstra

Edsger W. Dijkstra: A Dutch computer scientist and programmer who made fundamental contributions to the development of programming languages.

Relationships with Belief Culture and Ideology

The eye sees only what the mind is prepared to comprehend.
– Robertson Davies

Robertson Davies: A Canadian novelist, playwright, and critic known for his exploration of moral and mythic traditions in modern culture.

Culture is the widening of the mind and of the spirit.
– Jawaharlal Nehru

Jawaharlal Nehru: The first Prime Minister of India and a central figure in Indian politics before and after independence. Nehru was a passionate advocate for education and cultural understanding.

The spiritual life does not remove us from the world but leads us deeper into it. – Henri J.M. Nouwen

Henri J.M. Nouwen: A Dutch Catholic priest, professor, and writer who wrote extensively on spiritual life and social justice.

The highest activity a human being can attain is learning for understanding, because to understand is to be free.
– Baruch Spinoza

Baruch Spinoza: A 17th-century Dutch philosopher of Portuguese Jewish origin, known for his rationalist approach to ethics and metaphysics.

Relationships with Art and Creativity

Every child is an artist. The problem is how to remain an artist once we grow up. – Pablo Picasso

Pablo Picasso: A Spanish painter, sculptor, and co-founder of the Cubist movement, widely regarded as one of the most influential artists of the 20th century.

Art enables us to find ourselves and lose ourselves at the same time. – Thomas Merton

Thomas Merton: An American Trappist monk, writer, and theologian known for his explorations of interfaith understanding and social justice.

Creativity is contagious. Pass it on. – Albert Einstein

The creative adult is the child who survived. – Ursula K. Le Guin

Ursula K. Le Guin: An American author best known for her works of speculative fiction, which often explore themes of sociology, psychology, and environmentalism.

Creativity is thinking up new things. Innovation is doing new things. – Theodore Levitt

Theodore Levitt: An American economist and professor at Harvard Business School, known for his work on marketing and globalisation.

Art is not a mirror held up to reality, but a hammer with which to shape it. – Bertolt Brecht

Bertolt Brecht: A German theatre practitioner, playwright, and poet who developed the epic theatre movement, emphasising art's role in social change.

Global Relationships

The world is becoming a global village, and we are all neighbors. Our challenge is to learn to live together in peace. – Kofi Annan

Kofi Annan: A Ghanaian diplomat who served as the seventh Secretary-General of the United Nations, known for his advocacy of human rights and global peace.

The real voyage of discovery consists not in seeking new landscapes, but in having new eyes. – Marcel Proust

Marcel Proust: A French novelist, critic, and essayist best known for his monumental novel *In Search of Lost Time*.

The Internet is becoming the town square for the global village of tomorrow. – Bill Gates

Bill Gates: An American business magnate, software developer, and philanthropist, best known as the co-founder of Microsoft Corporation.

We have to acknowledge that we are all part of a web of life around the world. – Jane Goodall

Jane Goodall: A British primatologist and anthropologist, considered the world's foremost expert on chimpanzees and a prominent advocate for environmental conservation.

Every time you spend money, you're casting a vote for the kind of world you want. – Anna Lappé

Anna Lappé: An American author and educator known for her work on sustainability, food systems, and climate change.

Peace cannot be kept by force; it can only be achieved by understanding. – Albert Einstein

Art is the lie that enables us to realize the truth. – Pablo Picasso

We are the first generation to feel the effect of climate change and the last generation who can do something about it.
– Barack Obama

Barack Obama: The 44th President of the United States, known for his efforts to address climate change and promote global cooperation.

The soul is healed by being with children. – Fyodor Dostoevsky

Fyodor Dostoevsky: A Russian novelist, short story writer, and essayist whose works explore human psychology in the troubled political, social, and spiritual atmospheres of 19th-century Russia.

Our ability to reach unity in diversity will be the beauty and the test of our civilization. – Mahatma Gandhi

Mahatma Gandhi: An Indian lawyer, anti-colonial nationalist, and political ethicist who employed nonviolent resistance to lead India's successful campaign for independence.

Practical Applications and Exercises

The art of connection lies not in grand gestures, but in the quiet dedication to daily practice. – Octavia Butler

Octavia Butler: An American science fiction author known for her explorations of hierarchy, human nature, and social justice in her works.

Conclusion: The Living Reef of Relationships

Coral reefs are the nursery of the ocean, and if you kill the coral reefs, you'll kill everything else. – Dr. Sylvia Earle

Dr. Sylvia Earle: An American marine biologist, oceanographer, and explorer known as a pioneer in marine conservation and for her advocacy for protecting marine ecosystems.

Level 3 – Influence

You don't need a title to be a leader.– Mark Sanborn

Mark Sanborn: An American author, professional speaker, and entrepreneur known for his work on leadership development and personal growth.

The Nature of Influence

True influence doesn't push or pull; it gently tilts the floor, allowing others to move naturally towards positive change.
– Brian Mosley

Personal Agency and Influence

The most common way people give up their power is by thinking they don't have any. – Alice Walker

Alice Walker: An American novelist, short story writer, and activist. Walker is best known for her novel *The Color Purple* and her work on racial and gender equality.

The sharpest blade isn't the one in your hand; it's the choices you make. Every decision can cut through darkness, leading either to a path of light or into shadows. Choose to carve out a future that honours life, not one that slices it away. – Anthony Olaseine

Anthony Olaseinde: A British community activist and author from Sheffield, known for his impactful work addressing knife crime and fostering community connections. Olaseinde founded the organisation 'Always An Alternative' and authored 'One Knife, Many Lives', using his personal experiences to drive positive change in urban communities.

The Power of Alignment with Core Values

Your beliefs become your thoughts, your thoughts become your words, your words become your actions, your actions become your habits, your habits become your values, your values become your destiny. – Mahatma Gandhi

Influence in Personal Relationships

To handle yourself, use your head; to handle others, use your heart. – Eleanor Roosevelt

Eleanor Roosevelt: An American political figure, diplomat, and activist who served as the First Lady of the United States from 1933 to 1945, known for her advocacy for civil rights.

Influence in Professional Settings

The highest type of ruler is one of whose existence the people are barely aware. – Lao Tzu

Lao Tzu: An ancient Chinese philosopher and writer, traditionally considered the author of the Tao Te Ching and the founder of philosophical Taoism.

Influence in Communities

A small group of thoughtful people could change the world. Indeed, it's the only thing that ever has. – Margaret Mead

Margaret Mead: An American cultural anthropologist known for her studies of social structures in both Western and non-Western cultures.

The Butterfly Effect of Individual Action

Each time a man stands up for an ideal, or acts to improve the lot of others, or strikes out against injustice, he sends forth a tiny ripple of hope. – Robert F. Kennedy

Robert F. Kennedy: An American politician and lawyer who served as the 64th United States Attorney General and as a U.S. Senator, known for his advocacy for civil rights and social justice.

Influence Through Media and Technology

The power of the Web is in its universality. Access by everyone regardless of disability is an essential aspect. – Tim Berners-Lee

Tim Berners-Lee: A British computer scientist best known as the inventor of the World Wide Web, and an advocate for internet freedom and accessibility.

Ethical Considerations of Influence

Ethics is knowing the difference between what you have a right to do and what is right to do. – Potter Stewart

Potter Stewart: An American lawyer and judge who served as an Associate Justice of the United States Supreme Court, known for his pragmatic approach to constitutional law.

Practical Applications and Exercises

Stories have the power to create social change and inspire community. – Terry Tempest Williams

Terry Tempest Williams: An American author, conservationist, and activist known for her writing on the natural environment and social issues.

Stories of Influence

The purpose of life is not to be happy. It is to be useful, to be honorable, to be compassionate, to have it make some difference that you have lived and lived well. – Ralph Waldo Emerson

Conclusion: From Butterfly Wings to Global Waves

The true meaning of life is to plant trees, under whose shade you do not expect to sit. – Nelson Henderson

Nelson Henderson: While less well-known than some others on this list, Henderson's quote about planting trees for future generations has become widely celebrated for its wisdom on long-term thinking and legacy.

Level 4 – Collective Wisdom

We are a way for the cosmos to know itself.
– Carl Sagan

Carl Sagan: An American astronomer, planetary scientist, and science communicator, known for his ability to make complex scientific concepts accessible to the public.

Historical Perspectives on Collective Wisdom

The whole is greater than the sum of its parts. – Aristotle

Aristotle: An ancient Greek philosopher and scientist, widely considered one of the founding figures of Western philosophy and a significant influence on many fields of study.

Cultural Perspectives on Collective Wisdom

Wisdom is like a baobab tree; no one individual can embrace it.
– African proverb

Everyday Wisdom in Depth of Community

The true voyage of discovery consists not in seeking new landscapes, but in having new eyes. – Marcel Proust

The Role of Art and Symbols in Conveying Collective Wisdom

Art is not what you see, but what you make others see.
– Edgar Degas

Edgar Degas: A French artist famous for his paintings, sculptures, prints, and drawings. He is especially identified with the subject of dance and is regarded as one of the founders of Impressionism.

Collective Memory and Its Influence on Present Reality

The past is never dead. It's not even past. – William Faulkner

William Faulkner: An American writer and Nobel Prize laureate known for his novels and short stories set in the fictional Yoknapatawpha County.

Distributed Intelligence in the Modern World

Never doubt that a small group of thoughtful, committed citizens can change the world; indeed, it's the only thing that ever has.
– Margaret Mead

Practical Applications of Collective Wisdom

The aim of argument, or of discussion, should not be victory, but progress. – Joseph Joubert

Joseph Joubert: A French moralist and essayist, remembered primarily for his posthumously published *Pensées* (Thoughts), which influenced many later French writers.

Stories of Collective Wisdom in Action

Great stories happen to those who can tell them. – Ira Glass

Ira Glass: An American public radio personality and the creator and host of the radio and television show "This American Life".

Conclusion: Exponential Wisdom

Individually, we are one drop. Together, we are an ocean.
– Ryunosuke Satoro

Ryunosuke Satoro: A Japanese writer and poet known for his aphorisms and short, insightful quotes that often touch on themes of unity and collective strength.

Level 5 – Connection in Business

What Sheffield says today, the world says tomorrow. – Herbert Asquith

Herbert Asquith: A British statesman and Liberal politician who served as Prime Minister from 1908 to 1916. His quote reflects Sheffield's historical importance and pioneering spirit.

The Power of Connection in Business

Coming together is a beginning, staying together is progress, and working together is success. – Henry Ford

Henry Ford: An American industrialist and founder of the Ford Motor Company, known for revolutionising factory production with the assembly line.

Purpose: The Core of Business Connection

The greatest danger for most of us is not that our aim is too high and we miss it, but that it is too low and we reach it. – Michelangelo

Michelangelo: An Italian Renaissance sculptor, painter, architect, and poet, widely considered one of the greatest artists of all time.

Values: The Foundation of Business Connection

To be successful, you have to have your heart in your business, and your business in your heart. – Thomas J. Watson Sr.

Thomas J. Watson Sr.: The chairman and CEO of International Business Machines (IBM), who oversaw the company's growth into an international force from 1914 to 1956.

Agency: Recognising Individual Responsibility

The price of greatness is responsibility. – Winston Churchill

Winston Churchill: A British statesman who served as Prime Minister during World War II, known for his leadership during wartime and his eloquent speeches.

Leadership: Guiding with Connection

A leader is best when people barely know he exists, when his work is done, his aim fulfilled, they will say: we did it ourselves. – Lao Tzu

Vision: Crafting a Compelling Future

The very essence of leadership is that you have to have vision. You can't blow an uncertain trumpet. – Theodore Hesburgh

Theodore Hesburgh: An American Catholic priest and educator who served as president of the University of Notre Dame for 35 years.

Integrity: Building Trust in Business Relationships

The supreme quality for leadership is unquestionably integrity. Without it, no real success is possible, no matter whether it is on a section gang, a football field, in an army, or in an office. – Dwight D. Eisenhower

Dwight D. Eisenhower: The 34th President of the United States and a five-star general in the United States Army during World War II.

Community: Powerful Belonging and Shared Purpose

The greatness of a community is most accurately measured by the compassionate actions of its members. – Coretta Scott King

Coretta Scott King: An American author, activist, and civil rights leader who was married to Martin Luther King Jr.

Initiative: Driving Connection Through Action

The way to get started is to quit talking and begin doing. – Walt Disney

Walt Disney: An American entrepreneur, animator, voice actor, and film producer who founded The Walt Disney Company.

Conclusion: Integrating Connection for Business Success

The most important part of leadership is what happens when you're not there. – Ken Blanchard and Randy Conley

Ken Blanchard and Randy Conley: Blanchard is an American author and management expert, while Conley is a leadership and trust expert. They often collaborate on leadership topics.

Solving The Five Dysfunctions of a Team

A team is not a group of people who work together. A team is a group of people who trust each other. – Simon Sinek

Simon Sinek: A British-American author and motivational speaker, known for his work on leadership and organisational culture.

Trust is the foundation of real teamwork. – Patrick Lencioni

Patrick Lencioni: An American author and business management expert, best known for his books on team management and business leadership.

All great relationships, the ones that last over time, require productive conflict in order to grow. – Patrick Lencioni

Consensus is horrible. I mean, if everyone really agrees on something and consensus comes about quickly and naturally, well that's terrific. But that isn't how it usually works, and so consensus becomes an attempt to please everyone.
– Patrick Lencioni

Great teams do not hold back with one another. They are unafraid to air their dirty laundry. They admit their mistakes, their weaknesses, and their concerns without fear of reprisal.
– Patrick Lencioni

If you could get all the people in an organization rowing in the same direction, you could dominate any industry, in any market, against any competition, at any time. – Patrick Lencioni

Conclusion: Forging the Connected Enterprise

If you hire people just because they can do a job, they'll work for your money. But if you hire people who believe what you believe, they'll work for you with blood, sweat, and tears. – Simon Sinek

Level 6 – World Peace

If we have no peace, it is because we have forgotten that we belong to each other. – Mother Teresa

Mother Teresa: An Albanian-Indian Roman Catholic nun who founded the Missionaries of Charity and devoted her life to serving the poor and sick.

Philosophical and Ethical Foundations of Peace

Peace is not an absence of war, it is a virtue, a state of mind, a disposition for benevolence, confidence, justice. – Baruch Spinoza

The Role of Empathy and Compassion in Allowing Peace

If you want others to be happy, practice compassion. If you want to be happy, practice compassion. – Dalai Lama

The Impact of Education and Cultural Exchange

Education is the most powerful weapon which you can use to change the world. – Nelson Mandela

Nelson Mandela: South African anti-apartheid revolutionary and president, known for his advocacy of reconciliation and social justice.

Economic and Social Justice as Pillars of Peace

Peace is not just the absence of conflict; it's the presence of justice. – Martin Luther King Jr.

Martin Luther King Jr.: American civil rights leader whose nonviolent approach to activism transformed the struggle for equality in the United States.

Environmental Sustainability and Peace

The environment and the economy are really both two sides of the same coin. If we cannot sustain the environment, we cannot sustain ourselves. – Wangari Maathai

Wangari Maathai: Kenyan environmental political activist and the first African woman to win the Nobel Peace Prize.

A Personal Mission for World Peace: Cascading Connection

If we are to teach real peace in this world, and if we are to carry on a real war against war, we shall have to begin with the children. – Mahatma Gandhi

"My life is my message." – Mahatma Gandhi

Stories of Peacebuilding

There is no way to peace. Peace is the way. – A.J. Muste

A.J. Muste: American clergyman and political activist known for his work in the peace movement.

Level 7 – The Future of Humanity

The future belongs to those who believe in the beauty of their dreams. – Eleanor Roosevelt

Technological Advancements and Human Connection

The most important thing in communication is hearing what isn't said. – Peter Drucker

Peter Drucker: Austrian-born American management consultant, educator, and author.

The Evolution of Community in a Digital Age

The Internet is the first thing that humanity has built that humanity doesn't understand, the largest experiment in anarchy that we have ever had. – Eric Schmidt

Eric Schmidt: American technology businessman and software engineer, former CEO of Google.

Growing Global Empathy and Understanding

To understand the world, you must first understand a place like Mississippi. – William Faulkner

Environmental Sustainability and Human Connection

We do not inherit the Earth from our ancestors; we borrow it from our children. – Native American Proverb

The Role of Education in Shaping a Connected Future

The mind is not a vessel to be filled, but a fire to be kindled. – Plutarch

Plutarch: Ancient Greek historian, biographer, and essayist.

Ethical Imperatives in a Hyper-Connected World

The more elaborate our means of communication, the less we communicate. – Joseph Priestley

Joseph Priestley: English chemist, natural philosopher, and theologian who is credited with the discovery of oxygen.

Maven: A New Paradigm for Digital Connection

The greatest achievements become possible when we venture off the charted path and wander into the unknown. – Kenneth O. Stanley

Kenneth O. Stanley: a leading computer scientist known for his innovative work in artificial intelligence and evolutionary computation.

The Future of Work and Connection

> *The empires of the future are the empires of the mind.*
> *– Winston Churchill*

Growing Resilience in Connected Communities

> *I am because we are. – Ubuntu philosophy*

Conclusion: Our Role in Shaping the Future

> *The best way to predict the future is to create it. – Peter Drucker*

Conclusion: The Ever-Evolving Journey

> *To be human is to need others, and this is no flaw or*
> *weakness. – David Whyte*

David Whyte: Anglo-Irish poet and author known for bringing together the worlds of poetry, philosophy and organisational development.

Embracing Change and Growth

> *The measure of intelligence is the ability to change.*
> *– Albert Einstein*

The Power of Influence Revisited

> *The most powerful leadership tool you have is your own personal*
> *example. – John Wooden*

John Wooden: American basketball player and coach, known for his success and inspirational teachings.

Empathy and Compassion: The Heart of Connection

> *Compassion is the wish to see others free from suffering.*
> *– Dalai Lama*

The Impact of Education and Cultural Exchange

Cultural differences should not separate us from each other, but rather cultural diversity brings a collective strength that can benefit all of humanity. – Robert Alan Aurthur

Robert Alan Aurthur: American screenwriter, playwright, and television producer.

Economic and Social Justice: Foundations for Connection

Injustice anywhere is a threat to justice everywhere.
– Martin Luther King Jr.

The Future of Connection in a Technological World

We are all now connected by the Internet, like neurons in a giant brain. – Stephen Hawking

Stephen Hawking: British theoretical physicist and cosmologist, known for his work on black holes and relativity.

Practical Applications and Next Steps

Do not wait for leaders; do it alone, person to person.
– Mother Teresa

The Cascade Effect: Your Role in Shaping Connected Communities

I alone cannot change the world, but I can cast a stone across the waters to create many ripples. – Mother Teresa

An Invitation to Continue the Journey

The journey of a thousand miles begins with a single step.
– Lao Tzu

12. Summary of Books Referenced

The journey of connection is one of continuous learning and discovery. The following books have been instrumental in shaping the ideas presented in this book. They represent a diversity of thought from relevant fields, each offering unique insights into the nature of human connection and community.

I've presented these as an organised list of book titles with a brief introduction to the author, and in a formally formatted bibliography in the next section. I hope this helps your own lifelong journey of connection.

Introduction: The Essence of Connection

Modern-Day Relevance: Bridging the Gap in a Disconnected World

Lost Connections: Uncovering the Real Causes of Depression - and the Unexpected Solutions – Johan Hari

Johan Hari is a British journalist and author known for his incisive explorations of social issues. His book *Lost Connections* challenges conventional wisdom about depression and anxiety, suggesting that these conditions are often responses to how we live rather than purely biological disorders. Hari's work encourages us to reconsider our understanding of mental health in the context of our increasingly disconnected society.

Connect: Building Exceptional Relationships with Family, Friends, and Colleagues – David Bradford and Carole Robin

David Bradford and Carole Robin, both long-time Stanford Graduate School of Business professors, bring decades of experience in interpersonal dynamics to their book *Connect*. Their insights stem from teaching the school's most popular course, "Interpersonal Dynamics", offering practical wisdom on building meaningful relationships in all areas of life.

Level 0 – Understanding Connection

Interpreting Symbols in Present Reality

The Body Keeps the Score: Brain, Mind, and Body in the Healing of Trauma – Bessel van der Kolk

Bessel van der Kolk, a pioneering researcher in the field of traumatology, has transformed our understanding of trauma's impact on the body and mind. His seminal work, *The Body Keeps the Score*, draws on over three decades of experience to illuminate the profound ways trauma shapes our physical and emotional responses.

The Crisis of Purpose

21 Lessons for the 21st Century – Yuval Noah Harari

Yuval Noah Harari, an Israeli historian and philosopher, has become one of the most influential thinkers of our time. His books, including *21 Lessons for the 21st Century*, offer sweeping perspectives on human history and potential futures, challenging us to reconsider our place in an rapidly evolving world.

Lost Connections: Uncovering the Real Causes of Depression - and the Unexpected Solutions – Johan Hari

AI Superpowers: China, Silicon Valley, and the New World Order – Kai-Fu Lee

Kai-Fu Lee, a prominent computer scientist and technology executive, offers a unique perspective on the future of artificial intelligence in his book *AI Superpowers: China, Silicon Valley, and the New World Order*. Drawing from his extensive experience in both the US and China, Lee examines how AI is reshaping our world and the implications this has for human connection and employment. His insights are particularly relevant to our exploration of technology's role in shaping future communities.

Distributed Intelligence

The Case Against Reality: Why Evolution Hid the Truth from Our Eyes – Donald Hoffman

Donald Hoffman, a cognitive scientist and professor of cognitive sciences at the University of California, Irvine, presents a revolutionary theory about the nature of reality in *The Case Against Reality: Why Evolution Hid the Truth from Our Eyes*. Hoffman's work challenges our understanding of perception and consciousness, suggesting that our view of reality is shaped more by evolutionary fitness than by accurate representation of the world. His ideas offer a fascinating perspective on how we perceive and connect with the world around us, potentially reshaping our understanding of human interaction and connection.

Interpreting Symbols in Present Reality

The Body Keeps the Score: Brain, Mind, and Body in the Healing of Trauma – Bessel van der Kolk

Understanding the Landscape for Positive Impact

Tribes: We Need You to Lead Us – Seth Godin
Seth Godin, a marketing pioneer and thought leader, has been reshaping our understanding of leadership and community building for decades. His book *Tribes* explores how the internet has transformed the way we form and lead groups, offering insights that resonate deeply with our mission of fostering connection.

Community: The Structure of Belonging – Peter Block
Peter Block, an organisational development consultant and community building advocate, brings a wealth of experience to his book *Community: The Structure of Belonging*. His work focuses on how we can create a more connected, interdependent society through intentional community building.

Practical Applications of Connection

The Four Agreements: A Practical Guide to Personal Freedom – Don Miguel Ruiz
Don Miguel Ruiz, a Mexican author and spiritualist, draws on ancient Toltec wisdom in his book *The Four Agreements*. His work offers a powerful code of conduct that can transform our lives and relationships, aligning closely with your focus on personal growth and authentic connection.

Daring Greatly: How the Courage to Be Vulnerable Transforms the Way We Live, Love, Parent, and Lead – Brené Brown
Brené Brown, a research professor at the University of Houston, has become a leading voice on courage, vulnerability, and empathy. Her book *Daring Greatly* challenges us to embrace vulnerability as a path to more meaningful connections,

resonating deeply with your emphasis on authentic relationships.

Nonviolent Communication: A Language of Life
– Marshall B. Rosenberg
Marshall B. Rosenberg, psychologist and creator of Nonviolent Communication, developed a communication process that has been used worldwide in personal and professional contexts. His approach, detailed in *Nonviolent Communication: A Language of Life*, offers practical tools for creating compassionate connections.

Level 1 – Personal Connection

Ego Is the Enemy – Ryan Holiday
Ryan Holiday, a modern Stoic philosopher and author, explores the pitfalls of ego in *Ego Is the Enemy*. His work provides valuable insights into how our self-perception can hinder genuine connection and personal growth.

The Four Agreements: A Practical Guide to Personal Freedom
– Don Miguel Ruiz

Lost Connections: Uncovering the Real Causes of Depression - and the Unexpected Solutions – Johan Hari

Self-Compassion and Acceptance

The Untethered Soul: The Journey Beyond Yourself
– Michael A. Singer
Michael A. Singer, a spiritual teacher and former software programmer, offers a transformative perspective on inner growth in *The Untethered Soul*. His teachings on mindfulness and self-reflection align well with your exploration of personal connection.

Building Trust and Intimacy

The Speed of Trust: The One Thing That Changes Everything
– Stephen M.R. Covey
Stephen M.R. Covey, son of the renowned Stephen Covey, builds on his father's legacy in *The Speed of Trust*. His work illuminates how trust forms the foundation of all relationships, both personal and professional.

<u>Balancing Independence and Interdependence</u>

The 7 Habits of Highly Effective People: Powerful Lessons in Personal Change – Stephen R. Covey

Stephen R. Covey, an internationally respected leadership authority and organisational consultant, is best known for his seminal work *The 7 Habits of Highly Effective People*. Covey's approach to personal and professional development has transformed the lives of millions worldwide. His philosophy centres on timeless, universal principles that foster both individual growth and effective interpersonal relationships.

<u>Navigating Conflict and Resolution</u>

The Four Agreements: A Practical Guide to Personal Freedom – Don Miguel Ruiz

Level 2 – Relationships

<u>Human Relationships and Emotional Depth</u>

The Whole-Brain Child: 12 Revolutionary Strategies to Nurture Your Child's Developing Mind, Survive Everyday Parenting Struggles, and Help Your Family Thrive – Daniel J. Siegel and Tina Payne Bryson

Daniel J. Siegel and Tina Payne Bryson, experts in interpersonal neurobiology and parenting respectively, offer groundbreaking insights into child development in *The Whole-Brain Child*. Their work provides valuable perspectives on nurturing connection from early childhood.

The Seven Principles for Making Marriage Work: A Practical Guide from the Country's Foremost Relationship Expert – John Gottman

John Gottman, world-renowned for his work on marital stability, brings decades of research to bear in *The Seven Principles for Making Marriage Work*. His insights into relationship dynamics offer valuable lessons for all forms of human connection.

Hold Me Tight: Seven Conversations for a Lifetime of Love – Sue Johnson

Sue Johnson, the primary developer of Emotionally Focused Therapy, offers profound insights into romantic relationships in *Hold Me Tight*. Her work, grounded in attachment theory, provides a fresh perspective on creating and maintaining deep emotional bonds.

Friends: Understanding the Power of Our Most Important
Relationships – Robin Dunbar
Robin Dunbar, an anthropologist and evolutionary psychologist,
explores the nature of friendship in *Friends: Understanding the
Power of Our Most Important Relationships*. His research on
social bonding and the famous 'Dunbar's number' offers
fascinating insights into the limits and possibilities of human
connection.

Friendship: The Evolution, Biology, and Extraordinary Power of
Life's Fundamental Bond – Lydia Denworth
Lydia Denworth, a science journalist, examines the biological
underpinnings of friendship in *Friendship: The Evolution,
Biology, and Extraordinary Power of Life's Fundamental Bond*.
Her work bridges the gap between scientific research and
everyday experience, illuminating the vital role of social
connections in our lives.

The Power of Positive Leadership: How and Why Positive Leaders
Transform Teams and Organizations and Change the World
– Jon Gordon
Jon Gordon, known for his positive approach to leadership,
presents transformative ideas in *The Power of Positive
Leadership*. His work resonates with your emphasis on creating
vibrant, connected communities through inspiring leadership.

Attached: The New Science of Adult Attachment and How It Can
Help You Find—and Keep—Love – Amir Levine and Rachel Heller
Amir Levine and Rachel Heller apply attachment theory to adult
relationships in *Attached*, offering valuable insights into how
early bonding patterns shape our connections throughout life.

The Body Keeps the Score: Brain, Mind, and Body in the Healing of
Trauma – Bessel van der Kolk

Daring Greatly: How the Courage to Be Vulnerable Transforms the
Way We Live, Love, Parent, and Lead – Brené Brown

Nonviolent Communication: A Language of Life
– Marshall B. Rosenberg

The New Age of Ageing: How Society Needs to Change
  – Caroline Lodge
  Caroline Lodge, in *The New Age of Ageing*, challenges
  preconceptions about later life, exploring how we can create
  more connected, fulfilling experiences for older adults in our
  communities.

Community Relationships

The Difference: How the Power of Diversity Creates Better Groups,
  Firms, Schools, and Societies – Scott E. Page
  Scott E. Page, in *The Difference*, presents compelling evidence
  for the power of diversity in problem-solving and innovation,
  aligning with your vision of inclusive, dynamic communities.

Daring Greatly: How the Courage to Be Vulnerable Transforms the
  Way We Live, Love, Parent, and Lead – Brené Brown

Bowling Alone: The Collapse and Revival of American Community
  – Robert D. Putnam
  Robert D. Putnam's *Bowling Alone* offers a seminal analysis of
  the decline in community engagement in America, providing
  crucial context for your work on revitalising connection.

Community: The Structure of Belonging – Peter Block

On Dialogue – David Bohm
  David Bohm, a theoretical physicist and philosopher, explores
  the nature of thought and communication in *On Dialogue*. His
  ideas on collective thinking offer valuable perspectives on
  fostering deeper understanding between people.

Relationships with Nature and the Physical World

The Body Keeps the Score: Brain, Mind, and Body in the Healing of
  Trauma – Bessel van der Kolk

Relationships with Technology

Atomic Habits: An Easy & Proven Way to Build Good Habits & Break
  Bad Ones – James Clear
  James Clear, in *Atomic Habits*, provides practical strategies for
  personal transformation that can be applied to developing
  habits of connection and community engagement.

The Future of Humanity: Terraforming Mars, Interstellar Travel,
  Immortality, and Our Destiny Beyond Earth – Michio Kaku

Michio Kaku, a theoretical physicist and futurist, explores potential trajectories for humanity in *The Future of Humanity*, offering a broader context for considering the future of human connection.

Relationships with Belief, Culture and Ideology

A New Earth: Awakening to Your Life's Purpose – Eckhart Tolle
Eckhart Tolle's *A New Earth* presents a spiritual perspective on personal growth and consciousness, complementing your holistic approach to connection.

Global Relationships

Alone Together: Why We Expect More from Technology and Less from Each Other – Sherry Turkle
Sherry Turkle examines the impact of technology on human relationships in *Alone Together*, providing crucial insights for navigating connection in the digital age.

Cosmopolitanism: Ethics in a World of Strangers
– Kwame Anthony Appiah
Kwame Anthony Appiah explores the possibilities of global citizenship in *Cosmopolitanism*, offering valuable perspectives on connection across cultural boundaries.

Fair Trade for All: How Trade Can Promote Development
– Joseph E. Stiglitz and Andrew Charlton
Joseph E. Stiglitz and Andrew Charlton present a vision for more equitable global trade in *Fair Trade for All*, touching on the economic dimensions of global connection.

21 Lessons for the 21st Century – Yuval Noah Harari

Practical Applications and Exercises

Relationship Breakthrough: How to Create Outstanding Relationships in Every Area of Your Life
– Cloe Madanes and Anthony Robbins
Cloe Madanes and Anthony Robbins offer practical strategies for improving relationships in all areas of life in *Relationship Breakthrough*.

The Five Love Languages: How to Express Heartfelt Commitment to Your Mate – Gary Chapman
Gary Chapman's *The Five Love Languages* provides a framework for understanding different expressions of care and affection.

Level 3 – Influence

The Nature of Influence

Tribes: We Need You to Lead Us – Seth Godin

Personal Agency and Influence

Drive: The Surprising Truth About What Motivates Us
– Daniel Pink
Daniel Pink, a former speechwriter turned influential author on work and behaviour, presents groundbreaking ideas about motivation in *Drive*. His work challenges traditional notions of what drives us, offering insights that are particularly relevant to fostering genuine engagement in both personal and professional realms.

Leadership and the New Science: Discovering Order in a Chaotic World – Margaret Wheatley
Margaret Wheatley, an organisational behaviour consultant, explores how principles of chaos and complexity theory can be applied to organisations in *Leadership and the New Science*. Her innovative approach offers fresh perspectives on leadership and organisational dynamics in our interconnected world.

One Knife, Many Lives: The Journey to Save a Generation
– Anthony Olaseinde
Anthony Olaseinde, the founder of Always an Alternative, uses his personal experiences and community work to explore the devastating impact of knife crime in *One Knife, Many Lives: The Journey to Save a Generation*. His book provides powerful insights into how individual choices shape lives, echoing the profound influence of personal agency in fostering safer communities and brighter futures.

The Power of Alignment with Core Values

The Empty Raincoat: Making Sense of the Future – Charles Handy
Charles Handy, a Irish philosopher and management guru, has been at the forefront of innovative thinking about work and organisations for decades. In *The Empty Raincoat* (known as *The Age of Paradox* in the US), Handy examines the contradictions of modern life and work, offering prescient insights into the changing nature of careers, education, and social structures.

Dare to Lead: Brave Work. Tough Conversations. Whole Hearts.
– Brené Brown

A **Bigger Prize**: Why Competition Isn't Everything and How We Do Better – Margaret Heffernan

Margaret Heffernan, an entrepreneur and author, challenges conventional wisdom about competition in A *Bigger Prize*. Her work explores how collaboration, rather than competition, can lead to better outcomes in business and society, aligning closely with your emphasis on community and connection.

Level 4 – Collective Wisdom

The Wisdom of Crowds: Why the Many Are Smarter Than the Few and How Collective Wisdom Shapes Business, Economies, Societies and Nations – James Surowiecki

James Surowiecki, a journalist and author, explores the wisdom of collective decision-making in *The Wisdom of Crowds*. His work offers valuable insights into how groups can make better decisions than individuals under the right circumstances.

Cultural Perspectives on Collective Wisdom

The Heart of Understanding: Commentaries on the Prajnaparamita Heart Sutra – Thich Nhat Hanh

Thich Nhat Hanh, a Vietnamese Buddhist monk and peace activist, offers profound insights into mindfulness and interconnectedness in *The Heart of Understanding*. His teachings on compassion and mindful living resonate deeply with your focus on kindness and connection.

Braiding Sweetgrass: Indigenous Wisdom, Scientific Knowledge, and the Teachings of Plants – Robin Wall Kimmerer

Robin Wall Kimmerer, a botanist and member of the Citizen Potawatomi Nation, beautifully weaves together indigenous wisdom and scientific knowledge in *Braiding Sweetgrass*. Her work offers a unique perspective on our relationship with the natural world and each other.

Everyday Wisdom in Depth of Community

Community: The Structure of Belonging – Peter Block

Turning to One Another: Simple Conversations to Restore Hope to the Future – Margaret Wheatley

The Role of Art and Symbols in Conveying Collective Wisdom

The Hero with a Thousand Faces – Joseph Campbell

Joseph Campbell, a mythologist and writer, explores the power of myth in shaping human experience in *The Hero with a Thousand Faces*. His work on the universal patterns in stories across cultures offers insights into shared human experiences and collective wisdom.

Collective Memory and its Influence on Present Reality

On Collective Memory – Maurice Halbwachs

Maurice Halbwachs, a French philosopher and sociologist, pioneered the concept of collective memory in his work *On Collective Memory*. His ideas about how societies remember and forget are crucial for understanding how shared narratives shape communities.

Realms of Memory: Rethinking the French Past – Pierre Nora

Pierre Nora, a French historian, examines the role of memory in shaping national identity in *Realms of Memory*. His work on 'sites of memory' offers valuable insights into how societies construct and maintain their sense of shared history.

Lies My Teacher Told Me: Everything Your American History Textbook Got Wrong – James W. Loewen

James W. Loewen, an American sociologist and historian, challenges misconceptions in American history education in *Lies My Teacher Told Me*. His work underscores the importance of critical thinking and accurate historical knowledge in shaping our understanding of society.

The Body Keeps the Score: Brain, Mind, and Body in the Healing of Trauma – Bessel van der Kolk

Distributed Intelligence in the Modern World

The Wisdom of Crowds: Why the Many Are Smarter Than the Few and How Collective Wisdom Shapes Business, Economies, Societies and Nations – James Surowiecki

Communities of Practice: Learning, Meaning, and Identity – Etienne Wenger

Etienne Wenger, an educational theorist, explores how communities of practice facilitate learning and knowledge sharing in *Communities of Practice*. His work offers valuable insights into how shared learning experiences can strengthen community bonds.

#Republic: Divided Democracy in the Age of Social Media – Cass Sunstein

Cass Sunstein, a legal scholar and behavioural economist, examines the impact of social media on democracy in *#Republic*. His work raises important questions about how digital technologies are shaping public discourse and social cohesion.

Practical Applications of Collective Wisdom

Deepening Democracy: Institutional Innovations in Empowered Participatory Governance – Archon Fung and Erik Olin Wright

Archon Fung and Erik Olin Wright explore innovative approaches to participatory democracy in *Deepening Democracy*. Their work offers practical insights into how communities can engage more effectively in decision-making processes.

Tactical Urbanism: Short-term Action for Long-term Change – Mike Lydon and Anthony Garcia

Mike Lydon and Anthony Garcia examine grassroots approaches to urban change in *Tactical Urbanism*. Their work aligns with your focus on community-driven initiatives and the power of small actions to create significant change.

Community: The Structure of Belonging – Peter Block

Mistrust: Why Losing Faith in Institutions Provides the Tools to Transform Them – Ethan Zuckerman

Ethan Zuckerman explores the erosion of trust in institutions and how this can lead to positive change in *Mistrust*. His work offers a nuanced perspective on the challenges and opportunities in rebuilding trust in our interconnected world.

The Wisdom of Crowds: Why the Many Are Smarter Than the Few and How Collective Wisdom Shapes Business, Economies, Societies and Nations – James Surowiecki

Level 5 – Connection in Business

The Power of Connection in Business

Leaders Eat Last: Why Some Teams Pull Together and Others Don't
– Simon Sinek

Purpose: The Core of Business Connection

Start with Why: How Great Leaders Inspire Everyone to Take
Action – Simon Sinek

The Empty Raincoat: Making Sense of the Future – Charles Handy

Values: The Foundation of Business Connection

The Empty Raincoat: Making Sense of the Future – Charles Handy

Dare to Lead: Brave Work. Tough Conversations. Whole Hearts.
– Brené Brown

Agency: Recognising Individual Responsibility

Drive: The Surprising Truth About What Motivates Us
– Daniel Pink

The Age of Unreason – Charles Handy

Leadership and the New Science: Discovering Order in a Chaotic
World – Margaret Wheatley

Leadership: Guiding with Connection

Leaders Eat Last: Why Some Teams Pull Together and Others Don't
– Simon Sinek

Wilful Blindness: Why We Ignore the Obvious at Our Peril
– Margaret Heffernan

Vision: Crafting a Compelling Future

Built to Last: Successful Habits of Visionary Companies
– Jim Collins and Jerry Porras
Jim Collins and Jerry Porras examine what makes companies
stand the test of time in *Built to Last*. Their research offers
valuable insights into how organisations can create enduring
success through strong cultures and clear values.

The Fifth Discipline: The Art & Practice of The Learning Organization – Peter Senge
Peter Senge introduces the concept of the 'learning organisation' in *The Fifth Discipline*. His work on systems thinking and organisational learning offers valuable perspectives on how businesses can adapt and thrive in complex environments.

The Age of Paradox – Charles Handy

Integrity: Building Trust in Business Relationships
The Speed of Trust: The One Thing That Changes Everything – Stephen M.R. Covey

The Empty Raincoat: Making Sense of the Future – Charles Handy

Dare to Lead: Brave Work. Tough Conversations. Whole Hearts. – Brené Brown

Community: Powerful Belonging and Shared Purpose
Communities of Practice: Learning, Meaning, and Identity – Etienne Wenger

A Bigger Prize: Why Competition Isn't Everything and How We Do Better – Margaret Heffernan

The Second Curve: Thoughts on Reinventing Society – Charles Handy

Solving The Five Dysfunctions of a Team
The Five Dysfunctions of a Team: A Leadership Fable – Patrick Lencioni
Patrick Lencioni explores the dynamics of effective teamwork in *The Five Dysfunctions of a Team*. His insights into trust, conflict, commitment, accountability, and results offer practical guidance for building strong, connected teams.

Level 6 – World Peace

Peace by Peaceful Means: Peace and Conflict, Development and Civilization – Johan Galtung
Johan Galtung, often referred to as the father of peace studies, offers profound insights into conflict resolution and peacebuilding in *Peace by Peaceful Means*. His work has been instrumental in shaping our understanding of structural violence and positive peace.

Historical Movements Towards Peace

The Story of My Experiments with Truth – Mahatma Gandhi
Mahatma Gandhi, the iconic leader of India's non-violent independence movement, offers profound insights into personal and social transformation in *The Story of My Experiments with Truth*. This autobiography chronicles Gandhi's journey of self-discovery and his development of satyagraha - the practice of non-violent resistance. Gandhi's philosophy, rooted in truth, non-violence, and self-reliance, provides a powerful model for fostering connection and driving social change. His emphasis on inner transformation as a precursor to societal change aligns closely with our exploration of personal growth as a catalyst for community wellbeing. Gandhi's life and teachings continue to inspire movements for peace and justice worldwide, offering timeless wisdom for those seeking to create more harmonious and equitable communities.

The New Russia – Mikhail Gorbachev
Mikhail Gorbachev, the last leader of the Soviet Union, reflects on Russia's post-Soviet journey in *The New Russia*. His unique perspective as a key figure in 20th-century history offers valuable insights into global politics and peace-making.

Philosophical and Ethical Foundations of Peace

Perpetual Peace: A Philosophical Sketch – Immanuel Kant
Immanuel Kant, an 18th-century German philosopher, laid the groundwork for modern concepts of international peace in *Perpetual Peace: A Philosophical Sketch*. His ideas continue to influence discussions on global governance and cooperation.

Ethics for the New Millennium – Dalai Lama
The Dalai Lama, in *Ethics for the New Millennium*, presents a compelling vision for global ethics rooted in compassion and shared human values. Drawing on Buddhist wisdom yet

speaking to a universal audience, His Holiness offers practical guidance for cultivating inner peace and fostering genuine connection in our increasingly complex world. This work provides profound insights into how personal transformation can drive positive societal change, aligning closely with our exploration of connection as a force for community wellbeing.

No Future Without Forgiveness – Desmond Tutu
Desmond Tutu, the South African Anglican archbishop and anti-apartheid leader, offers profound insights into reconciliation and forgiveness in No Future Without Forgiveness. Drawing from his experiences chairing South Africa's Truth and Reconciliation Commission, Tutu explores the challenging yet transformative power of forgiveness in healing deep societal wounds. His concept of 'ubuntu' - the idea that our humanity is inextricably bound up in others - provides a powerful framework for understanding connection and community. Tutu's work demonstrates how compassion and understanding can break cycles of violence and create pathways to peace, offering valuable lessons for fostering connection in divided communities.

The Expanding Circle: Ethics, Evolution, and Moral Progress – Peter Singer

The Role of Empathy and Compassion in Allowing Peace
Empathy: Why It Matters, and How to Get It – Roman Krznaric
Roman Krznaric, a public philosopher, explores the transformative power of empathy in Empathy: Why It Matters, and How to Get It. His work offers practical approaches to cultivating empathy in our daily lives and institutions.

Into the Magic Shop: A Neurosurgeon's Quest to Discover the Mysteries of the Brain and the Secrets of the Heart – James Doty
James Doty, a neurosurgeon and entrepreneur, shares his journey of self-discovery in Into the Magic Shop. His work bridges neuroscience and compassion, offering insights into the physiological basis of empathy and kindness.

No Future Without Forgiveness – Desmond Tutu

The Impact of Education and Cultural Exchange

Pedagogy of the Oppressed – Paulo Freire

Paulo Freire, a Brazilian educator and philosopher, revolutionised thinking about education and its role in social change with his seminal work *Pedagogy of the Oppressed*. Freire challenges traditional 'banking' models of education, proposing instead a dialogic approach that empowers learners to become active participants in shaping their world. His ideas on critical consciousness and education as a practice of freedom offer profound insights into how learning can foster deeper connections and drive social transformation. Freire's work resonates strongly with our exploration of how personal growth and community engagement can create positive societal change.

The Force of Kindness: Change Your Life with Love and Compassion – Sharon Salzberg

Sharon Salzberg, a leading figure in the field of meditation, explores the transformative power of kindness in *The Force of Kindness*. Her teachings offer practical ways to cultivate compassion in our lives and communities.

Economic and Social Justice as Pillars of Peace

Development as Freedom – Amartya Sen

Amartya Sen, a Nobel laureate economist, argues for a holistic approach to development in *Development as Freedom*. His work emphasises the importance of individual agency and social opportunities in fostering societal progress.

Banker to the Poor: Micro-Lending and the Battle Against World Poverty – Muhammad Yunus

Muhammad Yunus, another Nobel laureate, shares his groundbreaking work on microfinance in *Banker to the Poor*. His innovative approach to poverty alleviation demonstrates the power of economic empowerment in creating social change.

Doughnut Economics: Seven Ways to Think Like a 21st-Century Economist – Kate Raworth

Kate Raworth presents a revolutionary model for sustainable economics in *Doughnut Economics*. Her work challenges traditional economic thinking, offering a framework that balances social needs with environmental limits.

The Little Book of Restorative Justice: Revised and Updated
– Howard Zehr
Howard Zehr, considered the grandfather of restorative justice, provides a comprehensive overview of this approach in *The Little Book of Restorative Justice*. His work offers an alternative to punitive justice systems, emphasising healing and community restoration.

Environmental Sustainability and Peace
Small Is Beautiful: A Study of Economics as if People Mattered
– E.F. Schumacher
E.F. Schumacher challenges conventional economic wisdom in *Small Is Beautiful*, advocating for human-scale, environmentally sustainable economies. His ideas have been influential in shaping alternative economic models.

World as Lover, World as Self: Courage for Global Justice and Ecological Renewal – Joanna Macy
Joanna Macy, an environmental activist and scholar, explores the intersection of spirituality and environmental action in *World as Lover, World as Self*. Her work offers a holistic approach to addressing global challenges.

Level 7 – The Future of Humanity

Wholeness and the Implicate Order – David Bohm

Technological Advancements and Human Connection
You Are Not a Gadget: A Manifesto – Jaron Lanier
Jaron Lanier, a computer scientist and virtual reality pioneer, offers a critical perspective on digital culture in *You Are Not a Gadget*. His work challenges us to consider the human implications of our technological choices.

Understanding Media: The Extensions of Man – Marshall McLuhan
Marshall McLuhan, a media theorist, explored how communication technologies shape society in *Understanding Media*. His prescient insights continue to inform our understanding of digital culture and connection.

The Evolution of Community in a Digital Age

Imagined Communities: Reflections on the Origin and Spread of Nationalism – Benedict Anderson

Benedict Anderson examines the origins and spread of nationalism in *Imagined Communities*. His work offers valuable perspectives on how shared narratives shape community identity in an increasingly globalised world.

Rewire: Digital Cosmopolitans in the Age of Connection – Ethan Zuckerman

Growing Global Empathy and Understanding

The Expanding Circle: Ethics, Evolution, and Moral Progress – Peter Singer

Peter Singer, a renowned Australian philosopher and ethicist, · presents a compelling case for expanding our moral considerations in *The Expanding Circle: Ethics, Evolution, and Moral Progress*. Singer argues that our capacity for empathy and ethical reasoning has evolved over time, allowing us to extend our circle of moral concern beyond our immediate family and tribe to encompass all of humanity and even other species. His work challenges us to consider the ethical implications of our actions on a global scale, offering profound insights into how we might cultivate more inclusive and compassionate communities. Singer's ideas on effective altruism and global ethics provide a thought-provoking framework for understanding our interconnectedness and responsibilities in an increasingly globalised world.

Cosmopolitanism: Ethics in a World of Strangers – Kwame Anthony Appiah

Learning for a Connected World

Deschooling Society – Ivan Illich

Ivan Illich, a philosopher and social critic, challenges traditional notions of institutionalised education in *Deschooling Society*. His radical ideas prompt us to reconsider how learning and knowledge sharing occur in communities.

Navigating the Digital Maze with Heart and Mind

Reclaiming Conversation: The Power of Talk in a Digital Age – Sherry Turkle

Maven: A New Paradigm for Digital Connection

Why Greatness Cannot Be Planned: The Myth of the Objective –
Kenneth O. Stanley and Joel Lehman
Kenneth O. Stanley is a computer scientist whose work
challenges conventional approaches to innovation and
creativity. In *Why Greatness Cannot Be Planned*, co-authored
with **Joel Lehman**, Stanley argues for the importance of
serendipity and open-ended exploration in achieving
breakthroughs. His ideas offer a fresh perspective on how we
can harness unpredictability to foster connection and
innovation in the digital age.

The Future of Work and Connection

The Shift: The Future of Work is Already Here – Lynda Gratton
Lynda Gratton explores the changing nature of work in *The
Shift*. Her insights into future work trends offer valuable
perspectives on how connection and community might evolve
in professional contexts.

Growing Resilience in Connected Communities

A Paradise Built in Hell: The Extraordinary Communities That Arise
in Disaster – Rebecca Solnit
Rebecca Solnit examines how communities respond to disasters
in A *Paradise Built in Hell*. Her work reveals the potential for
crisis to catalyse extraordinary social cooperation and
connection.

Conclusion: The Ever-Evolving Journey

Pedagogy of the Oppressed – Paulo Freire

The Future of Connection in a Technological World

Homo Deus: A Brief History of Tomorrow – Yuval Noah Harari

Reclaiming Conversation: The Power of Talk in a Digital Age –
Sherry Turkle

13. Bibliography

ANDERSON, Benedict (1983). Imagined Communities: Reflections on the Origin and Spread of Nationalism. London, Verso.

APPIAH, Kwame Anthony (2006). Cosmopolitanism: Ethics in a World of Strangers. New York, W.W. Norton & Company.

BLOCK, Peter (2008). Community: The Structure of Belonging. San Francisco, Berrett-Koehler Publishers.

BOHM, David (1980). Wholeness and the Implicate Order. London, Routledge.

BRADFORD, David and ROBIN, Carole (2021). Connect: Building Exceptional Relationships with Family, Friends, and Colleagues. New York, Penguin Random House.

BROWN, Brené (2012). Daring Greatly: How the Courage to Be Vulnerable Transforms the Way We Live, Love, Parent, and Lead. New York, Gotham Books.

CAMPBELL, Joseph (1949). The Hero with a Thousand Faces. New York, Pantheon Books.

CHAPMAN, Gary (1992). The Five Love Languages: How to Express Heartfelt Commitment to Your Mate. Chicago, Northfield Publishing.

CLEAR, James (2018). Atomic Habits: An Easy & Proven Way to Build Good Habits & Break Bad Ones. New York, Penguin Random House.

COLLINS, Jim and PORRAS, Jerry (1994). Built to Last: Successful Habits of Visionary Companies. New York, HarperBusiness.

COVEY, Stephen M.R. (2006). The Speed of Trust: The One Thing That Changes Everything. New York, Free Press.

COVEY, Stephen R. (1989). The 7 Habits of Highly Effective People: Powerful Lessons in Personal Change. New York, Free Press.

DALAI LAMA (1999). Ethics for the New Millennium. New York, Riverhead Books.

DENWORTH, Lydia (2020). Friendship: The Evolution, Biology, and Extraordinary Power of Life's Fundamental Bond. New York, W.W. Norton & Company.

DUNBAR, Robin (2021). Friends: Understanding the Power of Our Most Important Relationships. London, Little, Brown Spark.

FREIRE, Paulo (1970). Pedagogy of the Oppressed. New York, Continuum.

FUNG, Archon and WRIGHT, Erik Olin (2003). Deepening Democracy: Institutional Innovations in Empowered Participatory Governance. London, Verso.

GANDHI, Mahatma (1927). The Story of My Experiments with Truth. Ahmedabad, Navajivan Publishing House.

GALTUNG, Johan (1996). Peace by Peaceful Means: Peace and Conflict, Development and Civilization. London, SAGE Publications.

GODIN, Seth (2008). Tribes: We Need You to Lead Us. New York, Portfolio.

GORBACHEV, Mikhail (2016). The New Russia. Cambridge, Polity Press.

GORDON, Jon (2017). The Power of Positive Leadership: How and Why Positive Leaders Transform Teams and Organizations and Change the World. Hoboken, Wiley.

GOTTMAN, John (1999). The Seven Principles for Making Marriage Work: A Practical Guide from the Country's Foremost Relationship Expert. New York, Crown Publishers.

HALBWACHS, Maurice (1950). On Collective Memory. Chicago, University of Chicago Press.

HANDY, Charles (1994). The Empty Raincoat: Making Sense of the Future. London, Hutchinson.

HANDY, Charles (1989). The Age of Unreason. Boston, Harvard Business School Press.

HANDY, Charles (2015). The Second Curve: Thoughts on Reinventing Society. London, Random House.

HARARI, Yuval Noah (2018). 21 Lessons for the 21st Century. London, Jonathan Cape.

HARARI, Yuval Noah (2015). Homo Deus: A Brief History of Tomorrow. London, Harvill Secker.

HARI, Johan (2018). Lost Connections: Uncovering the Real Causes of Depression - and the Unexpected Solutions. London, Bloomsbury Circus.

HEFFERNAN, Margaret (2014). A Bigger Prize: Why Competition Isn't Everything and How We Do Better. New York, PublicAffairs.

HEFFERNAN, Margaret (2011). Wilful Blindness: Why We Ignore the Obvious at Our Peril. London, Simon & Schuster.

HOFFMAN, Donald (2019). The Case Against Reality: Why Evolution Hid the Truth from Our Eyes. New York, W.W. Norton & Company.

HOLIDAY, Ryan (2016). Ego Is the Enemy. New York, Portfolio.

ILLICH, Ivan (1971). Deschooling Society. New York, Harper & Row.

JOHNSON, Sue (2008). Hold Me Tight: Seven Conversations for a Lifetime of Love. New York, Little, Brown and Company.

KAKU, Michio (2018). The Future of Humanity: Terraforming Mars, Interstellar Travel, Immortality, and Our Destiny Beyond Earth. New York, Doubleday.

KANT, Immanuel (1795). Perpetual Peace: A Philosophical Sketch. Various publishers.

KIMMERER, Robin Wall (2013). Braiding Sweetgrass: Indigenous Wisdom, Scientific Knowledge, and the Teachings of Plants. Minneapolis, Milkweed Editions.

KRZNARIC, Roman (2014). Empathy: Why It Matters, and How to Get It. New York, Perigee.

LANIER, Jaron (2010). You Are Not a Gadget: A Manifesto. New York, Alfred A. Knopf.

LEE, Kai-Fu (2018). AI Superpowers: China, Silicon Valley, and the New World Order. Boston, Houghton Mifflin Harcourt.

LENCIONI, Patrick (2002). The Five Dysfunctions of a Team: A Leadership Fable. San Francisco, Jossey-Bass.

LEVINE, Amir and HELLER, Rachel (2010). Attached: The New Science of Adult Attachment and How It Can Help You Find—and Keep—Love. New York, TarcherPerigee.

LODGE, Caroline (2016). The New Age of Ageing: How Society Needs to Change. Bristol, Policy Press.

LOEWEN, James W. (1995). Lies My Teacher Told Me: Everything Your American History Textbook Got Wrong. New York, The New Press.

LYDON, Mike and GARCIA, Anthony (2015). Tactical Urbanism: Short-term Action for Long-term Change. Washington, D.C., Island Press.

MACY, Joanna (2007). World as Lover, World as Self: Courage for Global Justice and Ecological Renewal. Berkeley, Parallax Press.

MADANES, Cloe and ROBBINS, Anthony (2009). Relationship Breakthrough: How to Create Outstanding Relationships in Every Area of Your Life. New York, Rodale.

MCLUHAN, Marshall (1964). Understanding Media: The Extensions of Man. New York, McGraw-Hill.

NHAT HANH, Thich (1988). The Heart of Understanding: Commentaries on the Prajnaparamita Heart Sutra. Berkeley, Parallax Press.

NORA, Pierre (1996). Realms of Memory: Rethinking the French Past. New York, Columbia University Press.

OLASEINDE, Anthony (2020). One Knife, Many Lives. Sheffield, Always An Alternative Publishing.

PAGE, Scott E. (2007). The Difference: How the Power of Diversity Creates Better Groups, Firms, Schools, and Societies. Princeton, Princeton University Press.

PINK, Daniel (2009). Drive: The Surprising Truth About What Motivates Us. New York, Riverhead Books.

PUTNAM, Robert D. (2000). Bowling Alone: The Collapse and Revival of American Community. New York, Simon & Schuster.

RAWORTH, Kate (2017). Doughnut Economics: Seven Ways to Think Like a 21st-Century Economist. London, Random House Business.

ROSENBERG, Marshall B. (2003). Nonviolent Communication: A Language of Life. Encinitas, PuddleDancer Press.

RUIZ, Don Miguel (1997). The Four Agreements: A Practical Guide to Personal Freedom. San Rafael, Amber-Allen Publishing.

SALZBERG, Sharon (2004). The Force of Kindness: Change Your Life with Love and Compassion. Boulder, Sounds True.

SCHUMACHER, E.F. (1973). Small Is Beautiful: A Study of Economics as if People Mattered. London, Blond & Briggs.

SEN, Amartya (1999). Development as Freedom. New York, Knopf.

SENGE, Peter (1990). The Fifth Discipline: The Art & Practice of The Learning Organization. New York, Doubleday.

SIEGEL, Daniel J. and BRYSON, Tina Payne (2011). The Whole-Brain Child: 12 Revolutionary Strategies to Nurture Your Child's Developing Mind, Survive Everyday Parenting Struggles, and Help Your Family Thrive. New York, Delacorte Press.

SINGER, Michael A. (2007). The Untethered Soul: The Journey Beyond Yourself. Oakland, New Harbinger Publications.

SINGER, Peter (1981). The Expanding Circle: Ethics, Evolution, and Moral Progress. Princeton, Princeton University Press.

SINEK, Simon (2009). Start with Why: How Great Leaders Inspire Everyone to Take Action. New York, Portfolio.

SINEK, Simon (2014). Leaders Eat Last: Why Some Teams Pull Together and Others Don't. New York, Portfolio.

SOLNIT, Rebecca (2009). A Paradise Built in Hell: The Extraordinary Communities That Arise in Disaster. New York, Viking.

STANLEY, Kenneth O. and LEHMAN, Joel (2015). Why Greatness Cannot Be Planned: The Myth of the Objective. New York, Springer.

STIGLITZ, Joseph E. and CHARLTON, Andrew (2005). Fair Trade for All: How Trade Can Promote Development. Oxford, Oxford University Press.

SUNSTEIN, Cass (2017). #Republic: Divided Democracy in the Age of Social Media. Princeton, Princeton University Press.

SUROWIECKI, James (2004). The Wisdom of Crowds: Why the Many Are Smarter Than the Few and How Collective Wisdom Shapes Business, Economies, Societies and Nations. New York, Doubleday.

TOLLE, Eckhart (2005). A New Earth: Awakening to Your Life's Purpose. New York, Penguin.

TURKLE, Sherry (2011). Alone Together: Why We Expect More from Technology and Less from Each Other. New York, Basic Books.

TURKLE, Sherry (2015). Reclaiming Conversation: The Power of Talk in a Digital Age. New York, Penguin Press.

TUTU, Desmond (1999). No Future Without Forgiveness. New York, Doubleday.

VAN DER KOLK, Bessel (2014). The Body Keeps the Score: Brain, Mind, and Body in the Healing of Trauma. New York, Viking.

WENGER, Etienne (1998). Communities of Practice: Learning, Meaning, and Identity. Cambridge, Cambridge University Press.

WHEATLEY, Margaret J. (1992). Leadership and the New Science: Discovering Order in a Chaotic World. San Francisco, Berrett-Koehler.

WHEATLEY, Margaret J. (2002). Turning to One Another: Simple Conversations to Restore Hope to the Future. San Francisco, Berrett-Koehler.

YUNUS, Muhammad (1999). Banker to the Poor: Micro-Lending and the Battle Against World Poverty. New York, PublicAffairs.

ZEHR, Howard (2002). The Little Book of Restorative Justice: Revised and Updated. Intercourse, Good Books.

ZUCKERMAN, Ethan (2013). Rewire: Digital Cosmopolitans in the Age of Connection. New York, W.W. Norton & Company.

14. Index

199]
See also: *Personal Growth, Innovation, Cultural Exchange*

Cultural Exchange [181-183] Cross-cultural communication [181-183] Cultural diversity [181-183] Global citizenship [181-183] Language and culture [181-183] Cultural preservation [181-183] Intercultural competence [181-183]
See also: *World Peace, Community, Empathy and Compassion*

Leadership [154-158, 209-210] Servant leadership [154-155] Transformational leadership [155-156] Ethical leadership [156-157] Distributed leadership [157] Women in leadership [157-158] Youth leadership [158] Crisis leadership [158, 209-210]
See also: *Influence, Trust and Integrity, Business Ethics*

Resilience [203-208] Personal resilience [203-204] Community resilience [203-208] Emotional resilience [204-205] Organisational resilience [204-206] Building resilience skills [204-208] Resilience and wellbeing [204-208]
See also: *Personal Growth, Community, Environmental Stewardship*

Innovation [200-202] Social innovation [200-201] Technological innovation [200-202] Sustainable innovation [201-202] Innovation in education [198-199, 201-202] Community-driven innovation [201-202] Innovation mindset [202]
See also: *Future of Humanity, Business Ethics, Education and Learning*

Trust and Integrity [158-160] Building trust in relationships [158-159] Trust in institutions [159] Digital trust [159-160] Integrity in leadership [159-160] Restoring broken trust [160] Transparency and trust [160] Trust and social capital [160]
See also: *Relationships, Leadership, Business Ethics*

Mindfulness [219-222] Mindfulness practices [219-220] Mindful leadership [219-220] Mindfulness in education [219-220] Mindful communication [220-221] Mindfulness and wellbeing [220-222] Mindfulness in daily life [221-222] Mindfulness and technology [220-221]
See also: *Personal Growth, Resilience, Empathy and Compassion*

Afterword: The Journey Continues

"The obstacle is the way." – Ryan Holiday

As I put the finishing touches on this book, I'm struck by the fact that in working so hard to bring this to you, I've spent less time with nature, walking through my city taking photographs, meeting with friends for a coffee or to support their ventures. I had to focus, otherwise this would have taken forever.

This simple act of focused disconnection shows that we can only ever do our best in tough circumstances. It's not easy, and that is fine. I realise that some of the ideas presented here might seem idealistic. In a world of noise and disconnection, the notion of building deeply connected communities might seem far-fetched. But I promise, every concept in this book is grounded in real experiences and observable changes I've witnessed in Sheffield and beyond.

My own journey of transformation through connection continues to unfold. Each day brings new insights, challenges, and opportunities for growth. I'm constantly amazed by the people I meet who are bringing their own inspiring messages to create positive change in the world. From the friends hosting peer support groups across Sheffield to those reaching the international stage to promote human flourishing and everyday citizenship, these everyday heroes remind me that the power of connection is very real and within reach for all of us.

Thank you for joining me on this exploration of connection. May your own journey be filled with rich relationships, shared wisdom, and the joy of building a more compassionate world, one connection at a time.

Brian Mosley is the founder and host of Love Sheffield, a community initiative dedicated to fostering connection and positive change in Sheffield and beyond. To learn more or to get involved:

- Visit: **www.LoveSheffield.net**
- Email: **brian.mosley@LoveSheffield.net**

Printed in Great Britain
by Amazon